CLOSE TO THE CHARISMA

CLOSE TO
THE CHARISMA

*My Years Between the Press
and Pierre Elliott Trudeau*

PATRICK GOSSAGE

McClelland and Stewart

McClelland and Stewart Limited
The Canadian Publishers
481 University Avenue
Toronto M5G 2E9

Canadian Cataloguing in Publication Data

Gossage, Patrick
  Close to the charisma

ISBN 0-7710-3396-6

1. Gossage, Patrick. 2. Press agents – Canada –
Biography. 3. Trudeau, Pierre Elliott, 1919– .
4. Government and the press – Canada. I. Title.

FC626.G67A3 1986   971.064'4'0924   C86-094008-X
F1034.3.G67A3 1986

Printed and bound in Canada by John Deyell Company

CONTENTS

Preface 9

PART ONE

1 The Langevin 15
2 The Paradoxes of French Power 34
3 Topic "A" 65
4 Under Some Distant Hedge 81
5 Election Politics 109
6 Mal de PMO 131
7 The Phony War 145
8 Campaign to Disaster 165

PART TWO

9 Resignation and Rebirth 179
10 Travails and Travels 196
11 The Langevin Revisited 213
12 Looking Out – The PMO and the White House 225
13 Looking In – Coutts and the Constitution 234
14 Washington and Peace, Trudeau Style 247
15 Postscript 264

Un honnête homme,
rien ne l'étonne.

FLAUBERT

PREFACE

*T*he differences between the governments led by Pierre Trudeau and the one we are now enjoying led by Brian Mulroney are so marked, so dramatic, in both style and substance, that the Trudeau era has taken on a nostalgic quality quite disproportionate to its closeness to us in the historic past. Certainly this was the feeling I had when I began to reread the diaries I kept during the years I worked as a press officer for Mr. Trudeau.

It was Patrick Watson who advised me in his kindly and paternal way to keep a diary when I first went to work at the Prime Minister's Office. I am glad I followed his advice. I discovered to my pleasure that these pages brought back the Trudeau era for me in a vivid way, and it seemed to me that they even threw some light on Mr. Trudeau's personality, particularly as it affected those of us on his staff who worked for him directly.

I found that my journals covered the period from the fall of 1976 when I joined the PMO through the election of 1979. Then the demands of the job took over entirely and I made only sporadic observations. These diary entries are, in a way, the heart of this book. I have added sort of book ends from my present recollections (some all too present) to round out the story and bring the reader through my Washington adventures with Ambassador Gotlieb and my final professional encounter with Trudeau after his retirement. In this newer material I attempted to do what I would have done had I continued keeping my journals – to write directly about how the events and people struck me at the time.

My comrades and colleagues in the Prime Minister's Office, and my friends and clients in the Ottawa press corps provided an engaging and usually attractive cast of characters for which I am grateful. However, one of the hazards of publishing one's diaries or other undiluted memories is that people are described as they are perceived in the heat of the moment, sometimes quite uncharitably. It would have considerably reduced what value this narrative has if I had tried to neutralize these observations. I pray those who feel hard done by in earlier pages will read on. I end up recording the good in all.

The story has a peculiar slant as it is told from the point of view of a media-relations officer somewhere in the no-man's land between the press and the Prime Minister. But I hope that by describing the strategies, frustrations, responsibilities, and accomplishments on both sides of the press-Prime Minister relationship, it may help some readers to understand better how and why this relationship affects our understanding of national public affairs.

Like so many political groupies, I put my home life on hold during the years I worked in the political battlefield. Luckily, it was still there when I was released from service. My stepson, Sean, and daughter, Susanne, were a lot older than when I joined up, and I had to regain their friendship on returning from my extended war. They generously accepted me back as a normal human being.

My wife, Helga, now tells me that she hates politics. But she suppressed her feelings while I was caught up in that life, and her quiet support and understanding of the demands of the job permitted me to live it fully.

My old boss, Pierre Trudeau, assured me he would read this book when it was published. I won't hold him to his word, but I know there are some passages he would enjoy. Neither he, nor any of the other characters who march through these pages have put their imprimatur on one word that follows and I would hardly expect them to. I have only checked a couple of quotations of French poetry with the former PM. He piped up with the exact references before I got out a full line!

However, there were some people who had to read and reread this book until they almost dropped. My principal editor and an old friend, Ramsay Derry, was badgered by my brother, Rick, over a game of squash to look at some of my diaries. He then suffered through some dreadfully typed excerpts, and despite the careless spelling and backwards prose believed there was a book lurking there. I am very grateful for his sometimes superhuman efforts to shape up my jumbled memories.

At McClelland and Stewart, Dinah Forbes brought further editing skills to the manuscript and Jan Walter exuded the kind of confidence that all first-time authors absolutely require. Kris Ahlberg in our little office word-processed successive drafts during long hours, and an old Ottawa press colleague, Andrew Cohen of *The Financial Post,* gave the manuscript a careful and constructive reading.

Pierre Trudeau had a stock reply to the standard question about what he had accomplished as Prime Minister. "I survived," he would say, and the interviewer would often take the answer to be shallow or flippant. It was neither, and I hope that this book will show why simple survival is indeed a measure of significant accomplishment in the brutal and electric theatre of prime ministerial politics.

Patrick Gossage
Toronto, July 1986

PART ONE

ONE

THE LANGEVIN

*I*n the late autumn of 1981, after five years and a few months in the Prime Minister's Press Office, I finally got up the nerve to tell the PM face to face that I wanted out. He pushed his chair back from that imposing desk in that imposing office, and asked, "How long have you been here, Patrick?"

"Since fall, '76," I said. "That's over five years."

"As long as that," he mused. "It seems like just yesterday you came. You were so *green!*"

Indeed I was. Never a card-carrying Liberal party member, my last political activity had been in 1958 when I knocked on a few doors in Rosedale for a Tory, David Walker!

My press credentials were unimpressive. I had been offered a legitimate, honest, reputable reporting job with the *Globe and Mail* in 1965 but I'd preferred a more glamorous research job with a new CBC TV show being mounted by Harry Boyle called "The Observer." After this stint at the CBC and a similar one at CTV, I had gone to Ottawa and joined the Research Branch of the Canadian Radio-Television and Telecommunications Commission in 1970. My only experience in print, the "senior" service in journalism, remains to this day the questionable honour of rising to the position of "telegraph editor" at the *Guelph Daily Mercury* while the regular editor took a vacation.

As far as intimacy with the Ottawa press corps went, my contacts hardly extended beyond Elizabeth Gray, whom I knew and liked then and still do. She used to call me at the CRTC occasionally as she followed broadcasting policy for various CBC radio shows.

When my wife, Helga, and I finally bought a house in Ottawa, chance threw us into a semi-detached, the other half already occupied by David and Cecilia Humphreys. They quickly became good friends, and David did add to my knowledge of Ottawa reporters as he was a veteran newsman, then with the Ottawa *Journal.*

Why then did I get the job of assistant press secretary (or was it "associate"? – we used to fight over those things) in the fall of 1976? Frank Howard, the Ottawa *Citizen*'s meticulous chronicler of the comings and goings of political aides and public servants, provided my first incentive. In his column in the spring of 1976, I read of leavings and upsets in the Prime Minister's Press Office and decided to investigate.

Someone I knew, Jean Charpentier, had been named press secretary to replace Pierre O'Neill who had gone to Africa (all old press secretaries seem to be banished abroad). A perfectly tuned Franco-Ontarian, who in all ways deserved his press nickname "The Count," Jean was famous for his impeccable manners and extravagant gestures. He once threw a gold Dunhill lighter worth hundreds of dollars out his car window into the snow when his lady companion objected to it because it had been given to him by a former object of his desire.

During the late sixties, I had spent many hours drinking with Charpentier when he was an elegant Radio-Canada TV correspondent between exotic foreign postings and I was on assignment to another Harry Boyle TV show in Ottawa. I now decided to sound him out. When I finally got an appointment, I was ushered for the first time into the precincts of the Prime Minister's Office, known more familiarly as the "PMO." Of course, the PMO wasn't one office, but was the generic name for the institution, scattered in various Ottawa buildings, that grouped the somewhat bloated political staff who served Pierre Elliott Trudeau directly.

Lounging comfortably in Charpentier's huge office in the PMO's prime real estate, the Langevin Block, I found his worldly and slightly fatigued airs as appealing as ever, and he allowed that it would be nice to have someone like me on board.

I had a cursory interview later with his boss, the ever-pacing Dick O'Hagan, who energetically occupied the PMO position created for him, Special Adviser on Communications to the Prime Minister. Generously framed, O'Hagan had a taste for well-tailored suits and expensive shirts and fully lived up to his reputation as a "clothes horse." Both his face and body seemed in a constant state of motion – responding with infectious enthusiasm to everything happening around him. I felt honoured to be given the chance to learn press relations at the feet of this veteran former press secretary to Prime Minister Pearson.

Three or so years before, I had met O'Hagan at the Canadian embassy in Washington when I accompanied Pierre Juneau, then my boss as Chairman of the CRTC, to a speaking engagement. The same Juneau was now nursing his Hochelaga by-election defeat in a somewhat make-work position in the PMO.* Leaving no lever of influence unpulled, I told Juneau of my interest in working in the Press Office and then left for a holiday.

My candidature was a long shot at best. I knew there were other more politically deserving, more experienced, and, in at least one case, distinctly more sexy (a lovely blonde to be exact) pretenders than myself. I resigned myself to more labour at the CRTC. But Juneau must have intervened, for I was hired. The call came at our summer cottage. I was stunned. I was even more so when, returning to Ottawa, I was told I could start virtually immediately.

I went to the Press Office and looked for my friend Jean Charpentier. He was not there. Dick O'Hagan told me in hushed tones that Jean was "not well"; that he had talked to his doctor and the prognosis was not good. I could occupy his office!

Like an understudy called into the leading role by the star's misfortune, I moved in to the big press secretary's office facing Parliament Hill, instead of the smaller one facing a back lane adjoining that of my fellow assistant press secretary, Ralph Coleman.

The first question I answered, in tremulous voice, was from Frank Howard of the *Citizen* probing Jean's situation: Would he ever be back, and what security did he have in the office? To the relief of all of us, Jean made a miraculous recovery and returned before I could do too much damage with my swelled head.

I crossed to the dark side of the hall and teamed up with Ralph

* Juneau had been appointed as Minister of Communications in August 1975 but was forced to resign two months later when he was unable to win a seat in a by-election in Montreal.

Coleman, an army officer whose record of service included a dangerous (for his liver) tour as an aide-de-camp to the Governor General. He fast became an understanding and competent friend whose military approach to organizational and logistical problems O'Hagan deservedly praised as bedrock strengths of the office.

Press Office Geography

From my arrival in the fall of 1976 until the Liberal defeat in the general election of May 1979 I toiled as assistant press secretary in the Press Office located in the Langevin Building, a venerable late nineteenth century yellowish stone structure honouring Sir Hector-Louis Langevin, a father of Confederation and Minister of Public Works under Sir John A. Macdonald. With immense windows and towering ceilings "the Langevin," as it is called, is firmly planted on the block between Metcalfe Street and Confederation Square and looks with determination over the sloping expanse of Parliament Hill. Its north-facing windows are the best vantage points for viewing July 1 fireworks and, in spring and summer, the daily march past for the Changing of the Guard.

The lobby of the Langevin is most impressive. The entrance off Wellington Street is framed by imposing heavy oak doors, and the lobby is carpeted with a sea of blue broadloom. Within a four-storey stairwell of magnificent proportions, broad steps part into double staircases winding up to the huge landing on each floor.

Anyone who wanted to get beyond the huge lobby had to deal with the deceptive good humour of Ernie, a rotund veteran guard who was barely visible behind his command post under the stair landing. After I'd settled in, Ernie would often poke his head into my office to tell me there were reporters outside who wanted to come in out of the rain or snow while they waited for a meeting to break up. I'd say jokingly, "Turn the dogs on them, Ernie." He would answer, "Oui, Monsieur Patrick," and let them in to lounge on the stairs!

The Langevin is home to the majority of the Prime Minister's senior staff, and houses about half of those brightest of mandarins who toil in the Privy Council Office. It thus provides under one roof the most important network of advice for the PM and Cabinet. The Press Office offices are just to the right of the lobby on the ground floor. At the far end of the floor were the English speech-writers, a couple of policy advisers, and other mysterious individuals. However, we shared the front half of the first floor with the "francophones" – the French speech-writers, the people who prepared the PM's trips to Quebec, and the political people for the province, headed by Gilles Dufault and, later, Rémi Bujold, and also the PM's old intellectual soulmate, Jean LeMoyne. Le-Moyne's large, rumpled physique and his poor physical health masked one of the most vital and athletic minds in the PMO.

Being cheek by jowl with a brilliant and witty group of Quebecers did colour our perceptions somewhat. We tended, as they did, to feel somewhat orphaned from the real political power centre – *The Second Floor*!

The Second Floor housed *the* PMO power networker himself, Jim Coutts, the chief of staff and principal secretary to the Prime Minister. Right above us on the same floor was Colin Kenny, a somewhat paramilitary type, and his Ontario political staff headed by Peter McGuire. Their contacts and influence exceeded even the importance of that province in confederation. Brian Flemming, a handsome Halifax lawyer, represented Atlantic Canada from his office on the Second Floor. Tom Axworthy, the up-and-coming political adviser for the West, delivered the policy and idea flesh for the bones of Coutt's political savvy and intuition. My real friend on that floor during those years was Marie-Hélène Fox, Francis Fox's smart and fashionable sister. She held a variety of positions, but when I arrived she had taken on the part-time assignment of assisting Margaret Trudeau to cope with her public engagements.

Mrs. Trudeau herself was in and out of the office. Although her last son, Michel, was still a baby,* there were enough housekeepers and a nanny to allow her to indulge her own pursuits which included photography and Japanese cooking. Early on I was ushered into a vacant office down the hall to meet her and to see her photos of her Japanese cooking. I had to advise her on which TV programs might be interested in these twin talents. Although I thought it obvious she was suffering from a bout of too many unfocused energies, there were no indications in the office that there were any problems with her marriage.

We used to joke about being out of the real power play of the

* Michel was born on October 2, 1975.

Second Floor. But, curiously, the Press Office was more credible and accepted in the Centre Block of Parliament Hill, the more or less permanent location of the Prime Minister and his immediate entourage, than it was on the Second Floor. (I say more or less permanent because there was an office suite for the PM and his entourage in the Langevin Building. He used it only in the summer when Parliament was in recess and its air-conditioned comfort appealed.)

Someone from the Press Office "staffed" the Prime Minister during all those movements when he might encounter the press who freely roam the halls, grounds, and neighbourhoods of the Parliament Buildings. As all such moves started in the Centre Block office, I got to know it and its personnel pretty well, particularly because I volunteered early on to "staff" Question Period in the House of Commons. In the days before Question Period was televised, someone from our office had to be there to note any exchanges that might interest the media. We were responsible for accompanying the PM out of the House and for noting or recording any exchanges he had with the scrum of waiting reporters.

So, I had a ritual that took me to that inner sanctum two or three times a day. Out I would go, across Wellington at the lights at Metcalfe, past the sometimes extinguished eternal flame, up by the green or white expanse of the Hill's lawns, into the Commons door, and up the stairs to the quiet carpet-lined shrine – the Arthur Erickson-designed elegance of Trudeau's office.

There, I might join briefly the humming activity in the office of Trudeau's legislative and caucus mastermind and sometimes confidante, Joyce Fairbairn, who was a former reporter herself and was open to press arguments. If I had an urgent press request, I would go next door to the PM's outer vestibule and into Bob Murdoch's (his executive assistant) cell of truth and intrigue off to the right.

Joyce shed brightness and colour on all her dealings. From her bright red lipstick shades to her array of rainbow fashions, she matched her packaging to her unfailingly upbeat view of even the most testy situations. Murdoch looked stooped and burdened by comparison. He was much younger than he looked, and his face was frequently somewhat contorted as he reacted to the latest challenge of being the first in line for prime ministerial changes of mood.

20

Often, I would visit the office facing Murdoch's, to the left, and say hello to Cecile Viau, the PM's longtime secretary, keeper of files and personal records – a woman of great patience and charity.

The geography of the Prime Minister's Office was a key to understanding how it worked. So, too, were the mechanical and physical facilities that, in many ways, controlled or dominated our lives. From where I sat on the first floor of the Langevin (right, as you walked into the imposing downstairs hall, then left, second office), I looked at a phone, an intercom, and a typewriter. Those instruments were really all I dealt with most of the day – the press officer's tools of the trade.

My young daughter Susanne used to come into that palace on weekends and play with the copier and typewriter. Once she was asked what her father did. She said, "Oh, he smokes and talks on the phone." She was quite right. We were slaves to the phone because we answered and returned all press calls the same day, if at all possible. This was Dick O'Hagan's hard and fast rule, and an absolutely basic one.

Susanne also loved to play with the intercoms between the offices. These were *the* indispensable mechanical gadgets in the office. All important PMO officers had a one- or two-digit number on its sleek red face. One touch, beep, and an important voice would come booming out. No hands needed. This unassuming little instrument got me into the Centre Block office of the PM's executive assistant, chief scheduler, and question-answerer, Bob Murdoch. Jim Coutts answered his directly, but you buzzed him with caution. Even "Pierre Trudeau," as he would identify himself, on occasion spoke quietly into my room through this device. Its buzz signalled that someone from inside the Prime Minister's Office, not from outside, had something important to communicate. We all respected the access it gave us. It meant we could put a press question on hold and converse right away with someone who knew the answer, then come back to the journalist sounding brilliant and informed. It was a godsend.

The other communications miracle at our disposal in the PMO was an old-fashioned switchboard with operators on duty twenty-four hours a day, every day. By dialing "0" on a PMO phone, or by calling the PMO switchboard from home, you were connected to an immensely helpful, veteran operator with a devastating knowledge of where people were, and their numbers, at her fingertips.

21

These wonderful switchboard operators would do the chasing themselves, then phone you back, 'I have Mr. so-and-so on the line, Mr. Gossage. . . ." What a miracle, what a wonder!

These women also decided who talked to the PM at home. The only way to reach him at Harrington Lake or at 24 Sussex was through the switchboard. As he used the operator as a buffer, she could easily come back and say he wasn't available. All the operators had little black books with the phone numbers of the PM's friends, and the latest record of whom he would or would not talk to. What ultimate luxury – having someone else keep your little black book for you! They would also perform a similar buffer service for beleaguered press officers. We could refuse to accept a call at two in the morning, and the switchboard would simply say we were not in.

The Press Office Point of View

My vantage point from my arrival in 1976 until the defeat of the government in 1979 was from just beyond the charmed inner circle. In these years as assistant press secretary, I did not attend morning "staff" meetings in the PM's office. These were the regular preserve of Jim Coutts, my boss Dick O'Hagan, and Michael Pitfield, who was Clerk of the Privy Council and the intellectual and bureaucratic dynamo of the Trudeau government.

Joyce Fairbairn saw the PM for a few minutes daily to brief him before Question Period; Bob Murdoch, his executive assistant, ran in and out with papers, briefing notes, and anxiously ushered others in and out. That was it – the sum total of the PMO staff's routine contact with Pierre Elliott Trudeau.

This system, together with the Langevin Building's geographic isolation from the Centre Block, meant that for the hundred or so prime ministerial troops who worked across the street, the PM, already a lone and somewhat shadowy figure, was doubly distant. The vast majority of those who worked for this prime minister in the Langevin Building had met him face to face perhaps no more than once or twice, most likely at the annual PMO Christmas party. There, the real footsoldiers crowded around him sheepishly, telling him that they'd worked for him for months or years doing such and such.

The active press officers – Jean Charpentier, the senior press secretary, and assistants Ralph Coleman and myself – probably saw more of the PM than anyone else, those with "regular" contact excepted. This was because, aside from covering all his "movements" on and off the Hill in Ottawa, we travelled with the Prime Minister, one of Canada's most enthusiastic travellers.

We might be next to the PM in the back of the silver limousine only rarely, but we were almost always in the next car, and one of us invariably flew in the Jetstar for out-of-town Canadian trips, or in the old Boeing 707 for overseas or foreign jaunts. This role as an immediate and constant buffer between the moving, travelling PM and accompanying or waiting journalists, provided us with our most precious insights, as well as our most privileged experiences.

We were very seldom out of "eye contact" when the PM was in public situations, and our vigilance in protecting the person of the PM from unexpected thrusts by microphones attached to inquiring reporters was legendary. Joe Clark's first disastrous overseas trip as Leader of the Opposition, the infamous "lost luggage" trip, showed him the value of such basic routines.

While we saw a lot of the PM as he moved about, shook hands, worked in various aircraft, did press events of one kind or another, and performed at a wide variety of functions, and while we chatted to him whenever possible, we were seldom involved in any discussions with him that related to what he did or said. For the most part, the Press Office saw grand policy decisions, important appointments, and other affairs of government and state only as material either to communicate to the media or to keep from their knowledge as best we could!

This accounts for our rather strange point of view on some monumental events. Others proposed, we disposed. We started as the face of Trudeau's office but, increasingly, as the years went by and the inevitable hostility grew between the media, the PM and his office, we became his and its press mouthpiece. Others in the PMO could and did say, "That's it, I'm never going to talk to those jerks [in the press] again" or, "So-and-so [a journalist] screwed me, I'm cutting him off." But those of us in the Press Office had to keep talking and smiling.

Thus, for press officers, only two kinds of relationship counted – those with the PM and those with Ottawa journalists, our "clients" as we used to call them, all members of that venerable Canadian institution, the Parliamentary Press Gallery. We were the middlemen, and, if either end of the relationship soured, we suffered. Sometimes we suffered horribly.

The goodwill of other PMO and Privy Council Office players was important to our job too. These were both the "officials" (never named!) who helped us get information to the press, who briefed them or us, and those political aides, technicians, and others who helped with press logistics, who set up camera platforms and press rooms.

But we really succeeded only when the man himself had something to say or do and was ready to let the press be the conduit to the public. This kind of success was irregular but, when it occurred, it was memorable. Over the years, the Prime Minister's face-to-face contact with reporters became increasingly formal and finally, increasingly rare. This is an apparently inexorable pattern followed by most prime ministers.

The "scrums" or random push and shoves with the PM in the corridors of the Parliament Buildings were banned in 1976 and replaced by weekly news conferences in the cozy theatre run by the press in the Wellington building across from the Hill. This strange state of affairs meant that an elected member of the Press Gallery executive, not a member of the PM's press office staff, chaired these sessions and chose questioners. Visiting journalists were amazed at how easily we accepted this democratic system.

Occasionally, when the PM had something brief to say to the media that did not merit a full-scale news conference, he would go to the basement of the Parliament Buildings to 130S, a kind of tiny, organized "scrum" room with fixed cameras, microphone positions, and lighting. Before the advent of television in the House, the Opposition leaders went there daily to give their version of Question Period on mike and on camera. Trudeau usually left the task of replying to these sallies to his ministers.

Organizing, prioritizing, persuading, and, finally, scheduling interviews with TV, radio, or print journalists either together or in groups, was a monstrous task in the Trudeau PMO. The "Interview Request File" was definitely the office's most swollen and lethargic paper collector. It was virtually a one-way dossier – *in* only! When I arrived, we were unfailingly chirpy with all requests, whether from various arms of the CBC or from a hotline show in Winnipeg. (We might have up to half a dozen individual requests from the CBC and an equal number from Radio-Canada at any one time. I would often say, "Why don't you get together? Might be easier." But that never happened.)

There were the "standing" requests from such important U.S. shows as the "McNeil-Lehrer Report" on PBS (*never* done), as well as one-shot rush demands that had to be turned around quickly. Some examples of the latter are amusing: "Hello – Mr. Trudeau's press office? This is so-and-so from the *Walter Cronkite news program on CBS*. [Emphasis added, as they say.] We want to schedule an interview with Mr. Trudeau today on such-and-such" (often in those days on whether Canada could survive separatism). We loved turning down the U.S. networks who wanted to treat the Canadian PM like the Mayor of Syracuse. The answer was always "no," with a reminder that the PM was busy running a country.

The other kind of rush request usually came from some hotshot newsman from a Toronto radio station who felt that he had a right to an exclusive "sound bite" from the PM for his upcoming newscast. Their requests went something like: "Hello, this is Randy someone-or-other from CF something in Toronto. Could you put me through to the Prime Minister? Won't take a minute. Just want to get a comment from him on tape about such-and-such for my noon newscast." This touching view of the accessibility of our number-one elected official did not move his heartless gatekeepers. The answer was always "no."

Requests from the "regions," as we arrogantly labelled anywhere outside the Toronto/Montreal/Ottawa area, were carefully kept for possible use "on the road" during the PM's Canadian travel. They were often easier to get onto the schedules that were prepared by the regional political people just upstairs in the Langevin (rather than by the PM's executive assistant across the road in the Centre Block). Travel, moreover, was, more often than not, politically motivated, and, in the years 1977–79, granting interviews was often seen as part of the process of wooing voters for the endlessly threatened forthcoming election.

There were a few fixed points in the interview year – the annual television "year ender" with CTV's Bruce Phillips. Trudeau kicked at this tradition each year, claiming there was no reason to do it just because it had been done for years. But during my time in the PMO he never wriggled out of the interview.

I started the tradition of taping them in the homey surroundings of 7 Rideau Gate, the government's official guest residence across the road from 24 Sussex Drive. We would set a fire, arrange the Eskimo sculptures just so, and have a drink and a mince tart in the salon while we waited for the PM to appear. Phillips was unfailingly courteous and conscientious. He even brought his daughter to one taping where she got a good dose of Trudeau's charm. These occasions were invariably serious and revealing.

When we were abroad at economic summits, or away on other important international trips and visits, CBC TV nearly always did a "News Special," and normally Don McNeil tagged along to collect material. He almost always got an interview. The extended format suited us, and the PM liked Don's apparent depth and his respectful manner. Later, after Don's departure for the U.S. television networks, David Halton maintained the tradition with equal success. We always offered Radio-Canada equal time, and they usually took it.

Finally, there was one wild-card interviewer whose requests were nearly always granted. They came from Vancouver, from that old curmudgeon, Jack Webster. Jack mounted a pretty heavy and successful lobby for his first interview shortly before the 1979 election. He flew in from Vancouver, and I set him up in a borrowed office on the second floor of the Langevin. Jack was as nervous as a coot. I went to the Centre Block to fetch the PM at the appointed hour and, before bringing him into the room, told him to let his hair down, be familiar with Jack, not take him too seriously and generally "get into it." Above all, he was to throw all challenges back at Webster and to call him by his first name.

The PM matched Webster gusto for gusto. Trudeau's "Come on Jack, do you really believe that . . ." became a hallmark of successive and ever more outrageous exchanges. He threw it back and Webster loved it. Soon we were doing Webster nearly every time we went to Vancouver. They were rare moments, and our travelling media loved them as much as the two participants – there was always some news.

Webster and Trudeau developed great respect for each other, and at one interview Jack proudly introduced his daughter to the

PM. After decades of not being in touch, Jack and his wife had only recently been reunited with her, so it was a terribly important moment for the old softy, and the PM responded warmly.

Aside from these easy-to-schedule interviews, it is fair to say that, all else being equal, a beautiful female journalist did have an edge in getting a positive response to an interview request. It was less difficult to persuade him to do "Canada AM" after Pamela Wallin started to do the Ottawa items, and later when she moved to Toronto as full-time host.

As for the rest, requests turned brown with age more often than not. They became embarrassing. The *Globe and Mail* gave up asking. Jeffrey Simpson finally got a twenty-minute, carefully controlled session with him during the 1980 campaign. Richard Gwyn never did get an interview for his major study of the Trudeau years, *The Northern Magus*, and says so in his introduction.

Programs like "As It Happens," which relied on the phone, were discouraged. We claimed the PM did not like the impersonal nature of phone interviews. We developed a hundred excuses for putting people off. It became tiresome. Then out of the blue, usually for political reasons, a couple would squeak through, and those at the bottom of the file would move up a few notches.

When we were not shadowing or buffering the PM on the road, or dealing with interview requests, or interviews or news conferences, we press officers sat with our ears to the phone, or to the aforementioned red intercoms. We all developed the most virile negative feelings toward the communications instruments which controlled two-thirds of our lives. We often logged hundreds of calls a day – all from journalists, each one potentially a minefield in which our mouths could get blown off in print or on TV or radio, as what we had said would be reported only hours later.

Radio stations even called from time to time with their tape recorders already running! We got pretty adept at detecting the "beeps" which, by law, had to be audible if a conversation was being recorded over the phone and advance permission had not been given. But we all got caught at least once thinking we were having a nice background chat, only to hear ourselves on radio later.

The content of these endless calls was often mundane. This is an important admission! Far from passing on detailed background on the great decisions of the day, we were often just detailing schedules for trips, recounting whether the PM had or had not seen someone or other that day, or, as in the memorable case of my first call from Richard Gwyn, giving the year of the PM's bulletproof limo and the number of miles it had on it! There were calls about nannies, about maintenance at 24 Sussex, about where the PM shopped for clothes, and so on and so forth.

In fact, all these trivial details are important information for journalists doing stories or making plans for which the PMO was the only source of information. In the widely criticized but still prevalent personality politics of Ottawa, all this is essential lubrication for the far more ponderous and less enthralling grinding of the machine of state. Ottawa, moreover, is a city of a thousand sources. Ministers and their aides talked to the press (or at least used to in the Trudeau era), as did higher-ranking civil servants. For a determined Press Gallery tracker, substance wasn't that difficult to come by.

But, it must be admitted, Trudeau was a huge star, a real personality, and, happily for those journalists who covered him, the source of a torrent of newsworthy ideas. What the press lacked to embellish their fascinated coverage of him were the private details of his life that were deliberately kept secret. We alone were in the position to measure out such details. We did so with fearful prudence and considerable anxiety. That Trudeau was only very rarely impatient with what we did divulge makes me think we fulfilled this odd mission quite adequately.

Only one aspect of our daily lives "between the press and the Prime Minister" is still missing – the Press Club. This drinking and information-exchanging institution is not to be confused with the Parliamentary Press Gallery, whose membership is drawn exclusively from those who cover Parliament full time for reputable organs of information, and is far more exclusive than the roster of the Press Club. The National Press Club welcomed all whose life in Ottawa depended on information, as well as a few who just liked the cheapest bar in town. This is where, as one wag once said, "the Ottawa press drinks its own dirty bath water." While a bit exaggerated, this does give some flavour of the place.

At about seven in the evening, when the last telephone call of the day had been answered, I might drop into the Press Club on my way home. For those of us in the Press Office, it was an easy place to chat up our "clients," to compare notes informally, maybe to help with a difficult piece of speculation someone was trying to work up – the "would I be way off the mark if I said that . . . ?" kind of conversation. We often went there after hours, and, as a matter of pride, made a point of showing up when things were going badly.

I would try to linger only as long as necessary in the club at the end of the day. I did not always succeed. If the weather was nice, I would leave on my bicycle, coast down Sussex and turn up Mackay, which opens off Sussex just opposite the "residence" at number 24, where the PM would already be having his nightly swim with his kids. During those years we lived in New Edinburgh, a small community squeezed between the Rideau River and the domain of the Governor General.

My wife, Helga, saw little of a lively attentive husband for five long years. We had a young family, and by the time I dragged in their evening was already half over. I often sat down to a dinner kept warm in the oven while family routines went on without me.

Work had a way of following me home. As Ralph Coleman and I, of all the other Press Office types, were the most likely to be pleasant, the switchboard operators soon fastened on us as the best candidates for after-hours press, and even other persistent or annoying callers. "Mr. Gossage, will you take a call from so-and-so at the *Toronto Star*? They said it is important."

"Hi. So-and-so here. Just wondered if you have a reaction to the latest Gallup poll . . . to an air crash involving Canadians . . . to . . . " whatever.

So it would go. I would get an average of three or four calls every night – sometimes more. One black Christmas morning at about 1:00 a.m., a terrier on the overnight desk at Canadian Press called to demand I give him a list of the holiday destinations of all Cabinet ministers, then reviled me for not having them. As my voice rose in the dark bedroom so did my wife's anger. That was nearly the end of both my job and my marriage.

There were few perks attached to my job that my family could enjoy. We did get seats for galas at the National Arts Centre, and we attended the occasional reception for a visiting dignitary. Helga once met Vice-President Mondale – or did she? I would not necessarily know, and likely would not even be with her as I would be "working" these events. They weren't much fun for her.

The Prime Minister would be friendly whenever we ran into

him in the neighbourhood park, and we were invited to 24 Sussex once – when the PM was still with Margaret and needed somebody to run a videotape they wanted to see. I brought the wrong tape. When I met Trudeau years later, after his retirement, he remembered my screw-up and teased me about it!

A year after I joined the PMO, my wife bought a horse, American Rose. It saved her sanity during those years. Her weekend rides also gave me a quiet period to recover from the week and prepare for the next. On these quiet Saturday or Sunday afternoons, I normally sat at the dining room table and wrote my diary.

Indoctrination

Impressed by my lack of media savvy, Dick O'Hagan felt that I should have a full immersion as soon as possible after I joined the Press Office. His idea of rapid indoctrination was to get me on the road with the PM and as many unruly members of the Press Gallery as possible.

The Liberal government was very low in the polls at the time (about 28–29 per cent in the Gallup, an all-time record low for a party in power), and the newly elected Progressive Conservative Leader, Joe Clark, was still riding high. So the Press Office took the classic approach and decided to get the PM out to the "people," to get him in front of popular, enthusiastic crowds to show Canada he still had "it." An elaborate swing through P.E.I. (a Liberal stronghold provincially) and New Brunswick was launched in October.

Ralph Coleman had been assigned to accompany the PM and journalists on this complicated trip, but, part way through, was called away to do an overseas trip. Dick gloated as he told me that I would replace Ralph somewhere in P.E.I. "The best possible way to get to know the Press Gallery is to travel with them," he advised. He was right. The following days of that first autumn were an effective baptism. They also held some of the most memorable experiences of my years with Pierre Elliott Trudeau.

My first solo with the thirty or so reporters who trailed after the PM happened somewhere in P.E.I. where, behind the closed doors of a farmhouse, the PM was listening to farmers complain. The gaggle of reporters and cameramen were scattered about, relaxing in the yard. Someone told me that I should brief them on what was going on inside. I assumed this was routine, slipped in quietly, made a few notes, and later felt quite puffed up as the circle of reporters took down everything I said. Later, I realized they had not only quoted me, they'd also used my name.

The problem was that PMO press officers do not normally brief openly for attribution–not in the parliamentary tradition where only ministers are accountable. What I had thought was an effective exercise became my last of this kind. I learned quickly that it is safer and more effective to fill in details anonymously and less formally, and that every time your name is in the press is one less time your boss's name is.

On this trip the PM, his senior aides, and a few special reporters flew in two Armed Forces Huey helicopters, and the press officers and the rest of the media flew in a huge, unbelievably noisy, forty-passenger, twin-rotor Chinook transport helicopter. Crossing from P.E.I. to New Brunswick, we dusted from small town to small town, creating memorable events just by arriving. At Edmunston, we joined other cabinet ministers to hear briefs from several northern New Brunswick groups.

As the Chinook settled down on the football field of the high school where we were to have the session, there was a disconcerting change in the engine's pitch just as the ground was racing up to meet us. Something was amiss. It turned out that a bearing had failed in one of the giant rotors, and, as one of the crew said, "these babies fall fast!" To our immense relief, we landed safely.

After the lacklustre meeting in the sombre gymnasium was over, someone from the military announced that the Chinook was dead. We would have to cram as many of the press in one of the back-up Hueys as we could. The rest would have to follow behind later.

Reporters become very unpleasant very quickly when seriously inconvenienced. The crowd of thirty or so was soon in tight ranks around me, all shouting reasons why they should have priority for the few seats available in the Huey: "The largest newspaper in Canada can't be left behind"; "We are the biggest network"; "Canadian press has to have a photographer with the PM at all times"; "The French have to be represented"; "We have a death watch responsibility" (meaning the reporter feels obliged to be on board with the PM when the chopper falls out of the sky!); and so on.

I found myself suddenly infused with the authority that comes only when there is real conflict and crisis. I shouted for them to all shut up and ordered those who had arrived in one of the two Hueys to cross a line I drew with a stick in the sand of the playing field. I felt as if I was choosing teams at a summer camp. Then, turning to those who were left, I established some easily agreed-on priorities (Canadian Press's Mike Lavoie, for instance, who, as "pool," would take notes for those left behind) and soon had the right number running like mad to get into the back-up chopper. "I will get transport for the rest," I said bravely. "Wait here."

I told a man standing nearby watching this bizarre crossing-the-line ceremony that I needed his truck to get to the nearest airport "vite." He obliged, and soon I was renting a small fleet of light planes on the strength of my PMO calling card. I even sent the man with the truck, and another bystander with a car, back to the school to fetch the passengers, who I jammed into the rented planes. Soon we were airborn for Florenceville, our next stop.

The group who flew with the PM had only just settled in the huge, rambling motel when we arrived from the Florenceville airport. Almost immediately, I had to deal with an interview arranged for Isabel Bassett, recently married to John Bassett, and then working for CTV's "W-5" and trying to prove something. Her charms failed to work on the PM that late afternoon.

Dick O'Hagan, a native of northern New Brunswick, joined the tour that night and invited the senior journalists to his room to watch the U.S. presidential campaign debate. Despite my logistical success, I felt the re-establishment of hierarchies within the PMO, and retired to the bar to have a drink.

There I met the helicopter crew who were drinking in an unsettling way. But more important, I befriended Bruce Garvey, then working for the *Toronto Star*. A gritty old journalistic veteran, he had written a highly amusing piece called "Fear and Loathing in Northern New Brunswick," which poked a lot of cleverly written fun at our transport nightmares. Humour was obviously an indispensable ingredient of the job. I felt a bit more initiated.

There were other moments of hilarity. French-English tensions surfaced regularly in this period, just months prior to the election of the Parti Québécois in Quebec, and on this tour the PM had been asked several times for his thoughts. Somewhere in New Brunswick he had used a story about his mother-in-law, Mrs.

Sinclair, to reveal how silly anglophone fears of adapting to the French reality could become. He said, "Why, she even objects to French on cornflakes boxes!"

The francophone reporters travelling with us could not resist responding at the next mini-news conference with the PM. A huge box of cereal was bought and put right on the desk the PM would use for the conference. The PM came in and sat down, looked at the French in mock disgust and shock, threw the box rudely to the side, and exclaimed, "Not that stupid French again!" The press broke up. If he had the right props or was in a provocative situation that the cameras were watching, he could be counted on to perform.

The trip ended with a good feeling. Dick O'Hagan was right – I was launched.

TWO

THE PARADOXES OF FRENCH POWER

I *began a rather sporadic weekly diary a month and a half after coming to the PMO Press Office. It started with some inflated interpretations of what drove the French Canadians who had taken over Ottawa's mind, if not its heart. I felt that, if I was going to keep a record of these days, I ought to have something "important" to say. Later on, as my confidence and responsibilities grew, there was less and less time for what my father would call "intellectualizing," and I simply recorded events and feelings.*

The Quebec Intellectuals' Canada

December 5, 1976

The November 15 victory of Lévesque's separatist Parti Québécois marks the turning point in the saga of the Quebec intellectuals who, in the late sixties, opted for federalism and Ottawa.

This is a saga I have been watching for five years now. It has been my good fortune to work closely with some of the best representatives of the Quebec federalist group. First, I worked with Pierre Juneau when he was chairman of the CRTC. Then I was exposed to the cutting intellect of Fernand Cadieux through a friend at the CRTC, Rod Chiasson. Now I have a front-row seat from which to observe and to try and understand the PM and others, such as his sometime mentor Jean LeMoyne who is just across the hall from me in the Langevin.

As these intellects continue to have a large effect on the history of this country, it may be worth tracing my interpretation of their odyssey.

First, they are internationalists. Trudeau once said that it was too easy to stand in front of an audience and get the easy cheer with, "We are Canadians . . ." – this in reference to his recent performance at an ethnic evening in Toronto arranged by Johnny Lombardi.

Second, and most evident in my experience of the PMO, is their strange combination of deep commitment and vested interest in maintaining and enhancing the role of the francophone in the federal directory.

A recent Global television interview with Peter Desbarats and Peter Trueman showed the depth of this sentiment. Pushed to admit that, with the PQ victory, the anti-separatist battleground had switched to Quebec, the PM emotionally refused to be told to "go home to Quebec." He insisted the battle for French rights in the rest of Canada was as important as ever.

I also saw profound personal regret in Pierre Juneau, the former CRTC chairman and my old boss, that his fellow Quebecers rejected the legitimate role of Quebecers in Ottawa during the earlier dark moments of the Quebec-Ottawa confrontation on whether the federal or provincial government should control new communications technologies. He bitterly catalogued all that federal institutions like the CBC and the NFB had done to foster the self-expression of Quebecers, only to have their legitimacy questioned by the cultural leaders of that society.

It was sad to see the genuinely tragic demeanours of the Quebec federalists like Jean LeMoyne, Rémi Bujold, and Gilles Dufault as they watched the PQ victory engulf the screen in the Press Office on November 15. Are they really without a country? Or is Trudeau's dream of Canada as a homeland for Quebecers, with its necessary fraternal acceptance by anglos, still a sensible possibility?

But, as a friend pointed out last night, I am unfit to judge, as in Ontario, where I come from, questions of strong provincial loyalty are not relevant

So, they are internationalist, or at least anti-nationalist, and they demand a place in the federal polity. Third? I'd say is their admiration for a very specific kind of English-Canadian talent – people like Ralph Hart and John Bassett for Juneau, Jim Coutts, Michael Kirby, perhaps the Bronfmans, and God knows who else for Trudeau. Call them the successful entrepreneurs, manipulators, the folksy wheeler-dealers or fixers ("smilin' " Jack Gallagher of Dome Petroleum comes to mind), I only know that they do not represent English-Canadian reality at its fullest or best any more than the few francophones represent the same for Quebec reality. I cannot pretend to explain this strange union of divergent skills – priest and layman, lonely missionary, man of ideas and the shrewd or cunning or brilliant. Nor can I explain the attraction. Perhaps it's a longing for the possible. Perhaps Trudeau's teaming up with these anglophone opposites contributed to a unique fusion of strengths.

Inside the PMO

One of the more obvious things going wrong in the PMO, 1976 edition, is a fragmentation of effort and will. At the CRTC such fragmentation would be dismissed as petty office politics. Here it is wrapped up in the more critical question of who is to rule and why. It is more complex than the normal "court" structure that surrounds all powerful bureaucrats (in the CRTC, direct access to the chairman was *all* that mattered). The PMO is a loosely structured institution, and below the level of the PM and his principal secretary, Jim Coutts, there is an "everyone for himself" atmosphere. It did not surprise me that, after a month on the job, I still had not actually met Trudeau.

When I did, I was sent to film a clip with him for that redoubtable Canadian institution, "Front Page Challenge." Cabinet was having its annual think-in that day at the National Capital Commission's retreat above Meach Lake in the Gatineaus. I had to catch him during a break in the meeting.

I waited uneasily outside the meeting for the lunch break, shuffling in the hall of the old mansion and trying not to hear the secret Cabinet discussions.

Finally, a round of "ho hos!" signalled the break, and I went down into the timbered room. Where was the PM? I spied the one cabinet minister I knew, Monique Bégin, a boisterous former co-worker at the CRTC. I made a beeline for that single familiar, friendly face. "Oh, he's over by the bar," she said.

I introduced myself. The PM was very courteous and open. He has the ability to sense shyness and is gracious at setting the shy at ease. To my immense relief, he remembered his briefing note that set out who I was and what I wanted him to do.

He stood in front of the camera and convincingly read the cue cards I had prepared. He even made me feel welcome. But that's as far as it went.

I've found quickly, to my disappointment, that those who join the PMO thinking that work problems will be pleasantly discussed and resolved over cocktails (Trudeau, for starters, is notoriously ignorant of how to mix even the simplest drink) after work at the residence – perhaps even with spouses included – are sadly disappointed. Trudeau demands a lot of his staff but befriends them rarely. I've found that this simplifies life for both.

This came home to me during my first flight with him. It was after a couple of successful meetings in Dan MacDonald's P.E.I. riding. Unexpectedly, I found myself wedged next to the PM in the Huey helicopter for the half-hour ride back to Charlottetown and a press conference. I thought he would chat with Premier Alex Campbell who was only about ten inches away. I even thought he might have time for a briefing from me, since we were headed for a news conference and that was why Bob Murdoch, his executive assistant, had arranged for me to be aboard. This was not to be. I got barely a word in, and he gave me only the slightest recognition. He was short but pleasant with Campbell, made a few cuttingly frank comments about the forthcoming Federal-Provincial Conference, then sank quickly into private reflection, gazing intently out the tiny window as the fine P.E.I. agricultural land slid under us. Moments later, we swooped down into the parking lot of Keddy's Motor Inn. He swept into the news conference and performed magnificently despite the lack of briefing.

This lack of cronyism has led to the maintenance of the most amazing myths. There is a rampant impression amongst the Tories and also the media that the PM has stacked his office with his closest political friends. The myth imagines Trudeau plotting the next strategy with these cronies evening after evening at 24 Sussex. But I can see no evidence of this. Even the Pitfields do not appear to be part of any charmed, private dinner circle. Everyone in the office knows this impression to be a myth. But if, as Trudeau does, one keeps one's friendships to a bare minimum, it is easy for others to claim proximity, and who is to gainsay the claim?

As precisely as he orders his desk in his Centre Block office, Trudeau organizes his life into Sir William Osler's famous "watertight compartments." He works like a trojan from 9:00 a.m. to 6:00 p.m. spends a couple of intense hours with his family (no calls), and then returns to his papers (delivered in the infamous "bags" organized like a travelling office) from which he never escapes. He has told me he never takes problems into sleep, and I believe him.

I have already seen Trudeau put out enormous amounts of warmth and good will at party functions and public occasions. But he's made it clear that his staff is there to assist, each in a defined way, not to become personally entangled. Most here respect and understand this.

Trudeau can speak of atomization in contemporary society and not see that it's rampant in the office. There is no teamwork, and, of course, for all but a very few who ponder their privilege only in their own hearts, there is no connection with the top.

In this PMO it is more a question of who *dares* direct, advise, or influence, often with only the vaguest idea of what the PM might want. For the paradox of French-Canadian intellectuals is that they seem to have well-developed or predictable views on only a limited range of subjects.

In such areas as French-English relations, constitutional reform, and federal-provincial relations the PM's firm views are all too well known and consistent. In many other day-to-day matters, one has to try to read the rather insubstantial personality clues the PM offers to only a handful of his closest advisers and friends.

Moreover, we have not even kept up with the changing processes of government. The French-Canadian intellectual thrives on creative dialogue and debate. Too many of us still prefer direction from the top down.

Give and take seems as out of reach as individual gutsy decision-making for a generation of politicos who have not adjusted to the "new politics" – the more collegial system that can't get off the ground, has not set up its rules, or does not function simply because people like myself prefer to be *told* what to do.

Perhaps the speech-writers (so called) are the most cruelly disadvantaged by this system–Joan Forsey, Jim Moore, Jean LeMoyne. I saw LeMoyne almost in tears the day before a speech, text ready but having consulted with absolutely nobody.

Trudeau keeps his distance at all times. I had looked forward to the personal contact of briefing sessions, but I've found instead that written rather than verbal briefings are preferred. Perhaps Trudeau suffered enough nervous unstructured babbling from staff in the early years. Our briefs not only have to be written, they have to be exact. This demand for linguistic precision is an advantage to people like Michael Pitfield, who even speaks like a sparsely written two-page analysis. He briefs verbally, but few others dare. The rest of us struggle over memos, happy not to have our loose oral logic revealed to one of Canada's best minds.

Many of my press clients would agree that after a snapped response to an imprecise, wandering question at a news conference, they might have better spent their time writing a question and organizing their thoughts. Peter Desbarats of Global TV annoys his less perceptive colleagues regularly by doing just that and by eliciting revealing and cogent replies. He realizes you have to take Trudeau as he is. So do most of his staff. I am learning.

My dream world (the one that arrives at night) is now almost exclusively peopled by the PM and my fellow "aides." Usually I am blowing the one important opportunity of speaking up before the PM – presumably the once-in-a-lifetime occasion to redirect the ship of state!

The Media as Irritant

December 12, 1976

It's been less than a month since the landmark election of a sepatatist PQ government, and the stage is reserved tomorrow for Trudeau to confront Lévesque in their first meeting at a federal-provincial conference. This meeting will surely have important historic consequences. We bemoan the media for characterizing it this way, even if, in our hearts, we know they are right.

I now realize that Trudeau sees the media as an irritant in the great transactions of government. ("Why should I tell my secrets to that?" he once told the microphone of one of our sharper radio reporters as he plucked it from the reporter's hand and dropped it disdainfully on the floor.)

Even Ralph Coleman, after lobbying for a week for more access by the press to the federal-provincial conference, threw up his hands in disgust when, through Dick O'Hagan, it became clear that the PM would not be "stampeded by the press" into providing a paranoid public with a glimpse of personal encounters – a glimpse that could deeply alter their view of the nation's future.

The Press Office looks peculiarly impotent on this issue. We either have no case, or have not argued it properly. We have no strong or consistent advocate for our position. For his own reasons, Jim Coutts has decided to play no role in this non-debate. But what of Keith Davey who is alleged to care about this kind of thing? I am convinced that basic public communications policy between campaigns has not been thought out and is largely shaped by the unchallenged views of the PM himself.

The PM has clear and classic views of the proper role of the fourth estate in a democracy, but since the practitioners here in Ottawa seldom reach his standards, he is quickly frustrated. His key advisers don't even go that far. They neglect almost completely any consideration of tactics to deal with the scrambling practitioners of sounds and images who represent the daily media in Ottawa.

I'm led to believe that only during elections is the press, this necessary evil, dealt with on any regular basis. For the rest of the time, the seat of my pants would seem to be all the guidance required in the daily mediation of events and attitudes. The exercise of power in this PMO simply has little to do with dialogue with the press. This is an intellectual decision and is the side of the francophone in power that affects me most. It's a serious blind spot, however, as bad communications management is hampering nearly every PMO activity.

There is nobody to *lobby* for any coherent, alternate strategy. This was made eminently clear this week in a decision which will be a turning point in our relations with the media and, hence, the country. After a three-month gestation, we finally submitted, with extraordinary trepidation, a media *strategy* to the PM. On Friday, Trudeau remarked that one of its ideas, a weekly press conference, might be okay. It might at least pattern in some way his media activities, as well as serve as a trade-off for being left alone by the press pack in the corridors (the infamous "scrums").

But, instead of jumping decisively on the breakthrough and throwing it back as a developed proposal to the PM, we pondered, talked, second guessed, and worried about how the PM might react or behave. What could have been a turning point became instead a group trauma – certainly not group therapy! But we did manage to put this part of the proposal into effect. Ad-hoc corridor encounters between the PM and the press, the "scrums," are to be replaced by weekly press conferences. So, a situation of growing mutual disrespect between the media and the PM is to be resolved – not because of the intervention of press officers through their positions of competence and trust, but because of a sweeping trade-off – by the PM in effect saying, "You leave me alone and I'll see you once a week on my terms."

This represents a misunderstanding of the role of that sector of the Gallery with which I most closely identify, the "actuality" media – radio and TV. Scrambling, superficial, sometimes lazy, even inarticulate, they serve directly the vast majority of the public who are seized by the moment and its personalities, not by the trends in national life and the complexities of exercising leadership. As we used to say at the CRTC, those reporters who simply amplify the most sensational thing they see or hear are more part of society's problems than of their solutions.

In any case, the PM's deep despair and distaste at the Toronto lunch last month with media leaders, where "heavies" lectured him and showed basic impoliteness (among many other things that could be said), and his outburst of bile in front of Dick last week make me wonder if this office with this PM can exercise any instrumental function at all!

I dream about it. We are on a rack and it hurts, and I am wasting what expertise I have. It's a lonely job where every small moment of credibility, trust, or useful exchange with the media happens against a full background of neglect, misunderstanding, and appallingly self-serving leadership in the office. An example: everyone senior to Press Secretary Jean Charpentier covered themselves and preserved their freedom of action by making him sign the letter to the Press Gallery that announced the end of "scrums" and the institution of weekly news conferences. Charpentier was not involved in this decision and, in fact, disagreed with it. But this is normal PMO practice – find a "goat" to deliver the bad news.

I am at the moment only a peripheral player. I have to admit I am flattered at being patronized by such as the PM's executive assistant, Bob Murdoch, and delighted at being treated as a pleasant neophyte by veteran journalists such as Hugh Winsor and the dean himself, Richard Gwyn.

As a parentheses, Gwyn's "Decline and Fall of the Trudeau Empire" in the November 27 *Canadian* was seen as a journalistic milestone. I found it simplistic and tendentious. Also, as Gwyn confided to Ralph Coleman shortly after, the book from which this was an early excerpt was entirely premised on a defeat in the next election. Needless to say, it would not be published if Trudeau won!* Such is the state of contemporary Canadian political letters.

On a completely different level, we are driven by a new and perhaps fatal abstraction from the mind of the Prime Minister – that Quebecers should somehow feel at home in all of the Canada their ancestors explored and opened to commerce and religion. Perhaps we have all forgotten the importance of simply taking people as they are and working from there and of backing away a bit from the ideal.

We may have to back off. For there is a gut-wrenching reality for English Canadians to confront once and for all, namely a self-confident people in Quebec. "Phone me when you know who *you* are," Quebec nationalist and TV personality Lise Payette acridly tells a somewhat plaintive and uncomfortable Peter Gzowski on his first late-night Johnny Carson TV imitation, "90 Minutes Live." This showed up for all time our puny liberalism – we WASPs who think we are "nice." Do we have a matching conviction about the value of Canada and federalism? Do we have that level of self-knowledge? I doubt it; and as Gzowski looked crestfallen, I felt it.

I remember feeling the same lack of conviction as I worked out speech lines for Juneau at the CRTC. For me the speeches were academic. But Juneau had the conviction. Did I believe Northrop Frye's dictums about the regional roots of unity and identity and the strength of the pluralistic cultural experience? Did I think they had much emotional valence with the majority of my white *anglais* friends? I didn't. But those from Quebec leading the country have clear convictions on these questions and are moving on and out.

* Trudeau lost, but won again in February 1980 before Gwyn put his book, *The Northern Magus*, finally to bed later in 1980.

42

The Federal-Provincial First Ministers' Conference – the first one with Lévesque – is now over. As is usual at the opening of these conferences, there was a photo session in the middle of the horse-shoe table in the Conference Centre at which the premiers, the PM, and aides sit. The photographers and reporters crowded in, asking questions, doing catch-as-catch-can interviews. The PM banged his gavel, signalling that the meeting was to start in closed session. Sean Moore, the Conference Centre's unflappable media officer, and I had the unenviable job of clearing the room of media.

But this time a few of them sat down on the floor and refused to be moved. They staged a sit-in for an open conference! Marjorie Nichols from the *Vancouver Sun* and Charles Lynch of Southam were amongst the more celebrated Gallery members in on this act of civil disobedience on behalf of the Canadian public and freedom of information. Amazingly, the Conference backed down – partly. They performed some *pro forma* speechmaking for the press and cameras, then retired to an upstairs room for the real bargaining.

There was something vaguely demeaning about seeing Lynch squatting in front of the rolling cameras and refusing to move when the conference went into closed session. But it was a great moment for him, I suppose. While the "protest" had all the theatrics of a demonstration for a critical, life and death cause, the substance of the issue was hardly at that level.

The PM gave an amazing press-conference performance. He was obviously in command. Lévesque, despite disgusting and amorous advances, not just from the French press, but from some civil servants who should know better, will come out as the self-serving irritant he is. The other premiers referred to Lévesque as the "new boy" at the photo session. He was pushed so hard at the PM's dinner for the premiers last night at 24 Sussex that he finally said there was only one thing he wanted for Quebec, and that was *out.*

This notion doesn't fit in at all with the new idea of "negotiated federalism." It scares the other nine and makes the *front commun* seem a selfish expedient for Quebec. But, can Quebecers afford to be taken right out of where the action is?

The thought of the PM sitting silent through the heated dinner discussion I find bemusing. Goodness, he does hold the cards, and he knows it. These premiers are good politicians, good bargainers. They know the game. Like MPs, they haggle for goodies to bring home to their constituents. By definition they can't ever be really satisfied. Yet Bill Bennett, the best businessman of all, having saved face by his public bitching about the conference agreement, rushed to the PM secretly afterwards to say okay to the deal. Trudeau at least was *honest* about the real bargaining.

The Weekly News Conference

December 19, 1976

Sunday night. A warm visit at friends, and the solid beauty of a festival of lessons and carols at the Cathedral makes it difficult to look back on the week of anxiety, foolish games, and blatant self interest.

Briefly, I've had my worst experience to date with the PM. His New Year's message taping was a screw-up from beginning to end. I had booked the wrong day! I was master of ceremonies as sweaty aides rushed to perform the cover-up and to get him out of his bad mood. But, I felt curiously detached. I found it hard to identify this temperamental performer as the Prime Minister. He was worrying he had not had time to wash his hair, that he couldn't read the prompter, that the English text was difficult. Dick was beside himself and listed all the misfortunes of the day in a huge memo for posterity. There, it's out of *my* hair, was the memo's real message. Bob Murdoch, to his credit, takes these things in his stride. He is a remarkable individual for all his fussing. With the PM, he's cool as ice.

The next day we faced the fall-out of our ill-advised note to Charles Lynch on weekly press conferences. It provoked as much childish, self-serving breast-beating from activist Gallery members as I ever hope to see. Dick's equivocations were almost as good a show. The press's promotion of some sort of democratic right to ask the PM questions whenever they want turns any theory or practice of delegatory democracy upside down. I do fear for the games of brinkmanship played by some in the Gallery. They want to force issues with no other mandate than one of the numer-

44

ous platforms our overloaded information system provides. This is a long discussion.

I still cultivate the hope that the more civilized circumstances of weekly news conferences will build some lines of mutual respect between the office and the media; that, over time, the PM will realize that the press is not a lump of aggressive faces, lenses, and microphones, but a human collective that includes those with whom dialogue and exchange can be engaging and fruitful.

A long, frustrating experience on the front line faces me, however. I need patience, patience, patience. My life extends far beyond the borders of this deadly game. And if I can let the calm conviction and reflection from the other part of my life continue to suffuse my job, instead of the other way around, then I will be able to contribute. Perhaps this is part of the PM's genius. I've certainly seen signs of it.

One footnote: this week, the French-language network of the CBC, Radio-Canada, which for years has been seen to harbour separatist feelings, has started to describe Ottawa's actions as emanating from "l'état central." Such nuances (suggesting that Ottawa is capital of the "central state" and foreign to Quebecers) drives the federalist Quebecers in this town crazy.

End-of-Year Interviews

December 26, 1976

Christmas has come and gone, marked by one of those clever breaks between public and private life for which Mr. Trudeau is so celebrated and suspected. Secrecy surrounds his holiday plans. It would seem that only he knows, so tight-lipped are those who do. Security. Well, on Friday one of his Mounties asked *me* if I knew whether the PM was going to Midnight Mass! At Thursday's first news conference, he had to be reminded to wish the assembled gang "Merry Christmas." Clearly, this season belongs to him, *not* to the public.

This week, Trudeau psyched up for two remarkable television performances. Both play tonight. Bob Murdoch told me that before the Bruce Phillips interview on CTV the PM was alone, pacing in his office, for over half an hour. In response to Phillips's persistent questioning, it was an effort of will for him to patiently ring the changes of his classic approach to federalism in the face of the PQ victory. He was straight, however. The public hadn't taken his "prescription" on how Quebecers needed to be treated to feel at home in Canada seriously before, and he wasn't going to leave any room for doubt this time, even if it was the same old "prescription."

To take a brief, unofficial stab at interpreting the impact of Trudeau's year-end interviews: first I'd say that no public leader uses the word "clobber," as the PM did to describe what had to be done to Lévesque's PQ, without attracting a sizeable amount of attention. Second, there were his warnings of the possibility of civil war. This was too strong for any but the *Toronto Sun*. Only in the U.S. was this the uniform press lead – anything more subtle we can only assume they wouldn't understand.

There was not much punditry or interpretation by the press. The real gravity of the situation weighs lightly on the well-padded Canadian breast. Only the francophones actually compare and analyse self-inflicted wounds.

His excursion to CFVO in Hull for the TVA (the largest private TV network in Quebec) taping of his French year-ender had an entirely different atmosphere, even though the message was similar in many respects. Jean Bédard and his boss, Monsieur Lapointe, were both respectful, worried in a gut way Phillips could never show. Trudeau used every debating trick to dismantle the separatist argument. Too bad this was the week Lévesque expunged the word separatist from PQ usage. But the PM's arguments do not change. He even trotted out one he'd used on Quebec militants at the first post-election pep talk – the "infinite divisibility" one. (If Quebec can separate from Canada, why can't the English part of Montreal separate from Quebec, and so on.)

The arguments were rational, empirical, and well delivered. He sat on the edge of his seat, using characteristic gestures – open hands inward to lapels (thumping his body mike). But, the arguments don't touch those whose deepest longings have been touched by the promise of self-fulfilment and absolute control of their own destiny. It is a dream, of course – perhaps the same kind of dream that makes Quebecers the heaviest investors in lottery tickets.

Trudeau disparages these deep aspirations, confusing them with his own and those of his colleagues who, because of privilege and sophistication, can find rewards on the larger Canadian stage. This privilege is given to few, and so when he talks about the whole of Canada as a "home," in the sense of the geography one's ambition can encompass, whether in business, government, the arts, or what have you, he speaks outside the legitimate aspiration of all but a select few.

Meanwhile, I have some grounds to suspect that deals are being made. If, as he said, the separatists have to be "clobbered" provincially, the rebirth of the provincial Liberals can hardly be left to chance. Drapeau saw Trudeau secretly on Friday. God help us if federalism requires his support at the price of Montreal's onerous share of the Olympic deficit!

January 5, 1977

This is a quiet week. We'll have to start planning some rudimentary strategy to quiet the somewhat childish criticism of our first press conference. It all looked too pat. It is a lot to expect journalists to ask topical aggressive questions of the scrum kind in the atmosphere of punditry that pervades the weekly prime ministerial news conference.

Geoffrey Stevens (*Globe and Mail*) suggested today that the PM is just another politician and somehow shouldn't get front-page/lead-item treatment just because he answers questions at a news conference. This is the heart of the press/PM dilemma. It's manifest in Ken Colby's well-remembered anxiety when threatened with missing part of the New Brunswick trip after the Chinook broke down. He called this absolute necessity to be glued to every public act of the PM the "death watch."

No breast-beating by Stevens or the *Globe* is going to change the fact that this man is, one, the Prime Minister, two, a star in his own right in a country that has few national heroes in any true sense of the word, three, that he chooses to fight on the big issues and, four, that his views on federalism will remain the most personal and articulated of any public man.

This rationale aside, I must admit that the end of the daily press exposure of a beleaguered PM, warts and all, was a political decision backed, I suspect, fully by Coutts. When Coutts speaks, as

47

he did recently at a "Programme Committee" meeting, of emphasizing TV, he means controlling the media, particularly TV, and there is no doubt of that.

The Syd Bibby offer that Senator Keith Davey promoted of open TV air time on CHCH Hamilton may be accepted as a political necessity with little thought of the backlash.

This is the Davey/Coutts/Kenny dream. But it lacks thought – and here I buy the Charles Lynch/Terry Hargreaves (CBC) argument that some of the PM's best lines come from "scrums": that a political figure is legitimately tested in challenge, response, the working out of policies, to quote Trudeau himself, in the "marketplace of ideas." However imperfect the press, their interaction on a more regular basis with the PM does represent one facet of that marketplace.

January 8, 1977

Here I am, alone on a Saturday night, laden with the half-resolves that must be the sickness of my generation. Half not smoking, half hung up on my family, half convinced of what I'm doing in life. I don't feel comfortable among the true believers; yet, I am absorbing their belief. I am, at the moment at least, a container, a sponge; not a formed piece exacting loyalty or respect for my opinions. It's so easy today to be half involved in a lot of things.

I have a Toronto TV-producer friend who is the epitome of a generation that indulges the best this fantastic consumer age has to offer with apparently little real strength or commitment. His only real commitment beyond family is to that very careful and civilized indulgence which makes and defines his life. Searching for oneself is a luxury of the post-war generation.

An Ottawa friend admits proudly that the life of the floating bureaucrat suits him, characterized tellingly by the ability to have three drinks at noon and not worry about the effect on the afternoon. Now, we both admitted last night, we can't have those three. But not because of any decision that the afternoon's work is too important, simply because a far more exacting routine has been imposed on us. Such are the demanding half-realities of political existence.

Today was of a sparkling white purity – enough to make mortals fear their transience and insignificance. Yet, with terrible logic, on Monday I'll again be behind opaque venetian blinds at the office, fretting my dream life into actuality. Unable, almost, as Pierre Billon (an aide to Gérard Pelletier) so eloquently articulated at lunch on Friday, to impose form on that which really concerns us.

"Do you have access to Trudeau?" Billon asks me, arriving twenty minutes late for lunch. It takes me forty-five minutes to find out why he asks. Poor Billon. The insane manner of executing institutional bilingualism in the federal civil service is his cross of sorts. He gave me the headline that must *never* appear – one million a head for the 350 who got through language school training and were successful enough to use their newly acquired language skill!

Trudeau has not been told the truth. I hear him tell his franco-compatriots on his year-end TV interview that French units exist. They don't. Designated, yes, but not instituted. If only things were as good as the Bibeau report painted them. Chrétien is the unwitting vehicle for the lies of his deputy minister. Bilingualism in the federal civil service, a keystone of Trudeau federalism, is crumbling sandstone.

Sure, I'm naive, but because the lines I am using to defend the PM's views on the federalist response to Quebec dissatisfaction are so fragile, I'm left only with admiration for the endless flexibility of political morality.

Last night, I talked with a friend who works in Clark's office. He was eloquent on the human comedy of high places. The Gallup poll was widely and deeply dreaded in Clark's office. That it showed a turnaround in PC support hyped the mood radically. Bill Neville delivered an inspirational sermon to the staff (he smokes heavily), then returned to a discussion of monumental triviality on some lost missive that was to have gone out to riding associates. "What are we doing right?" he asked.

And in our office, the disembodied voices on the intercom, the clipped exchanges, the pacings, the beads of sweat on Dick's brow as he asks some unseen spirit, "How do *I* know what the public thinks." Perhaps the mysteries of the public's fickle perceptions protect us all in some way from being too enamoured of our role in directing grand affairs.

It's clear to me that, in the act of constructing sentences, some order can be built. This is true for me at any rate. Much else is temporal and centrifugal. Thoughts can be linked convincingly enough to further pattern a further reality. I see this effect every day. Images (TV images particularly) may have a cumulative effect, but they are only consistently effective and noticeable if they are purposefully arranged over a period of time; in other words, if they are "propaganda." The individual sentences and slogans by which we receive and store complex events–"French in the air is unsafe," "government is wasteful and inefficient," "Joe Clark has no policies," "Trudeau is arrogant," "business initiative is killed by government," and so on–are the simple frameworks of ideas.

But, I have to believe also in long-range, dedicated, consistent effort–in the "work" as my old boss at the CRTC, André Martin, would say. Quebec Minister Claude Morin's ten-year campaign to prove the futility of negotiated confederation and Pierre Trudeau's equally lengthy perspective on nationalism and federalism are examples. These "works" are structured through language that proceeds from elaborate argument and logic, not just experienced like an arrow in the stomach.

Jean Charpentier came up with a good line the other day while explaining to me why he quit Radio-Canada and came to the PMO. "I did not think it was possible to grow old gracefully as a television journalist." How difficult to grow old gracefully unless one has had something of universal value to say – publicly.

January 15, 1977

The holiday is over. We are back in the thick of media negotiations, a bizarre exercise in inverse logic with the Prime Minister which invariably leaves us gasping and confused. This master logician won't be told in the same memo that there is danger of media overexposure on the "unity" question and then be encouraged to do two interviews in French. He took delight in using this internal contradiction to make our request look foolish. I shudder at the demand for clarity, precision, and logic he places on softer minds.

This week trivial housekeeping (literally) assumed inflated importance. This involved the life and times of the PM's household, supposedly a story not to be reported, and certainly not promoted if we are to believe the PM's well-publicized views on keeping private and public lives separate.

Nevertheless, since I first met Margaret Trudeau and advised her on some press or TV appearances which might feature her Japanese cooking and photographs, I've sensed there is ambivalence as far as Mrs. Trudeau is concerned. Clearly she wants a public life and role.

The incident last week involved a want ad she placed in a number of papers for a live-in babysitter. I fenced with the press on this somewhat ill-considered placing of 24 Sussex's household agenda on the public record, and continued to deal with persistent rumours of her pregnancy. I find it all distasteful. The press's interest reminds me all too clearly of the public's morbid appetites rather than of its intellectual curiosity.

It's amazing that so few recent leaders have succumbed to this easy path to the hearts and minds of the mass-media consumers. At any rate, I couldn't believe myself on the phone with reporters spinning positive reasons for Margaret's placement of lengthy ads in four papers. Marie-Hélène Fox added piquancy to the *reductio ad absurdum* of the affair Friday afternoon by squealing over the intercom to look out the window because we'd see Margaret on the way down!

Wednesday we held a sobering meeting on the Quebec speech (important because it is the PM's first foray into Quebec since the PQ election) with the francophones. The meeting was made more difficult than usual because of Jean LeMoyne's serious illness. It was strategy at its cold-blooded best. But at least there were signs of a reassuring reluctance to gutter fight with Lévesque at this stage.

Trudeau won't stand on a patriotic platform. He has said that it is too easy to stand in front of an audience and get the easy cheer with – "We are Canadians. . . ." He does not feel comfortable with the patriotic appeal. On a more profound level, he may not even understand its content. Patriotic nationalism is English and Tory – it has atrophied, granted, and as a residual sentiment it is totally foreign to the present francophone leadership.

The PM and those in the PMO like Jean LeMoyne, Rémi Bujold, and Gilles Dufault are now "fédéralistes" (almost a swearword – it was eventually made one and came out "fédéraste" like pederast). In a new and painful way they are cut off decisively from the mainstream of thought in their home province.

Gilles Dufault is convinced that our strongest argument against independence is economic. Yet both he and Rémi Bujold, in a somewhat impassioned exposition, told of the bitterness among the average Quebecer over English domination. Jean Charpentier, of course, pleads for his fellow francophones outside Quebec. Meanwhile, the PM is already working on his Quebec speech which will be a direct call to the members of the Chambre de Commerce to analyse federalism. I often wonder why, at this level, advisers bother–there is seemingly very little room in which to contribute on *his* issues.

Not that the enemy's weaker flanks have escaped analysis. The francophones in the office gloated over Lévesque's expected inability to pay for promised programs and over his intellectual dishonesty. In an interview in Mexico during his holiday, Lévesque announced that Quebec could be independent in three or four years, appealed to Mexico's example of economic and cultural survival, and then went, as a good provincial leader, to New York for cash!

Last night I went to an establishment dinner party at Gerry Robinson's (National Director of the Liberal party) coldly elegant Rockcliffe house. The party was a bit tense, I thought, everything a bit too refined for young power-fringers. But this is the success package for a man I can't help feeling is stretching himself to fill the key position he holds in a beleaguered party. Poor Gerry, he has so many bosses to report to, and, worse, their attentions to the party's problems are rare indeed.

John and Susan Hylton, friends from CRTC days when he was legal counsel (he's now a CRTC commissioner), were there. Funny to think that Pierre Juneau put us both where we are, with titles we wouldn't have dreamt of having in our Toronto incarnations. I openly share John's worries about a possible change of government, but underneath I was more worried by the lack of conviction in all that Liberal *bonhomie*.

In the office, we are one step closer to getting a better handle on what the media are really saying and doing. We'll soon have a professionally designed and operated monitoring service. I have largely worked out a system with another CRTC Research Branch graduate, Allan Fraser. We both want, more than anything else, to put the almost tactile messages of the electronic media into their proper place in our daily consideration. The new daily report, "Mediaday," will start with the summaries of the previous evening's television news and the morning radio. This is where the ballads of our age are written.

It's amazing how the electronic flow of news has continued without the daily prime ministerial input since the end of "scrums." In a way, that's the beauty of our modern newsgathering machinery. Only the pundits would comment on the PM's relative absence. No news is no food for the airwaves: the volume remains the same. There in no blank space in radio or TV newscasts where a prime ministerial "actuality" should be. Only the pundits are slowly starving!

January 29, 1977

The highlight of the week was the PM's big Quebec speech – his attempt to win the hearts and minds of Quebecers in the heart of enemy territory. The PM is on the offensive for the first time since November 15. He has the initiative in the great unity debate – he's upstaged Lévesque. Even Radio-Canada, in its commentary last night by the editor of *Montreal-Matin*, admits it. Gilbert Bringué and Paul Racine (Radio-Canada radio and TV) are shaken. This man can still deliver an emotional wallop. You could feel the tension in the Langevin Building all week.

The Quebec City trip didn't auger well a week ago. The PMO professionals were being circumvented by Lalonde, Ouellet, and who knows what other advisers. Speech writers like Moore and LeMoyne were being coldly ignored. Trudeau was fueling up on his own at private lunches. Wednesday was cleared of all his appointments. Yet he's produced no text, not even any notes. Finance was asked for notes. André Juneau told me that handwritten notes had been seen with blanks, "chiffres," for this or that. One prime ministerial head is inventing the whole thing.

Tuesday was Lévesque's night at the Economic Club in New York. He told the Americans that an independent Quebec is inevitable – "as natural and irreversible as growth itself" – and reassured them that it's not a radical socialist nation a-building, just a johnny-come-lately version of the thirteen colonies throwing off the last traces of foreign dominance. Nobody knows if it worked. Uncertainty is still the only certainty. The PM took off from there with the kind of logically orchestrated appeal few national leaders today can make.

There was the PM, finally delivering his speech in the Château Frontenac in Quebec City, flattened against the wall, no notes, only his watch curled in the palm of his hand, his eyes never leaving his audience of burghers. He was personal. He used every trick he knew – anecdote, indirect quote, satire, hyperbole, and the absurd (his best weapon).

The text itself was circular, laden with unfinished sentences. (I helped translate it late into last night and today.) It won't survive, but the moment will. Even if, as I suspect, he sees the "identity" of Quebec (whatever he means by that in the bilingual recesses of his mind) as somehow more linked to its place in Canada than to its self-actualization within its own borders.

This makes a nice analogy with his own life – one easy to express personally. It's easy to appreciate rationally the rectitude of this approach. It will work for that part of the post-war bulge in Quebec who are making it in the normal North American way. Unfortunately, a lot of that bulge has rejected that normal way and would spit in the faces of their contemporaries who have joined Bell Canada or gone to Alberta where the money is. I don't know who is right.

The Langevin Building was wonderfully silent on Friday, speech day. Its halls echoed faintly with Trudeau's television voice. Jean was so relieved when half a dozen reporters sought him out "unsolicited" to tell him it was Trudeau's best speech ever.

Tonight on TV the Opposition rails, knowing in their guts that they aren't even on the stage where the two stars are fighting it out. Everybody loves it. The real argument is academic to most, so why not sit back and watch the fight? This is the best all-Canadian-content show since the October crisis of 1970. Broadbent even screamed that Canada's future was being reduced to the whims of two personalities. Precisely. Clark is caught blaming Trudeau for separatism. Will anybody buy that now?

On it goes. The office is mainly on the chickenshit circuit. Ralph and I amuse ourselves in our adjoining offices shouting "chickenshit" everytime we get a call that qualifies: "Can we interview the new nanny?" "When will such-and-such appointment be made?"

Trying To Make News

February 6, 1977

How strange the media are about their own trade. They take words at face value if it suits the occasion even when they don't believe them. I was struck this week by the very activist role of certain news outlets – the very deliberate editorial role played even in the basic act of newsgathering and reporting, and the search for prominence for the resulting story.

A week ago the Extraparliamentary Opposition List hit the headlines.* Its existence was not known until now. I have to admire the tenacity of the press in smoking out the story. I was shocked to see an actual copy of the list – I knew lots of names on it! But it is like exegesis; you have to have lived the fears of the time to understand why government felt it needed this kind of information.

At the first news conference after the list was out, the PM had things to say about the New Left at the time the list was made. His remarks did not quell the fever of indignation the story had generated. In truth, nobody on the list had suffered. I brought this to the attention of a couple CBC guys: no response. News is often moral and ethical.

Thursday, Trudeau thoughtlessly shrugged off any suggestion in the House that people with police files should be able to see them and clear their names. He said it was logically absurd – after all, there may be "thousands, millions of them." I groaned as he said this. Would it be a story on its own? Not quite. John King (*Globe and Mail*) asked Trudeau if he knew of the U.S. Freedom of Information Act which permits just what Trudeau was dismissing. He did not, and his reply was somewhat flip to boot. King snapped his notebook shut and walked out of the news conference, the story virtually written. He made the *Globe and Mail* front page on Friday.

One could argue that King's piece was hardly a news story. It was more of a paste-up which fitted a journalistic mood and, because freedom of information is the pre-eminent press story, it gained front-page prominence.

---

* This so-called "blacklist" named a host of members of left-wing organizations in the late sixties and early seventies and was compiled by the RCMP for Jean-Pierre Goyer when Solicitor General. It was distributed to Cabinet.

The only antidote in the business is to pump out solid news with all the ardour and passion that the Opposition pumps out the bad, the innuendo, the bile. We tried just that on Tuesday with the signing of the Memorandum of Understanding on Maritime Offshores Resources. We tried to set up the Commonwealth Room in the Centre Block like a reception room in the Elysée Palace. It did look good. As anticipated, the press wanted to know why Quebec and Newfoundland weren't there, not why the other three provinces were! Trudeau was not very well briefed and not amused. The story did get some play, but one can't help having some sympathy with the PM when he says that you are damned if you do, damned if you don't.

My, we are in a hypersensitive period. The Queen's Jubilee and the attendant symbolic recognition of the event caused friction – and gave the media another good story! "God Save the Queen" and "O Canada!" were sung in the Chambers, and a couple of Quebec MPs remained glued to their seats. It made the *Globe and Mail* front page the next day. The fact that several members of the Press Gallery behaved the same way was not reported. Then yesterday, Prince Andrew was off to Harrington Lake to visit the PM. Should the PM have pictures taken with him? The implications of this for the Quebec press were actually the subject of some discussion with the Quebecers down the hall – happily in the end it was seen to be okay.

Thoughts on Power

February 13, 1977

This week embodied all that is schizophrenic in the Prime Minister's office and my involvement in it. It showed that the greatest single problem for those who have power is to remain humane and deeply motivated. A number of incidents illustrated to me the collision of the ambitions and the value structures the PM's power edifice is built on – largely, I still like to think, despite itself.

Perhaps the most striking incident was the candid admission from one of the RCMP security officers we work with that he was the chief investigator behind the infamous Extraparliamentary Opposition (EPO) "Blacklist." We were driving back from an advance to the Niagara Peninsula, and just coming off the Burlington Skyway, when out this pops from the officer in the front seat. I was thunderstruck. The stuff of our moral anxiety, and the press's moral outrage for the past weeks had been this man's assigned *work*! Of course he had nothing but confidence in the relevance and accuracy of that investigation. In fact, with not a little bit of vanity, he allowed that poor old Frank Oberle, the Opposition hit man on this, was slightly off track. Later, to satisfy my direct curiosity about his present work, he simply said, "right wing." What can I say!

Of course he is only a foot soldier; but, along with an army of other blinkered young men, he is responsible for the PM's physical security when travelling. Had he become at all friendly with the man after nearly ten years of this? "Oh no, it's not my place!"

Had I not been exposed to the PM's own staff advance people in action during the past two days, I might have taken this exposure to the values of the force more calmly. But, loosed on hotel personnel, party workers, and other instrumental types, these PMO heavies display all the same blind singlemindedness of their badge- and gun-toting buddies.

I hasten to add that I like them. Colin Kenny has been particularly supportive of my green self from the beginning. But their motivations bother me, as does the careful wrapping they provide the PM which threatens to reduce his personal imprint on events to small proportions indeed.

Late Thursday night in Toronto, safe from politicos in the home of my rock critic friend, Ritchie Yorke, I thought I had it worked out – visually at least. We were talking about Pierre Juneau's painful attempt to be elected in Hochelaga.

I had spent two days doing political work in Juneau's office helping design his campaign (read, public strait-jacket) and I realized how little room for expression a real personality has in politics; how victimized he can be by willful political advisers whose values may be totally different, even opposed, but who can get things done!

My visual image is of layers, or of a funnel. The politician is the container, or is buried beneath layers of outer goop. Only those with the most solid character core, like Trudeau, survive to provide any leadership at all. What makes the rest tick? What does motivate the spear carriers? I was haunted by this question. Is it just being in the magic aura of power – is that all? We get off on it, alone, on the road. "We are from the PMO." "Yes sir!"

But that zeal is minor. It is no more than a sort of paramilitary dedication. Is it really possible to find that sort of thin-lipped loyalty in my or the post-war generation? Apparently it is. Power is so fragile, so hard to put one's hand on in this office, why is it so important?

Brian Flemming, the political adviser for the Atlantic region in the PMO, appears attractive, up, open. But there is no mistaking: he wants to be elected and to be a Cabinet minister. Although he serves well, he has another agenda in the PMO. His ambition requires vanity; a desire to be talked about. A crew from Atlantic Television waits in his outer office to film another item about the Halifax native in the PMO.

Who are you Patrick Gossage, and how can you help me? Well, according to Colin Kenny, I am a "breath of fresh air" – then I get the diatribe about those who don't wear "boots," who don't feel a military dedication to the boss. Oh dear! I wonder about the ambitions of the old regime as much as about the new: Clark's slick athletes awaiting their turn at the Canadian olympics of power!

Maple One in Toronto

February 19, 1977

Maple One in Toronto. I was tremendously amused yesterday by my discovery on following the PM's limousine into Ottawa from the airport in the police car, that the code word used for the PM in Ottawa is "Maple One." It is such a fitting symbol for the man/office as object/property, and it provides marvellous insight into the real organizational principles of the trip to Toronto and Niagara I've just experienced. This now becomes the story of Maple One and the search for excellence.

Maple One found Torontonians unusually ready to listen. They were even conscience stricken by the thought that their friends in Quebec might choose to leave Canada. They were ready to be told by the PM of their negligence of French-Canadian realities. Lots of evidence of what Ritchie Yorke calls "late flowering nationalists." Everywhere Trudeau went – high school sessions, a giant ethnic worship service – all applauded his ten-year-old insights.

I am beginning to think something is happening, attitudes are shifting. The young are by nature fair and open, and perhaps find any role in being more "understanding" appealing. Businessmen, such as those gathered at a banquet at the National Club organized by Peter Newman where CEOs pleaded with the PM to "please be our saviour," want at once a prophet and mediator. At last they see the possibility that Quebec's aspirations might constrain profit, and they want the PM to do something about it!

On the way back in the Jetstar, an amazingly jolly PM mused in French about the dinner with Toronto's corporate elite. He said flatly he was not prepared to be their saviour. Colin Kenny, a day later, bemoaned Trudeau's tendency to ignore those who come asking for help. I hardly think he is indifferent to real need, but corporate crybabies certainly came to the door for a loaf and got a stone!

As for the Liberal establishment, my first real exposure to its Toronto core was at the remarkably electric retirement dinner for Mitchell Sharp. They are seeing their world fall apart and it hurts. They have had only fifteen years of warning since the Quiet Revolution that their hegemony was going to have to be shared, plus nine years of the PM telling them bluntly, if humorously, about "French Power"! Now he is saying, "move over and make more room in Ottawa."

The easy power bonds of Liberal back slapping that we saw at the Sharp dinner are becoming less important. As Chrétien said, in a somewhat embarrassing token performance there, "Everyone says bonjour now!"

Lévesque is saying Trudeau no longer represents Quebec, if he ever did. It hurts the Liberal establishment. Quebec used to be "delivered" to the federal Liberals. Now nothing is sure.

Thursday night I found myself in a late-night truth session with the PMO "boys." It was quite a performance: cutting up past colleagues; Colin saying how impossible it was to make friends in politics; gossiping about Trudeau when he was single (the famous Barbra Streisand date engineered by Vic Chapman) – political locker room talk.

Then at 4 a.m. or so, Allan Ferguson from the *Toronto Star* called. Did I have any booze? – of course. The Royal York always leaves a complimentary bottle for PMO staffers. He arrives with three buddies on their last legs. I made it through all this. I coped even with the hooker we caught on the PMO's sixteenth floor plunging towards the Royal Suite. We managed to divert her by calling her in through our open door. Scant hours later, Trudeau and Bill Davis were having an elegant breakfast just yards away.

On Thursday night at the Sheraton Centre we attended a huge reception for ethnic Canadians, the brainchild of Johnny Lombardi. Thousands and thousands of invitations were distributed inviting mobs to hear the PM. Rivers of humanity rolled into the Grand Ballroom to hear Trudeau. Nearly every non-WASP Canadian that ever drew breath in Toronto was there clutching an invitation.

I felt conscience-bound in the name of public safety to dam the river and relieve the crush, if only temporarily. Patrick Gossage, crowd control! What next? This is not done, I am told, by those more expert than I. A quick assessment of the crowded hall, of the bars open, but for little business, reassured me. Three thousand people waited patiently and silently, jammed against the stage. They were quiet, disciplined; no hassling. I'll never forget that hush. This was reverence indeed for Maple One as object/office.

Later, a member of the U. of T.'s radical intelligentsia heckled the PM in mid-speech. But he blew the chance of a lifetime to whip the crowd into an anti-racist frenzy. He was greeted only by polite boos. This was the new Canada. Trudeau told them about *two* languages. They applauded. Oh for more thousands so ready to accept the didactic PM!

Today the PM is in Washington for his visit to President Carter. I am not. I am among those spurned who have to watch his speech to Congress on TV. We listen hushed as he lifts the overwritten text off the page.

Washington Hype

February 27, 1977

This was Washington-hype week. The results were so positive that election rumours have started. The PM's Congress performance seems to have softened even the hardest-hearted senators. To top it off, CTV's Bruce Phillips was able to cajole President Carter in a TV interview into admitting that he personally would prefer a united Canada! What a boost. Take that, Lévesque!

The PM appeared to be in a great mood throughout. Even the fact that the trip had included hangers-on like Jean Drapeau hardly moved a critical press pen. Margaret and Mrs. Carter chewed over their abiding interest in mental health issues.

Everyone was flushed with excitement, and the coverage showed it. Only old Dalton Camp threw a few dew drops of cold water on it, days later. The fact that the trip rated only a social page item in Washington was defended by O'Hagan. These "grosses langues" (big tongues), as le Devoir's Lise Bissonnette labelled the Washington social columnists, are powerful journalistic figures.

Separatism and Radio-Canada

The Radio-Canada separatism affair, which escalated again this week, may have more far-reaching impact than the Washington hustle. The knife edge the PM has walked for weeks on this subject finally became so sharp that he couldn't balance on it anymore. On Friday, a decade's bitterness about Radio-Canada's Quebec nationalist leanings (leanings which, by the way, contributed greatly to making it such a force in Quebec's cultural and political renaissance) boiled to the surface.

At his news conference, the PM carefully avoided first-person accusations, but nevertheless endorsed his Cabinet colleague's right to snipe at Radio-Canada, and marked the separatist leanings of the majority of its newsmen as "common knowledge." Jean Charpentier and I found this hard to take, especially as we knew he had told his ministers to cool their anti-Radio-Canada ardour in Cabinet. This fact leaked in the morning, and we were happy to confirm it to other enquirers. But the damage was done – shooting the francophone news messengers could begin in earnest.

Yet I understand only too well the frustration of federal francophones who watch Radio-Canada treat their pronouncements with the vague detachment and slight disdain normally associated with reporting from small foreign capitals, while Quebec government announcements are piped out whole with breathless enthusiasm.

Gilles Gosselin, Radio-Canada's Toronto correspondent, simply says the views of the majority have to be represented. But federal attacks only increase the alienation of the francophone reporter from the main currents of Canadian life. I can see it. The immensely attractive Madeleine Poulin will not join CTV for more money and a bigger audience out of a loyalty anglos find difficult to understand.

There is little doubt that the CBC, the principal instrument Canadians have for understanding each other, is out of service. Nevertheless, overt political pressure, far from turning Radio-Canada around, will simply turn it more in on itself. Whatever the political allegiance of Radio-Canada newspeople, they are journalists, and I feel, with fading conviction admittedly, that what bias is on display now will eventually self-correct. Perhaps now, the fact that they have to defend their professionalism will reinforce some balance.

In any case, our job in the Press Office has been made that much more difficult. Another gap has opened between our knowledge of the media and the PM's daily responses to these alien messengers. What can we say to him?

Other than this, the week was full of the usual chickenshit, the fall-out from the Washington trip – how many favourable letters, phonecalls, and so on arrived after the speech to Congress. Lots did, it turns out. So, when Coutts calls to find out "how we did," we can all confidently say "just fine."

March 7, 1977

This has been freedom of the press week. The government has decided to investigate Radio-Canada newsgathering. On Friday we announced that we will lay the crescendo of accusations against Radio-Canada on the doorstep of the federal broadcast regulator, the CRTC, for investigation. Few events could have rocked me more.

So, insensitive attacks on a supposedly independent public information organization are to be probed by a public organization that has limited credibility! All my ingrained newsman's principles are offended. In the PMO, the press seems to be viewed as a passive instrument with little, if any, role in public affairs.

I am in the unenviable position of knowing all too well the media's shortcomings – particularly those of this Gallery. Yet I believe profoundly in the role of a free and inquiring press, however far its daily activities stray from that ideal. Of course, what galls those few in this PMO that would agree with me is that such a far-reaching decision affecting the press was taken without reference to the professional advice available in Cabinet and the Press Office.

O'Hagan returned impotent and downcast from a staff meeting in which de Montigny Marchand, an elegant number two or three to Pitfield in the Privy Council Office, and others hammered out the formula. Dick couldn't believe their indifference to his basic arguments about the dangers of the case. The Communications Committee of Cabinet, including Don Jamieson and Romeo LeBlanc, were not consulted at all.

Information about a serious Cabinet split on the issue was small comfort, as was the generally apathetic reporting of the event. Perhaps I should be satisfied that the Cabinet hawks will be somewhat muted, but I see other ambitions satisfied. Apparently CRTC Commissioner Roy Faibish wrote Trudeau proposing the solution adopted. Now all the displaced francos at the Commission can get back at a society's expression in which they no longer have a voice.

CRTC Chairman Harry Boyle was not personally consulted by Trudeau but was shown a letter by de Montigny. Great stuff, but who is dealing the cards?

Perhaps forces are being shaped that will affect all of us. Perhaps the mood of the fragile media messengers is a key element in the public's evolving perception of this government. Like the politicos, they know the public cares little about press "rights." But another credibility gap has opened between the press and the PM, and we will live with its subtle and no-so-subtle manifestations.

I will continue to argue that media love affairs with ideologies are short-lived and self-correcting, that the flow of images is beyond analysis, and that only their cumulative impact can be discussed.

Portrait Intime

On Monday, Alain Stanké (a friend, a Quebec TV personality, and a publisher) interviewed the PM for the TVA special on Trudeau. It is to be a "Portrait Intime" of the man and his family. Stanké was superb. He made the PM laugh and drew him out more than I thought the PM would allow. Trudeau came off as a self-contained man willing to say why under Alain's expert probing.

Two pieces are worth noting. First, Trudeau's unwillingness to admit to any warm, ongoing personal relations. Stanké pushed all the buttons – he mentioned Pelletier hoping to get a glimpse of the human being who likes old, comfortable relationships. But, no dice. Trudeau said such relationships are great when there is a shared working *cause*, but hard to maintain after.

Second, his dislike of parliament – the House at its normal worst, not the institution. On this he was simply descriptive. People shout, scream, and are insincere. It is noisy and you don't learn much. This came out of a discussion of how much he dislikes loud noise! Even his son Justin knows enough to turn down the car radio.

But the PM's genuine marvel at children came through. "Alors la vérité, la beauté, tout ça, ça me rejouit. Et on trouve cela chez un enfant, cette créativité, cet être qui se forme, qui se crée, qui apprend à vivre et je suis émerveillé de voir tout cela."*

This alone will make the documentary as memorable for the audience as it was for Alain and me. It proved to me that good research and respect for the man and his ideas are the essential ingredients for a good interview.

---

* Truth, beauty, these make me rejoice. And you find that in a child – that creativity, the being forming itself, learning to live. And I marvel to see all this.

64

This was how Trudeau's Centre Block office looked when Gossage joined the PMO in 1976. Here, Trudeau's executive assistant, Robert Murdoch, briefs him at the end of the day. (Page 20) (*Les Editions Internationales Alain Stanké*)

This is a more telling image of the PM's office – stark and somewhat foreboding when one entered for a meeting. (Page 20)   (*Mike Evans*)

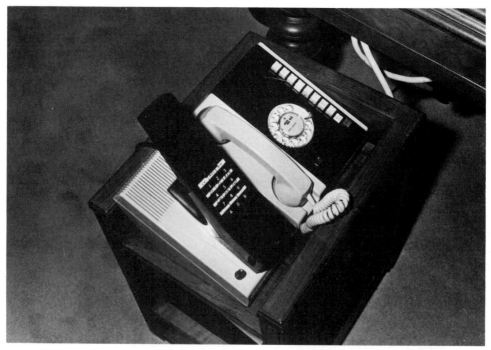

This was the PM's phone and intercom setup. (The intercom is on the left.) The PM used it with great effect. "Pierre Trudeau here" would come booming in and receive instant attention. (Page 21)   (*Les Editions Internationales Alain Stanké*)

Gossage often rode his bike to work in Ottawa. Here he is trying to run down the photographer. (Page 29) (*Fred Chartrand*)

Trudeau found Gossage's interventions on behalf of the press tolerable at best. Here, Gossage is trying to charm his boss into saying something to them following a federal-provincial conference. The position of Trudeau's shoulders conveys the impatience he undoubtedly expressed. (Page 43) (*Fred Chartrand*)

A photograph of the PM giving the press the finger during the 1978 Bonn summit was widely reproduced. Here, led by CBC reporter, Mark Phillips (second from left), and CTV's Peter Lloyd (far right), a group of reporters playfully gesture right back a couple of days after the incident. (Page 141) (*Fred Chartrand*)

Ted Johnson and Bill de Laat chat with Gossage on the ferry to Victoria during the 1979 election campaign. They were the young and relaxed duo who set up the PM's western events. Johnson later became Trudeau's executive assistant after the 1979 defeat turned into a 1980 election victory. (Page 164)

On the 1979 campaign plane, Marie-Hélène Fox and Gossage occupied the seats that marked the border between the PM and his staff in the front of the plane, and the press at the rear. (Page 169) Gossage is displaying the "broken wing" he suffered retrieving a Frisbee from the roof of a press bus. (Page 171) (*Rod MacIvor*)

TOP: The 1979 election campaign touched down in Ottawa every Saturday evening for a precious Sunday off before departing again Monday morning. One father and two sons fully enjoyed this homecoming on the tarmac beside the DC-9. (Page 173) (*Bob Anderson*)

TOP LEFT: Gossage listens as the defeat of the Liberals becomes obvious in the crowded ballroom of the Château Laurier on election night, May 22, 1979 – "Black Tuesday." (Page 167)

FAR LEFT: This is one of Trudeau's infamous "bags" – his nightly Calvary stuffed with the responsibilities of running a nation. The bag was an ever-present reminder for him at 24 Sussex, at Harrington Lake, in aircraft, and in cars that these burdens are removed only when you cease being Prime Minister. (Page 182) (*Les Editions Internationales Alain Stanké.*)

LEFT: Jim Coutts and Keith Davey ponder the sliding fortunes of the Liberal party during the 1979 campaign at one of the regular Sunday staff sessions. These meetings were supposed to instill a weekly dose of confidence in the staff on their one day a week off the road. (Page 173) (*Patrick Gossage*)

A pensive and beleaguered Leader of the Opposition waits for his driver in the days just prior to his November 22, 1979, resignation. Gossage's smile is wearing thin. (Page 185) (*Fred Chartrand*)

THREE

Topic "A"

*M*ost of my early months at the PMO were spent learning the ropes and trying to achieve some credibility
with a few of the press. Relations with the Gallery were in flux
because of the change in access to the PM, effected by the institution of weekly press conferences and the turmoil over Radio-
Canada's alleged separatism in its newsroom.

*Aside from rumours of Mrs. Trudeau's pregnancy, and her ear-
lier unsuccessful flirtation with public and TV appearances, the
PM's home front had provided little material for the press or problem for the office. Margaret Trudeau was known to us mainly
because she occasionally dropped into the office. We saw her, and
she was friendly. We knew she talked with some Press Gallery
members on a friendly basis, particularly Claude Hénault from
United Press. But this was seldom reported.*

Margaret Intervenes

March 16, 1977

My life, and the country's, has been upended by the worst kind
of pack journalism – not to put too fine a point on it. This was
Margaret's week. It started last weekend with her ill-thought-
out appearances at two Rolling Stones concerts in Toronto.

I've had to deal with a river of calls. I've had to invent a "policy" on Mrs. T. on the spot and without aid. The most senior PMOers washed their hands and covered their tails, at the expense of those on the front line, or so it seemed to us. It is hard to review a week of anxious, apologetic, or acid calls – hundreds of them. All of them wanted official confirmation of where and when, or some other amazingly personal aspect of the Trudeaus' life. I could not say a word, and became famous in the *Toronto Sun* and elsewhere for imaginative variations of "no comment."

It was a futile, frustrating game. I found it especially frustrating in dealing with British or German callers (they share a racy tabloid tradition, *au secours*!) who did not respect or know the cozy rules of the game which keep me safe and unquoted in Canada. I found that even inflections in my voice (a "*worried* aide confided") become fit material for the European wire services, which fed this information back in reprints that found their way into the Canadian papers with amazing speed.

The experience helped me sort out a lot of things. In particular, I sorted out the friends and professionals in the trade from the exploiters and vultures who fall on your every word. Has lust for personal knowledge of the great become the only common currency, the real edge of competition, which worries even the mighty *Toronto Star*, the esteemed *Globe and Mail*?

Syd Margles of Standard Broadcast News eased into *the* question at Thursday's news conference, and we had the pleasure of hearing P.E.T. praise his Press Office's mute role!

All else is overshadowed by the vagaries of the PM's wife, and the traumatic effect her wanderings have on all those who dote on the moods of power.

Last Sunday I spent some time on the phone with two senior PMO types searching for some grain of reality in the sea of vicious rumour in which I found myself swimming with the rest of my colleagues and clients. One of them had met Margaret at 24 Sussex on her return from Toronto. The other had talked directly to the PM. The result was simply denial; at worst, choked silence. Mistrust and suspicion are the hallmarks of this kind of coverup.

Coverup of what anyway? At least the lady in question had the courage to say in public that she had had enough! There was no such candour or even willingness to discuss what should be said by the faceless aides.

I'm not doing the week justice. Nor am I doing justice to what people like Bob Murdoch (who is a friend of Margaret's father) must be going through. I've taken a posture I am ashamed of – even with our neighbour, David Humphreys, who phoned on behalf of a friend, a British reporter, for confirmation or denial of Margaret's attendance at the dinner for British PM James Callaghan, whose visit to Ottawa ran smack into the Margaret story. I found myself doing a Watergate coverup on this innocent, even legitimate question. How humiliating! It took at least two days to kill even the simplest errors. But it is a self-generating scene.

On such sleazy stories, the global flow of dirt homogenizes all media output to the lowest common denominator. Someone's slip in reply to a question from a British paper is self-righteously played back with a London dateline in the *Globe*, then reported on radio here. So it goes, and we measure our breathing.

March 29, 1977

I have just been listening to "just folks" from cities and towns with unlikely and unpronounceable names talking "across the fence" to President Carter in his recent historic two-hour phone-in. Dreams of electronic populism afflict us these days.

Between agonizing over Margaret's latest adventure (does she have a black eye?) about the only planning we do is to borrow tactics from the U.S. – Carter envy. O'Hagan is busy clipping and circulating all evidence of the methods and techniques Jimmy Carter uses to convince the U.S. public he knows them and shares their concerns. O'Hagan is eternally ebullient.

My desk is piled with slick sheets of manipulative ideas. The latest is from Barry Callaghan suggesting, among other things, that his father, Morley, be interviewed by Trudeau in a sort of "Civilization" series hosted by the man himself, not on art but on the PM's roots. These ideas float about – somewhat confused dreams which I am sure distract from, even illuminate, the insolvables of getting out basic information to the hungry press/public.

The Good, the Bad, the Ugly

There have been so many developments recently. They coalesced neatly around the Liberal workshop we attended with the PM in Toronto last week. It was, as a marvellous Jamaican cabby told me, "a good way to see the good, the bad, and the ugly."

The good were the party youth I met. They were fired up by being part of the winning team – at least for the moment – and ready to be charmed by the PM. Oh, and ready to make giant efforts to prove their acceptance, even *love*, of the French fact, thus dramatically disassociating themselves from an older, more cynical generation.

As for the PM – well, he is not so much the bad, but the alone, the ascetic. He caressed his solitary leadership alone in the Constellation Hotel, while Kenny, Coutts, and others plotted and planned coups of one kind or another, most of which, like the meeting with Premier Davis, didn't come off. They counselled an inspirational speech for Saturday night that in the PM's hands became a gossamer history lesson delivered to a seminar of the faithful. The sergeants cannot move the general an inch.

At the little reception I arranged for the press the same mood carried, and I saw a rare side of the PM acting like a young man showing deep respect for an older teacher. It was the monk-like old Liberal warrior Senator Maurice Lamontagne (an adviser and minister in the Pearson era, and someone who inspired the Trudeau generation with his views of bilingualism) who won this from Trudeau. He intercepted the PM's flow of ideas while my press clients sat on the floor at their feet, listening with rare attentiveness. Trudeau, again, turned the mini-news conference at the end of the workshop into a seminar.

For me, the ugly was certainly the press. The pundits particularly, scenting not news but moods, not digging but sniffing, not reporting but suggesting. And now that the nineteenth-century idea of maintaining marriages in public life is shattered, the PM's mood seems as important to them as it is to Jim Coutts or to any of the rest of us courtiers who, as Bob Murdoch so aptly put it the other day, "live vicariously through him." In a way the pundits, who have the leisure to observe, do too.

At any rate, Dick and I were assured today by one of the PM's handlers that he was unusually and extraordinarily unpredictable. Well, gossip, not policy, is the lifeblood of politics and politicos these days. The PM talks of the consensus-making function of the party, but all I heard, or should I say retained, was the ad man Jerry Grafstein's idea to access TV directly, which I tagged a "telelib," and a New (?) Liberal from the U. of T. asking me what Trudeau wore to bed!

Topic "A"

April 5, 1977

Is the state of the PM's marriage really the most important issue in the country today? Perhaps dulled by flaccid economic events, even torpor in the Ottawa-Quebec duel, reporters and the country seem to be lying in wait for the story with the greatest popular currency – the *break-up.*

It certainly beats last week's budget. Poor Finance Minister Don Macdonald, faced with stumbling questions from the press of the "please give us the lead for our stories" variety, was only able to provide turgid bureaucratese. Trudeau strode into budget night's electronic event, paused to smile with Marchand, and disappeared into the night in a plain cop car. That part of the machine can run without him.

John Warren of CBC, a bright-eyed veteran, admits that he has been assigned to deliver Big Mac (Donald Macdonald) to his upstart junior colleague, Ken Colby, after the news conference. "Nice reward for eighteen years' experience," he mutters. We all serve the star system in one way or another.

On Friday, my old pal from CBC days, Jim Reed, arrives from Toronto to do the Margaret story. He gives me the usual "take me into your confidence" bit, laced with some cant about the "public's right to know." Later, on Saturday, I got the "she's sick" line – "just tell me and we'll leave her alone." That attempt and Suzanne Howden's plaintive call from a rainy New York stakeout outside the apartment where Margaret was supposed to be staying, begging me to tell her Mrs. T. had gone to L.A., show how deeply journalistic traditions and ethics are menaced in such situations.

The bottom-line rationalization is that everyone is trying to show that Trudeau's performance is being hampered by marriage "difficulties." This was Craig Oliver's rather maudlin conclusion on a "W-5" piece.

Marjorie Nichols of the *Vancouver Sun* holds endless court in the press club, spinning variations on Margaret's preference for garter belts as was revealed in her *People* Magazine interview. Richard pundit Gwyn takes full advantage of his old *New York Times Magazine* connections to assert that it is "official" – Margaret is taking up her career and ceasing public duties as Trudeau's wife. Even George Radwanski of the *Financial Times* can't resist asking personal questions at the regular news conference today. In all, Trudeau faced nine questions on his personal life – one-third of his weekly time with the media.

I am, perhaps, over reacting to the emotional pressures of the past weeks. But today even O'Hagan was wondering if what Dalton Camp calls "Topic A" isn't central. Are we ourselves falling victim to the very gossip we have been at such pains not to feed?

But when I saw Hugh Winsor's gothic face loudly fuming about Margaret's privileged position as a photographer, and Trudeau's reply that he isn't a gentleman, I can't help feeling some sympathy for both – Winsor for having to ask the question and Trudeau for having to answer!

Then there is the *Citizen*'s Frank Howard, full of professional pangs about not following up and writing on his earlier hunch that Margaret was using her free airline pass for her latest travels. Perhaps it's simply just the best thing to happen to the Press Club and to the Press Gallery's penchant for navel gazing. But it's the worst thing that has ever happened to those who live vicariously in the PMO and to whom the PM's moods are like stock-market information to a broker.

April 13, 1977

Sitting in the Press Club today, I got up to go to the washroom and passed the Grays, John and Elizabeth, one of the more charming, if oblique, pairs in the Gallery galaxy. They want me to "top" a particularly vulgar putdown I used on Marjorie Nichols a few days back to neutralize a rather venomous gossip session. What can I say? I try to do a little number on bad snow conditions in Utah where the PM is on a skiing holiday, but no dice. I at least got a laugh.

Easter and the unfailing sun and hope of Easter Sunday were quickly darkened by a barrage of phone calls. Margaret has left town again, this time for Boston. I am appalled how easy it is for the press to know her itinerary – Air Canada, the RCMP, even the Consulate all lend the press a hand. I was alone and at sea.

Finally I talked to the ever ingenuous RCMP Inspector Guy d'Avignon with the PM in Snowbird, Utah, and was able to confirm that the PM was still there and knew of Margaret's travel plans. I can now talk with knowledge and can quell the usual horror rumours that I have to hear out with my well-bred patience. My upset didn't last long. When I talked to Trudeau today, I reverted quickly to respect.

So, all in all, a somewhat barren few days. There was little input, and the output was stretched to the snapping point particularly by the Jack Horner saga.* Jim Coutts, who helped mastermind the deal to get this Conservative to cross the floor to join the Liberals, is, like his boss, in warmer climes. A young reporter from the Ottawa *Journal* wants to know what, if anything, was offered to make Horner switch sides. I tell him, in the absence of real information, that Bob Lewis has a good piece in *Maclean's* and to read it!

The PM Nobody Knows

April 26, 1977

A long-faced senior PMO colleague announced knowingly and dramatically today that the rumours of the PM's homosexuality, allegedly spread by Mrs. T. herself, could bring the government down. This ultimate madness seems as good a place as any to continue the saga of the PM that nobody knows.

Today's lunch was typical. Two ad agency types were giving staff the pitch to package Trudeau like soap, and were getting increasingly impatient with Jim Coutts, who was predicting the PM would say, "Why should I?" Why indeed?

Why should he deliver on cue the blockbuster speech others had promised and pushed him into? On our recent foray to the prairies, he preferred to save his inner fire for an unadvertised special with a crowd in Saskatoon that didn't expect it, and was bland where fireworks were required in the televised speech so carefully planned for the Canadian Association of Broadcasters (CAB) convention in Winnipeg.

---

* Jack Horner, a veteran Tory, ran unsuccessfully for his party's leadership in 1976. A sore loser, he made no secret of his distaste for Joe Clark. The Liberals, coveting a representative from Alberta, invited him to join them. He was immediately made Minister without Portfolio, and then Trade Minister, but lost his seat in Alberta in the 1979 election.

71

Confound all adversaries, even your own staff. Why not?

At the CAB convention we wanted him to sizzle because we had elaborately arranged for live TV coverage of the speech, claiming it would be of "significance." He was awful. I took a lot of crap from my CAB friends – "when you need us next time, we may just not be there." They were let down. I commiserated with CBC's Anne Medina and went to bed exhausted and discouraged; the helpless observer of the inevitable when you promise more than you can deliver.

In Saskatoon he was brilliant, if demagogic. I couldn't believe it. He was everything we had wanted him to be the night before. He spoke at a sort of indoor pioneer village. I pushed him down that long Disneylandish fake main street of turn-of-the-century prairie buildings (indoors in a hangar!) He pressed the flesh. The crowd was warm, polite, and receptive. I handed him a tiny boy right at the front who he was about to miss and he was sweet with the tot. Then he leapt onto the unlikely platform of the rebuilt railway station. Legs apart (his election "gunslinger" pose Ralph Coleman assures me), forefinger thrusting out and down, looking beyond the indifferent gaggle of cameramen, he delivered his absolute best to the crowd.

That he rose to the heights of *mépris* for his PQ enemies (calling them just that, the enemies of Canada) is not important. What is important is the irrepressible spirit of the man – determined to be himself against all advice, all odds, all ambition.

The next morning, a frozen-faced PM greeted our breakfast attempts to have him change his mind about a local news conference. No dice. He obviously felt he had said his bit. He didn't even look up from his breakfast.

Later, returning in the plane, landing gear just up from a wartime strip in Battleford, he took my compliment on the Saskatoon performance ironically. "Ah, the best of the best, eh?", reminding me with no uncertainty that we should not second guess his performances. I won't ever again.

As if to prove the point, the PM absented himself on Saturday from the yearly epic of fake press-politician bonding, the Press Gallery Dinner. A *grippe diplomatique* perhaps (but more likely a sincere revulsion for that evening's display of drunken bonds between press and politician) this is one highly visible symbol of a larger reality he rejects. He would not have been disappointed. The Gallery president had been drinking, and Jim Munson (a radio reporter and sometime hero of the Gallery who forever asks the PM about the legalization of marijuana at press conferences) shouted throughout the speeches. Then the whole reeking crowd of penguins retired to see the yearly satirical show about Ottawa events. I drank too much.

May 16, 1977

Today at a launch for the Canada Games on Parliament Hill, in brilliant sunshine, Mrs. T. appears *en famille* giving sweet comfort to the heavy hearts who find agony in the domestic trials of our leader.

A more charming demonstration of bliss one could not have imagined after weeks of black rumour. There they were, with children, unaffected by ceremony or rank. A human family! This is written as if by a doting courtier – somebody for whom a furrowed PM brow draws up unspoken wells of sympathy and concern. It has been a long road for the PMO – high-coloured salon sympathy has been on its finest display. Now where to attach it? What if this is just a normal rocky marriage, and we are witnessing only the normal grand passions and dramatic cycles of romantic self-deception?

Innocents Abroad

I am just back from ten days in Europe, my first trip minding the media abroad, at the London Economic Summit and NATO heads of government meeting.

A few observations: Trudeau's performance on the international stage is firmly in the hands of Ivan Head, Trudeau's personal adviser on foreign affairs and an ally who was unfailingly helpful with pestering press office questions. His sandy hair and professorial demeanour hide a powerful ego, however. In London, Head had an army of External Affairs' advisers to back him up.

Foreign trips are a giant, but not unamusing, escort job. The press officer's job is to make sure the media road show gets to events on time, gets hotel rooms, and is fed scraps of information (including clippings). In Paris, CBC's Ken Colby asks me politely to make a phone call for him. Of course I oblige – I am here to serve. This sounds like sour grapes. It is not meant to be. My job, in a real sense, depends on the press's relative inability to do its job without at least logistics assistance. Nevertheless, we have a problem when we make trips almost too attractive for internationally unsophisticated Ottawa-based journalists.

Our travelling press behaved, on the whole, like children. In London, many were unable to leave the hotel without help, and few had any certain view of the story or how to get it. A handful went to the international press centre to compare notes with colleagues from other summit countries. We provided a suite in the Hilton with an open bar and this became the scene of boyish and girlish confidence-building until all hours.

In Paris, the angst was even worse. The French language was strange to many of our anglo reporters (*sic*) and so, horror of horrors, the newspapers were inaccessible! In London the English-speaking reporters watched the BBC news and pored over the papers we provided, amazed at the cursory treatment Trudeau was given. David Halton and Joe Schlesinger (stationed in London and Paris respectively as the CBC's overseas pros) cringed at the behaviour of these bush leaguers from back home.

It all became a bit pathetic. On the trip's last day, following the Summit and a visit to President Giscard d'Estaing, at the news conference in Canada's elegant Paris cultural centre, Trudeau refused to be led further into a tiresome litany on Quebec by our mono-themed press colleagues. The press acted like hurt adolescents. Munson almost begged him to react to some particularly acerbic comments about the federal government from Lévesque (perhaps all his desk saw as potentially newsworthy from this part of the trip) at the fag end of the particularly frustrating forty minutes. All Trudeau had to say was, "Sorry to disappoint you!" The press contingent was furious and so was I – at them!

The francophone contingent posed special problems. A long-standing grievance broke to the surface in London with the first English-only briefing by Ivan Head. In a bedroom of the Hilton suite, an angry caucus of the francos faced me with serious charges. I knew they had a case. The fact that the PM's adviser has difficulty communicating in the other official language is hard to take.

Poor Jean Charpentier had to break the news of the revolt to Ivan and suggest that he be joined at his briefings by a bilingual External type. Ivan responded with an expletive deleted, and that was his last group briefing.

The shoe was on the other foot in Paris, when a briefing by our ambassador, Gérard Pelletier, was more in French than in English. There was an outburst from Steve Scott, this trip's over-extended Canadian Press slave. (Canadian Press files stories to meet the newspaper deadlines of its member papers from coast to coast, so the work is never-ending for their reporters.) Scott's having to "beg" the good Ambassador to repeat in English sparked the francophones to point out that this was precisely the kind of treatment they had been suffering for years! *Dialogue des sourds.*

Well, I picked up lots of new French slang including *jouer au flipper* (play the pinball machines) and stored up a lot of strange memories. I especially remember one very civilized meal arranged by the civilized John Honderich. The equally sophisticated *le Devoir* writer, Lise Bissonnette, helped leaven the lump immensely.

On these trips, a lot is squeezed from the PM, our remarkable and only source. On the London-Paris jaunt, the briefings were like sideshows rather than excerpts from the real performance. Only the PM delivers. The press may not believe his version of these meetings – but they did not seek out any other sources!

Staff members of most Canadian political leaders have cut their political teeth in election campaigns and are most skilled and happy in the campaign mode. Two or three years into a mandate they start to live in a constant state of election promotion, preparation, and preparedness. This panic over elections that never took place suffuses the pages that follow.

There were three hugely enjoyed false alarms for the real general election of April-May 1979 in which Joe Clark defeated the Liberals. The first of these three spirited PMO build-ups for an election started in the fall of 1977. Then there was a preparation for one that could have been held in the spring of 1978, the normal four years after the 1974 victory. Finally, the fall of 1978 seemed to provide another window, and we had another false campaign.

Poet Campaigner

May 22, 1977

Trudeau, last week's international statesman, is this week's poet campaigner! I experienced lots of culture shock on this general election preview swing through Quebec and P.E.I. – a few glimpses of the man's ability to lead and attract. It happens everywhere. Jean Charpentier told me the story of following behind him in Paris while he shopped on foot, and how the people who did not know him nevertheless stopped to look. This is the remarkable impression I've received on this domestic swing watching him repeatedly on platforms at close, press-eye view. It was hard to take one's eyes off him. He looked both commanding and vulnerable.

He displayed a lot of natural grace with the islanders in Kensington, P.E.I. – a weathered, rumpled crowd of rustics and rurals singing an off-colour song, which was endlessly elaborated by the press corps satirists on the three-hour flight back.

This flight has already entered gallery legend for other reasons – largely to do with the length of flight, the normal availability of beer, and the absence of washroom facilities on the older Otter. One particularly hardworking and sensitive Canadian Press reporter, of course, became the one who could not wait and, in close proximity to some female reporters, found relief in the air sick bag! Not much humour here, but there was a lot of hearty amusement at the time.

Back to the tour. It was an easy success for the PM, not just in P.E.I. but also in the events that followed in Quebec City – particularly at the packed, respectful arena at Laval University. But, there was much fear and apprehension displayed during the drive to the arena. It showed in Bob Murdoch and Gilles Dufault's white knuckles as we silently listened to the crackling RCMP radio. What, no news from agents on the spot about demonstrators? Then, once in the hall, our relief when there was no heckling and nothing was thrown. The PM spoke from his heart at this university, which has more separatists per classroom than any other, and was warmly applauded.

The hook in all this is the possibility of the PM succumbing to pressure for a fall general election, fought with only the Trudeau presence – magnetic though it may be – and only one reply to the complex problems facing Confederation – language equality.

This message was confused by at least one minister less generous than his boss. He was not above using fear to make his point. Thanking the PM at Mascouche on Friday, his threats that there would be "loss of freedom" under the PQ sounded cheap coming from the same platform at which Trudeau had just been appealing to love and generosity.

Back at Langevin, I enjoy the paradox of the top political strategists, Coutts, Davey, and Axworthy, discussing election plans that will assure Quebec's future in Confederation in the only language and outlook they really know – English! A weird scene.

"Stratégie," Rémi Bujold, our energetic Quebec operative in the PMO moaned, "Nous n'avons pas de stratégie!" He was reacting to news that Lévesque was holding his weekly news conference almost on top of ours scheduled for 3:30 p.m. – an easy and effective way to compete for news space. This shows up the latent amateurism in our office. I am part of the "second wind" of an old administration. Everything points to the questionable wisdom of gearing up now for a fall election.

The press seem increasingly easy as far as we are concerned. They are sometimes unbelievably lazy. An interview the PM did in Paris with *le Monde*, available ten days ago, quoted the PM as saying he would not lift controls until the next election.*

I showed this to Big Mac's (the Finance Minister) aide, who blanched. No reporter picked it up, however, until yesterday. The office then released a typed version and, finally, the existence of the line became widely reported!

I look after the care and feeding problems. The Press Office finds itself in the ridiculous position of dragging the press after a campaign-oriented PM without the logistics or organization available in a real one. We limped after the PM's 550 m.p.h. Jetstar coming back from P.E.I. in a 190 m.p.h. Otter!

To return to the original theme: Trudeau's eyes twinkled on Thursday when he denied rumours of a fall election. Help!

---

* Wage and Price Controls were introduced in October 1975 for a three-year period.

Separation and Goodbyes

May 30, 1977

Friday was the day of days for maudlin sentiments, hushed gasping. Margaret and Pierre are to go their own ways. Everyone is caught up in the drama. The touching announcement, using first names only, and, at the Press Office's urging, on the PM's personal, not the PMO's stationery (about our only involvement, save physically getting it out to the press), catches everyone in shocked surprise.

I am sure our politicos see the image of Trudeau as a single father as sure vote-getter. With some horror, Jean Charpentier sees the prospect of hungry women reporters (Radio-Canada's Catherine Bergman aroused more than casual enquiries from the PM following Thursday's news conference) taking advantage of his interest in blatant charms. Peter McGuire sees trips with the kids (already requested) as great new attractions. Dick O'Hagan, showing veteran wisdom, simply doesn't want to know!

Meantime, a fresh and chippy PM had big hellos, even small talk, for everyone as he strode out of 24 Sussex across to Rideau Gate this morning for a meeting with the President of Mauritania. He was even driving the Mercedes again!

On Wednesday, we threw a stagey goodbye party for Gilles Dufault, who is leaving his Quebec political duties in the PMO for a job in Montreal. Even he thought the lavish finale at the Rideau Club a bit "cou cou." It started with a respectful circle of his friends, admirers, and detractors listening to eulogies from the PM, Lalonde, and others in the echoing Confederation Room on the Hill. People who I have heard Gilles curse, and who he has warned me about, came to pay tribute as only the politically motivated can. Gilles was teeth from ear to ear.

Then the senior PMO staff moved to the sombre and musty "Blue Room" of the old Rideau Club to continue the farewell – Coutts presiding. Again, a group not exactly suffused with mutual love, but nonetheless paying lavish and largely effective lip service to solidarity. This was combined, of course, with lushly expressed selfless dedication to the unseen but not unfelt presence of the PM. Everyone had to speak, as is the routine whenever Coutts and Davey are in charge.

The one PMO staffer we knew would run if there was an election,

Brian Flemming, was notably ill at ease, mumbling that he didn't have time to make notes! The rest of us bumbled along more or less amusingly. Ralph and Bob were particularly good. Coutts reserved the apex of the evening for himself with his hilarious imitation of Paul Martin Sr. Tears were rolling down my face. He is a seasoned professional performer.

Once finished, the group dispersed with amazing speed and lack of lingering congeniality.

June 14, 1977

The next campaign-style excursion is to the Gaspé – an endless advance in RCMP vehicles last week. Rémi Bujold (who has ambitions to run in his home riding on the peninsula) led the way, finessing adequate family stopovers and visits including an absolutely charming evening with his mother in St. Luc near Carleton.

We overdrank two nights running with an endless succession of Rémi's former classmates. If Ottawa federalist Rémi was made to feel the gap with his old pals, the problem was a hundred times worse for me, the *anglais*. But booze does help and I was commended for being *"pas si pire,"* staggering back to the motel at dawn.

My experiences in PQ Quebec have been not so much of solitudes as of situations where, on both sides, your *humanity* is tested.

The trip to Pierre de Bané's riding further up the peninsula is *pour payer les dettes*. This is turning into an epic down-home holiday. The PM will arrive in the midst of a shrimp festival in Matane. Help! My negative thoughts soon disappear as I enjoy the real enthusiasm of the festival organizers who are looking forward to this unexpected publicity bounty. The PM is a real event in small-town Canada, and we have fun being the operators who simply push the logistical buttons that turn it all on.

How cheap of the media to criticize Clark's recent western tour where few showed up. He isn't a star and doesn't have the PMO infrastructure, so the best advance team in the world isn't going to bring a whole town out, as will happen next week when the helicopters blow down on Ste.-Anne des Monts. These are the images I'll take away from this job, and I will be happy to take almost no credit for the density of enthusiasm.

Election rumours are fizzling somewhat. The great meeting with the PM and strategists Coutts and Davey occurs Friday, and the good money says the PM will be hard to convince. Thank God the Ontario election entrails are hard to read. No easy support for the idea of an early election there.

On the other hand, several key advisers (Rémi, Flemming, perhaps Coutts himself) are themselves anxious to run and feel the magic elixir of delegated power and personal public adulation flowing through their veins. How objective is their advice? From backroom to front-door, politics can write strange careers. The real reason for grand decisions may be as tied to the personal timetables or frustrations of key aides as it is to any so-called science of politics.

FOUR

UNDER SOME DISTANT HEDGE

Gaspé and Holiday

July 4, 1977

I can still hear the scream of helicopters in my ears and still dream of prime ministerial disasters. The last three weeks have more than prepared this soldier to leave the front line – but he is somehow unable to put it out of his mind.

Talking to Jean Rivard, a radio reporter from Télémedia, about the last day of the Gaspé trip which felt like yesterday to me, he said, "Oh, you mean two weeks ago!" The Gaspé circus was like that – unbelievably compressed. I went there ahead, and spent two full days nailing down details in Matane until my stomach finally settled. Then I took the bus for the Mont Joli airport to pick up my press clients arriving from Ottawa. It is unlikely I will ever again have such a wholesome group of forty or so.

We lodged the press at a wonderful seaside motel called la Belle Plage. I swear that the excellent food and pleasant rustic accommodation helped create a spirit of contentment. There was actually a temporary suspension of griping and bitchy reporting.

To my surprise, all the details worked out. The bus arrived on time, events came off, and the PM's middle child, the natural and photogenic Sacha who came along with the PM, kept film cranking.

I felt the bizarre satisfaction that comes when the press's and the PMO's interests coincide – when we are both being had and love it!

Later I saw Bill Fox's (*Toronto Star*) item on that day – an admitted piece of front-page fluff. Many newspapers that day sold themselves with still photos of the single parent and child. Fox's pieces was boxed around one, and why not? It's not news perhaps, but it communicates. Every newsman wants front page for his story, and more often than not, does what is required to adjust or goose it up to get it there!

What a strange business. We press officers charm and stroke the reporters, take them right to the event and give them the best position, provide newsworthy material (by any number of definitions!), hand it to them on a platter, make sure the least possible effort is required to get the story out (press rooms, phones, and so on), even arrange the charter flight to get the film or tape back for TV deadlines, and – *voilà* – the trip is a success!

The next day our helicopters chugged up the Gaspé peninsula and dusted into what I considered a privileged experience – tiny Ste.-Anne des Monts. The three-helicopter landing alone will provide talk for months to come. The PM told us of walking and cycling the Gaspé alone as a young student. Now, with one phone call, his aides can lay on a fleet of military helicopters for the same trip.

In the chartered Hawker Siddeley on its way back to Quebec from the Gaspé, lobster was served and jangled nerves were settled. Everyone was accounted for, including the neat little guy from Radio Carleton who knew he had hit the big time! The visiting crew from Australia was in high spirits, even though the beer was all gone. Even CBC's Mark Phillips stopped being a brat.

At Quebec we threw off bags, lightened the load by a few, and arrived in Ottawa in time for all TV purposes – except for Global's Marjorie Walters, who was greeted by her driver saying that her item had been cancelled – the only real downer.

One significant motif ran through the trip. Had the Federal Government's language paper, as interpreted by Secretary of State John Roberts, gone soft on Lévesque? The *Globe and Mail* had said *yes* in screaming headlines just as the trip started. To his credit, Jeff Simpson, their young and conscientious correspondent, and a recent parliamentary intern, had agonized over it.

Trudeau had been at his professorial best explaining Roberts's unfortunate misinterpretation in his news conference in the Matane studios of Radio-Canada. This episode taught me you have to get it right the first time – the press is not interested in playing a correction the way it played the original story. By the third kick at this particular can last week, the press wasn't interested at all, even though the PM virtually hung Roberts out to dry. It's one time out in this business.

One final more optimistic note in a week when June 24 (Quebec's St. Jean Baptiste Day) and July 1 (Canada Day) reduce an ideological debate to the power and simplicity of flags and slogans. On June 23 we had a big mixed dinner with the press at the Belle Plage in Matane. At one table for twelve, half were English, half were French-speaking. All, but all, of the anglos at the table spoke French. Jean Charpentier was mystified and impressed. The corny unity slogan for that year, "Canada I want to shake your hand," had come to that table. We enjoyed good food, the Entre Deux Mers, and good play between the iconoclastic Quebecer, Jean Rivard, and my Franco-Ontarian colleague, Charpentier. All of the anglos were *trying*.

Holiday Musings on Power

July 8, 1977

Holidays. This year in Plymouth, Mass., with our friends the Humphreys.

I have chosen the easy route. Unlike the Canadian establishment (as if the comparison is in any way relevant whatsoever!) who always holiday so that business continues to be done, I'm isolated from anyone who cares at all about the corridors of power in Ottawa. Only David Humphreys and Helga with their occasional asides remind me that five-hundred miles north there is an island of national fever (perhaps a swamp would be more appropriate) to which my energies seem irreversibly dedicated.

Yesterday, during a Boston excursion, I finally persuaded my small family audience to foresake the joys of Harvard Square and walk the hundred yards to Episcopal Theological School where I spent a year trying to become a priest in 1961-62. How cold and monastic it looked after a fifteen-year absence. "I blew it," I thought, despite the deserted, cheerless facades and the nondescript architecture. From the small, ordered office of the Dean under the heavy Gothic arches of the main academic building, I had self-consciously set out away from institutionalized curacy into journalism. I felt then I had compassion and could communicate, and tried to convince Dean Coburn that the two callings were similar! They did not turn out that way.

July 8, 1977

Now I am part of the "cozy with power" syndrome that repulsed me as recently as last night when I realized (David Humphreys said it much better than I) that the famous Ottawa editor Grattan O'Leary's life was not about journalism at all – it was about mutual admiration and intimacy with power. Is my life not about press relations, but about intimacy with power?

At any rate, how many today in the Gallery, removed by decades as they are from O'Leary's time when the senior press were consulted by prime ministers, still dream the same dream? I think of Mike Duffy, bubbly, chubby, but petulant, confessing how hurt he was that Trudeau had never personally recognized him in the hundreds of scums he had thrust his mike into. Now he, like many others, doesn't even come to news conferences. He finds them too structured and competitive, I suspect. The ambition of a one-on-one with the top man fades slowly. "What do *you* think, Mike?" will never be uttered, at least not by this prime minister (to Duff or to any of the other reporters who feel as he does).

In the PMO, a chance for a one-on-one with himself is all that counts. Jim McDonald, a shadowy Press Office figure who is sort of an assistant to Dick, tells me proudly how much the PM likes the briefing notes he works up for Dick to give the PM for the news conferences, but complains that it is ridiculous that Dick should go up and meet the PM and walk with him across to the press theatre. Why not him? He did the notes!

From the perspective of Plymouth, Mass., Ottawa and its backyard battles matter not a damn. At the Bartletts' (our landlords and neighbours in this summer "compound") cocktail party for the Canadians, I am asked a few *pro forma* queries about Margaret and there it ends.

We scan the papers. Peter Ward is in the *Boston Globe* writing on pipeline matters, and a New York tabloid has Prince Charles in Regina on an RCMP horse. *Maclean's* is brimming with attacks, not just on Lévesque's policies, but on the mealy-mouthed Liberalism that has allowed it to happen! The latter piece, by the "dean of Canadian historians," Donald Creighton, lies on the coffee table, the best possible evidence of the faint domestic squabbles of the mouse family under some distant hedge.*

Yet, being in Boston yesterday reminded me of all that is worthwhile and worth protecting under that hedge. It is more peaceful, and is a courteous and quiet society, even if it is politically expedient to draw it otherwise. We do have a collectivist genius – in labour, even business, and in our urban societies. A Boston radio ad for a Boston harbourfront apartment building that touts its ultra-sophisticated security systems, says it all. We may be more or less irrelevent to the world, but we are not irrelevent to ourselves. We musn't make this error.

Down the road we will fight Canadian elections, perhaps referendums, that are almost totally apart from our everyday experience. They will be fought on alleged conflicting racial moralities and ideologies that are more the product of theorizing than the results of our practical experience or wisdom or observation.

At the centre of these struggles will be the "battle for the hearts and minds of Quebecers." But the content of the battle up to now has been largely abstractions: symbols like francophone sovereignty vs. assimilation; the impossible concept of making Quebec completely French again ("francisation"!); the PM's warnings about the dangers of a stifling ethnocentricity in Quebec.

Grievances seem somewhat imposed – on both sides – yet there is no denying the fervour of Trudeau's basic beliefs, or of Lévesque's. The battle, however, is about visions that are like the air we breathe, almost never analysed. But they are personified in the PM and in Lévesque.

The press dreamed up a good series of symbols for the Trudeau of the Gaspé trip – "poet, statesman, father"! On the other side is the caricaturist's Lévesque. Both speak dreams. Trudeau quotes

* This controversial piece by Donald Creighton urged English Canada to be more aggressive in defending its rights in the face of threatened separation by Quebec.

poetry – even in Ste.-Anne des Monts – perhaps to try and establish some mystical bond with the people in the Dodge Chargers. Lévesque and his chief theorist, Camille Laurin, spout Marxist-Freudian psychiatry to those who dream of CB radios and *quatres par quatres* (four-wheel-drive vehicles).

Perhaps real problems, such as the economy and unemployment, have become so intractable, our societies so basically unmanageable, that only the grand ideas that unite people are suitable today as the stuff of politics.

Despite this self-indulgent introspection, the holiday is infused with long, hot brightness, with the children who delight in exploring – Sean's diving for lobsters and Susanne's rock and sea glass collecting. Helga's beloved sea finally charms me too, and I forget the silent clearness of the northern Ontario lakes I holidayed on for so many years. The old blue Buick floats us on day excursions to beaches and, returning, we become the northern darlings of the strange American colony in the Bartlett "compound."

July 19, 1977

*"The true doom of the media barons at all levels is to believe the media, thereby infallibly encompassing their own destruction."**

For what it is worth, I have been brooding on this line. A fundamental question surely: whether you "believe" your own work – or I might have said whether you believe your own lies, if you engage in deliberate falsehood.

When I think of the Tom Goulds, the Bruce Phillips, the Richard Gwyns, the Geoff Stevens (the recipient of a long drawn-out, hand-delivered letter of sympathy from the PM on the tragic death of his teenage son) and especially my friend, the *Star*'s Peter Lloyd, I feel there is scant deliberation on this question.

There is a principle that operates to which all, in one way or another, fall victim – that of investing one's own work with infallibility; of taking a craft, which is about all most journalists practice, and treating it as revealed truth. I want to hear just a few of them less sure of themselves, less certain of their interpretations; for once hear them say, "This is a really hard one to call."

* Malcom Muggeridge, *Chronicles of Wasted Time*, The Infernal Grove, Collins, 1973, p. 54.

I am more than ever convinced that, in the news business, it is the straight and careful chroniclers who are worthy of their hire and worth helping as much as possible. Hurray for Canadian Press!

This is all very heavy on a hot night filled with heaviness. The night an election could have been called. It is marked in my mind. Funny, I don't feel that much relief that there is no phone call. This holiday has largely to do with kids, with my wife, and with vistas I can't capture. The three weeks' rest is enough and I need a new challenge.

July 25, 1977

A few personal notes on the day before my birthday. My life this year has felt like a hurricane in a breadbox. I have put out huge amounts of sheer energy in an environment so closed that it could be seen to encompass no more space than that between the telephone on my desk and my ear.

Trips open these horizons. Although the interaction is the same, there is a different kind of confinement in the restricted package of PM, aides, and trailing press corps. Contacts with the rest of Canada are brief as the country slides by bus, aircraft, or helicopter windows.

Aside from continuing this exotic life, it is hard to see where a junior press officer goes. There are a lot of bodies between me and being number-one flack. One thing is sure, if Dick leaves, he is unlikely to be replaced permanently – there is only one Dick.

Jean Charpentier seems tired and, I suppose, might step down after two years. He is secure and could do a lateral move into the public service. Of course there would be other ambitious candidates, but I am in position. And I don't mind being last choice. I was for my present position, I almost forgot!

I could jump back into journalism. Or could I? There is little precedent, and there would be a lot of retraining and laundering. And I would start, as usual, from a meagre position. I have not forgotten meeting the once-powerful adviser/speechwriter to the former minister of communications, Eric Kierans, one Frank Howard, covering a community meeting for the *Citizen*. It could happen to me. (Yet, he quite quickly became Ottawa's chronicler of civil service comings and goings.)

All this reflection seems now like such a luxury as I plunged right back into it on return from holiday. Now the PM is, finally, on *his* vacation, following ten full days of action.

We are into the unity debate. The first thing I hear conjures up a wonderful image. *Le Devoir*'s Lise Bissonnette was a guest of "Présente à l'écoute," a daily Radio-Canada phone-in program, for a wrap-up on the parliamentary session. Total confusion from callers. Her conclusion stressed Ottawa's alleged irrelevance, which she tagged with the great line that about all everyone in Quebec was interested in was "la tête de Trudeau" (like the head of St. John the Baptist!). What a great artifact to provide common experience on both sides of the Ottawa River.

This image did not apply to a thoroughly charming if exhausting weekend in St. John's, Newfoundland, to open the Canada Summer Games. The best part was the joy of seeing the PM caught up with everyone else in the warmth and authenticity of the opening. The night before, he had virtually refused to go. Change of plans and planes because of the CATCA strike! But Bob Murdoch, his "conscience," prevailed and there he was, not so much a star as a spectator.

It was a "unity" opening. There were all sorts of stretched analogies from all speakers, including a bilingual plea to God from the Archbishop. It was the first appeal I have heard since the crisis that puts the Deity squarely on the side of one bilingual nation – joining President Carter's endorsement of a united Canada in his Bruce Phillips TV interview.

Strange how the man can be relevant or irrelevant depending on the situation. He was puzzled by the calm, even indifference, in the athletes' cafeteria where he sat eating his meal on a tray with a minimum of buzzing about. Yet at the dress-up reception, he was mobbed by the begowned matrons and bemedalled legionnaires of St. John's.

I am fascinated by the tenacity of unsound ideas in our office. Now it is the buildup to sell a fall election! If at once you don't succeed . . . . The PM is still fighting it off. But Jim Coutts's persistence is legendary. Now Trudeau has agreed to have another go after three weeks of holiday reflection. "No" is not good enough for these persistent suitors. As Colin perceptively remarked the other day, everything that happens is turned into an argument for an early election.

Rumours that Jim Coutts will run provokes new jockeying. Dick O'Hagan, we are told, is slated for principal secretary.

The "Election That Never Was"

August 26, 1977

"Bullshit!" Perhaps the loudest I have ever said it on the phone. This to counter another Gallery rumour that Friday was the day for an election call. Our office has been at a rolling boil all week.

We know the thumbscrews Coutts and Davey applied on Monday, Tuesday, and again on Thursday. Jim has been looking frantic for the first time this year. It almost is like a plot – the promised jobs, the elaborate ruses to keep things hushed. Monday is to be decision day, and even as I confirm this with Peter McGuire, Colin Kenny's trusty assistant, Doug Small's story for Canadian Press that Monday indeed is to be the day is clanking out on the wire machine in our office. Who talked to him?

It is a sultry August day. Helga has taken Susanne, her friend Donna who teaches at Carleton University, and the neighbour's daughter, Jennifer, to the sea for a bonus vacation. Alone here, virtually alone at work, I am re-reading Alain Stanké's transcript of the "Portrait Intime" interview with the PM of last year and savouring its striking passages on solitude.

I think of the PM facing this lonely decision pushed on him by advisers who know little of his inner life. I think of the personal timetables that influence the majors in this chess game. I think of Trudeau who seeks the peace, as he says in the transcript, to know the name of every tree and flower, to count the blades of grass and "planter des radis"!

My secret (I could never admit it) friend in Joe Clark's office is bullish about an election. He suggests a minority Liberal government at worst from their point of view. He is probably right.

We talk about Quebec. Perhaps what Lévesque is attempting is to get Quebec back to a simpler, more uniform society. He does not want non-Quebecers like me, or Alain Stanké (of Lithuanian background) for that matter, as French-speaking equals. The purity thing is frightening. The PM's vision is better and more generous – but this fall isn't the time to take it to the people.

Meanwhile, until the election decision is made, everything is at a standstill. Bob Rabinovitch of the PCO tells me Cabinet agendas are sketched through September but are being held until, as we say, "the shoe falls."

Last night when I called Coutts to tell him the nature of press speculation, he said, "Just tell them I'm on vacation, and Davey is on holiday." This must be one of the most sleepless holidays of his life. Coutts and Davey know they face ridicule in stories about the "election that never was" if it doesn't come off.

"Well, that's the way the cookie crumbles," and with that Colin tells me the decision has been made. There will be no election call. "The election that never was" scenario had come true. We are in Dick's office. Colin is almost in mourning. In twenty-four hours I've taken hundreds of calls, feeling, not knowing but saying, "things are quieter . . . ." Now I see the outcome on Colin's face.

A different gang is taking credit for the decision. The PM's riding president takes credit for masterminding an eleventh-hour intervention by Marchand that helped hold off the hawks! Who knows?

Lessons

September 1, 1977

In the middle of last week's election turmoil the PM got a haircut at the Hair Place, a ridiculously public venue looking out on an upstairs mall. He was discovered. A Canadian Press photographer arrived and took the photo. A passing CBC type was overheard saying "that's just the way Margaret likes it" and it was reported as a statement from a press aide. The PM was furious. CP apologized – they got it wrong. A note with the CP apology goes up to the PM and rocketed back with his "more evidence of a meddlesome press" neatly written in the margin!

Lise Bissonnette called about the election and confidences flowed. She was convinced the line was tapped. It all makes me give much thought to the future. I think of the spring visit of the offensive young RCMP Security and Intelligence type who knew that some of the Toronto boys in the PM's bodyguard had betrayed confidences to me. He solicited my help in identifying potential leaks. I see details of my life filed, my calls recorded.

But I have to stick to this breadbox – there is too much going on.

90

September 13, 1977

It's fascinating to look inside the PMO after watching "Washington Behind Closed Doors" on TV, an exaggerated dramatization of White House intrigues. But the ranting Robert Vaughan, who played the tight-phrased President's keeper, did have shades of the PM's executive assistant Bob Murdoch! I saw Vic Chapman, Trudeau's original executive assistant, today and he said that he recalled President Nixon's Haldeman as a "nice guy"!

I was amused to find in a borrowed copy of Theodore White's *Breach of Faith* that the only underlined passage referred to what is called the "Chappaquiddick Theorem" – that there is no good time for a political figure to tell bad news except *right away*! A good lessson. I wonder if and when it may be useful to me.

Meanwhile, last week provided a different sort of lesson. How to find advantage in passing over that fine line that divides Press Office communications from outright manipulation? Presumably, putting the emphasis on "good news" falls somewhere in between.

It started a week ago Friday, when down the grand staircase of the Langevin Building swept *the* top Canadian and *the* top American who are trying to negotiate a gas pipeline deal to bring Alaskan energy through Canada to the lower states. The unlikely pair – Allan MacEachen and the U.S. Secretary of Energy, James Schlesinger, already had a draft agreement and only presidential approval and ratification awaited.

But the Americans had a testy ratification problem. Carter's wholehearted acceptance and support counted for a lot to get the agreement through Congress. The following week, the PM would attend a Carter Panama Treaty signing circus in Washington, which could provoke the same Senate opposition as the pipeline deal might. It was clear by Schlesinger's reservations in the scrum that a final accord was not in the bag for Carter and Trudeau's Thursday bilateral meeting.

Despite our caution, the Canadian press was convinced the deal was in the bag. Why else would Trudeau go to Washington? Parochial punditry couldn't accept the simple courtesy of our presence at a grand hemispheric gathering.

Tuesday the Carter administration put up a balloon on the pipeline deal. Yes, clicked over the wire, sources who refused to be named said Carter would accept the deal since the terms were great for the U.S. Well, this U.S. position, which characterized the deal as being a Canadian cave-in, got there first and it stuck. The press wrote that the U.S. had come out on top in the negotiations.

In Washington, Ralph and Jean had nothing to say. They gave no solid indication that a Thursday-morning announcement was on. There was no way to counter the U.S. balloon. Our key people were not even there. On Thursday morning, the PM was finally read a Carter-prepared "joint announcement." Dick couldn't even advise Jean, who had left for the White House with the Canadian media, and without proper accreditation, of course.

Following their meeting, Carter and Trudeau acted out a well-controlled love-in for the press. But only on Friday did the Canadian side of the deal and what *we* had won come out.

Patrick's theorem – *only the first shot counts*. The press is little interested in getting out your side of a story the next day, if your views were not in the first shot. But how should we get our interpretation of events out in such cases? Clearly, the next time I should simply leak on my own initiative. Maybe I should let my sense of fairness override my distaste for such manipulation.

On Friday, a long-awaited product of the famed Tellier Group (a high-powered group chaired by the handsome Paul Tellier to study constitutional alternatives and promote unity) hit the streets.* This was Trudeau's constitutional initiative on minority language rights. A turgid letter went out to the Quebec premier elaborating on the proposal's overt "special status," "opting in" formula for Quebec.

The *Globe* had the story a day before. Again the first shot was hard to top, as was Lévesque's outright rejection. Perhaps Lévesque has said "no" once too often. Even Geoff Stevens praised the PM's flexibility this morning in the *Globe*. I was amused by

---

* In February 1977, Trudeau named Paul Tellier, then Assistant Deputy Minister of Environment, to head an internal group to address "new challenges to national unity." Its mandate was to co-ordinate activities by the federal government on national unity.

In May, Trudeau asked Tellier to set up an interdepartmental committee to study the rights of French-speaking Canadians outside Quebec. In September, Trudeau proposed a constitutional amendment to protect minority language rights, guaranteeing freedom of choice in the language of education for all Canadians. Predictably, it was rejected by Lévesque, who said it diminished provincial jurisdiction over education.

Joe Clark's claim on the weekend that the PM expected it to be rejected all along. According to Dick, who spent a late Friday night meeting with the PM, Clark was right! Where was the truth for the press, let alone the public, in all this?

September 21, 1977

This week saw a surprise Cabinet shuffle. We had heard from Dick's own mouth on Thursday morning that it wouldn't go until next week.

The next day of cabinetmaking (the analogy is accurate – all the pieces have to fit just so) was a madhouse. Norm Cafik, the lone newcomer, was in, then out, then in again as we typed, cut, pasted, and retyped press releases. This is the stuff of ulcers. I tipped Ken Colby of CBC TV that he was on the right track in saying Cafik was in, then, when he was out, begged him to make like he had never heard me! Another first!

Mordecai Richler was granted a luncheon with the PM the week before. Gloomy over the decline of *his* Montreal, he is doing a piece for the *Atlantic Monthly*. Dick advised the PM that he should be reassuring. The PM allowed that he wasn't in a position since he was less than sanguine himself about the country's future. We are horrified at the idea of Richler writing a major think piece in a U.S. magazine that reveals this mood.*

Trudeau looks worn. A frantic bystander, I am doing my bit with *supreme de merde de volaille* or epicure chickenshit. Dick fumes behind a closed door and writes drafts of an opus on "media opportunities" that may never open the door for one. He is indefatigable. As he would say, "I've paid my dues," yet he struggles on.

At the nexus of a nation in considerable agony, I can see many failed opportunities and little teamwork or exercise of common sense. There has been a "study" of the PM's use of time and 90 per cent is "operational." Now more time is to be devoted to long-range thinking and planning, and the Cabinet shuffle reflects this. Fine, but who will look after nuts and bolts? Is it so complicated to decide that Quebec's language bill, Bill 101, discriminates against Quebec anglophones and should be fought? Yet any

* The highly critical and bleakly pessimistic piece that did appear in the *Atlantic Monthly* aroused much controversy and ill feeling.

federal action is stuck in the congested Cabinet machinery. Two weeks hence it has to go to the Priorities and Planning Committee of Cabinet again.

Journalism the Destroyer?

October 10, 1977

Last night, following a particularly tendentious "CTV Reports" which juxtaposed U.K. fascism, memories of concentration camps, and the present Quebec situation by subliminal analogy, I felt that it could well be a worthwhile mission to dedicate one's life to the improvement of Canadian journalism. It really has reached a low. Jean Charpentier feels that we may well see our country destroyed, not by our politicians, but by our press's polarization of the unity question.

This week's evidence: On Saturday at the Collège militaire royale de St. Jean, Radio-Canada's infamous C.-A. Deverieux is noted by the PM himself rolling his camera only during the couple of minutes in which the PM spoke English during a ten-minute speech in French. Sure enough only this clip is run on the French TV network that night, leaving the desired impression of prime ministerial insensitivity to Quebecers' aspirations.

Then, later, Téléscopie, a Radio-Canada television interview set up at the college for the PM. A more self-satisfied and clannish group of journalists I have yet to meet. The host, a prickly professional, had earlier expressed bitter paranoia at the PM "picking on Quebec." During the interview he asks, "Why" (and I have to believe he is sincere) "did the PM refer to Lévesque as 'l'ennemi' in a Montreal *Star* interview?" This became the theme of the whole interview. Trudeau rose to the bait. The host even got in a dig about the infrequency of his appearances on Radio-Canada, much to Jean's chagrin.

On future reading, this may sound insignificant, but my experiences with the media this week underline basic weaknesses in the national communications apparatus. In a word, it is polarized and parochial in a country where consensus-building is accomplished only through the fragile and discredited operations of political parties and the fragmented work of national radio and television networks. This is a country of tribal ghettos reinforced by tribal media.

We live in a dreamworld here where the Press Gallery pumps out information of "national" importance (meaning importance to both French *and* English Canada) for a smaller and smaller clientele, or, worse still, where this national flow itself is considered (at least in some quarters in Quebec) alien, even dangerous.

The "plot" mentality infuses the media outside Ottawa and the cozy confines of the Press Gallery. It can't be just that it sells, it must go deeper. Why else would CTV go to the brink of folly and exaggeration in setting out to prove the new "Special Forces" army unit at Petawawa was in fact formed to quell Quebec revolution? Radio-Canada's André Payette shot a sequence in St. Jean of the PM reviewing cadets to garland this same thesis visually.

Last week, Trudeau sent his "begging" letter to Lévesque. This, and his refusal to take Quebec's Bill 101 to a constitutional test or disallow it, were greeted, as predicted, by the French press, with the theme of "picking on Quebec" and, in the English media, of "abandoning" Quebec anglos. Nobody wrote the real story. We were given only views from different doorsteps.

Through all this the PM is pretty much the model of discipline, patience, and reserve. He did warm to teenage attention at the ball for cadets and their dates, and did, to my horror, bring someone lovely home on the Jetstar late Saturday night at the end of the trip. That is one side, but he watches the national crisis of desire to live together with outer detachment, devoting his intellect to the course he set for himself on this issue twenty years ago.

As Rémi said, he cannot be accused of not articulating a position. But in the short term it is of little emotional use. We will suffer more before anyone listens or even hears.

Last week, to illustrate how perhaps personal, not national, priorities may indeed be part of what we are all up against, I saw Margaret ducking out of a Head of State coffee party at 24 Sussex. She is obviously still in the picture, and I shudder to think of the effect she has on the PM's powers of concentration.

Trudeau Crusades

October 24, 1977

The image of privilege: MOT flight 901 from Ste.-Marguerite Station in the Laurentians to Ottawa and the PM's country place at

Harrington Lake – a red and white jet ranger helicopter that cruises only a few hundred feet above the silver treetops and burnished lakes and rivers. The undulating Laurentians lie to the north, to the south, Montreal, with cloud around the mountain. We swing up the Ottawa River at Hawkesbury and sweep up to the capital as if on some magic hydrofoil. Then, on a rush of air, across the Scott road to Meach Lake and down like a hawk to the lawn at Harrington.

All the while the PM sleeps in the tiny cockpit. Between sessions of staring with amazement out the plexiglass bubble, I ponder his drooping head in the front seat. He is exhausted and looks every day of his fifty-nine years. Moments before lifting off the golf-course landing-place in the Laurentians, he was, like me, a child on his first ride – smiling and jumping from side to side to make sure he missed nothing.

In the speech he had just finished, he returned to his twenty-year-old themes – present PQ activities perfectly fitting his earlier prophecies – and they are all about freedom, personal freedom. The speech required great concentration. It was on the new "clericalism" of the Parti Québécois and its followers who see some sort of lay salvation in a Quebec separate from Canada. This was an opportunity to talk before a non-metropolitan audience that he wanted to make use of, but his reason got the better of him. Most of his analogies bore little on lives as routinely lived – but the principles were crystal clear. His hearkening back to the stifling days of church authority, and his warning not to let it be replaced by separatist ideology, meant much to that crowd of older small-town lawyers and businessmen sipping their coffee in the timbered dining hall where he spoke.

But, now it is his weekend, and he is returning to his family, as I am to mine.

His three children, a nanny, and another woman are in a clutch at the edge of the lawn as we swoop down. With a sly smile he says goodbye to me as I hand him the inevitable token gift from the back seat.* We lift off outward along the lake and, through the bubble at my feet, I can see the pattern of kids on the grass, running, circling, one spread-eagle, around a youthful pied-piper

* The underground corridor which connects 24 Sussex with the pool house in the garden was crammed with scores of banal gifts and mementoes from such occasions.

Trudeau in the middle striding toward the house. Physical freedom found. An almost idealized image frozen in the still, late autumn beauty of the Gatineau.

Trudeau's own personal crusade for freedom is as noteworthy as his crusade against the "isms" that hem in his contemporaries. One element of this crusade appears as a remarkable unwillingness (or perhaps it is shyness) to take any keen or overt personal interest in others beyond the kind of quick and observant contact at which he excels – eye to eye. This is endlessly frustrating to those who might like to be a bit closer or be more indispensable to him. Even Dick O'Hagan talks of him with puzzlement. It means that Trudeau's idiosyncratic actions can only ever be noted, their motivations not understood.

For instance, nobody really knows, as you might with a friend, whether he wanted to see all the junk clippings about a tryst he was supposed to have had with a showgirl, Sandra O'Neill, that filled "Ottawa Today" last week. Joyce Fairbairn feels he must and Dick feels he musn't. Joyce gives them to Trudeau, and he feigns interest. It ends there.

He plays this mystery. If we build up a speech or event as we did in Winnipeg for the CAB, he will blow it. Downplay, as we did for the next night, and you have the second stringers scratching like mad.

Last week, his staff was biting their nails wondering what he would say on Leaders' Day in the House. Without consulting to any degree, he dropped his powerful idea of a national referendum on the constitution at the end of a ninety-minute lecture, as much as to say, "You thought I had nothing to say – hah!" We all run to catch up as he singlehandedly plays the issue.

How the other major issue of the past couple of weeks, the Queen's Silver Jubilee visit, fits into this, I am not sure. Certainly she was willing to lend the credibility only the sovereign can muster to a barely disguised political plea for unity – and to some pretty revisionist history as well! The story of this country is more than the simple overcoming of linguistic and cultural divisions; there are other major influences besides the "magic" of the creative tension between English and French. Until I came to Ottawa and found a few happy *working* relationships with

97

Quebecers (otherwise one's contacts tend to be sporadic and sentimental at best) I could not experience this magic tension.

The press was interested only in the self-answering question about "using" the poor Queen (for federal "propaganda" as Jean Rivard went as far as to say!). I am sure this was of little consequence to the PM. He bathed in the warmth she created (his phrase: "followed in her wake"), and the country took what it liked out of her articulation of Canada's nationhood.

In these times, attitude changes alone hold promise. When people like Bill Teshke, a senior economic adviser in the PCO, admit the traditional tools of government economic intervention by which society was advanced are now inoperative – an idea he dropped during an amazing pre-Speech from the Throne staff briefing – then perhaps it is more important to have a monarch stir things up symbolically.

We have to judge Trudeau and the staff's effectiveness by their ability to stir up people's basic thinking about themselves and their country. The referendum idea should be seen in that light. (What is ironic but has escaped the press is that he really doesn't want or intend to use a referendum.)

Meanwhile, as our boss strives to bring generous ideas to the Canadian people, I live through another attempt to bureaucratize our office in an endless game of retitling and reorganization.

Evidence of illegal RCMP activities in the late sixties and early seventies (including unauthorized break-ins, mail opening, electronic surveillance, and theft of Parti Québécois membership lists) surfaced in October 1977. This led to the appointment of a royal commission chaired by Justice David McDonald of the Supreme Court of Alberta later that year.

Watergate of the North

October 30, 1977

This is the weekend of the Canadian Watergate. I shudder at the convenient analogy. But I am all too aware that while phrases like "law and order" or "anti-subversion" are softer coming from the mouths of Canadian liberals, the national security fantasy so identified with Richard Nixon stands as a possible purgatory for any western democracy that plays with these ideas, however liberal it may claim to be. Anyone whose actions even remotely fracture the moral norms set by the media at the time of Watergate is judged by standards so fixed in the collective psyche that the consequences inevitably must follow the set scenario.

I registered a sense of doom on hearing the convenient justification for the RCMP keeping files of PQ membership during 1973. Oh yes, such illegal activities were nipped off by the PM, but after the fact, and, yes, "systematic" surveillance was frowned on at the time.

But the acceptance of data gathering as a preventive measure poses a moral dilemma that puts me quite on the other side of this pragmatic administration for whom I currently give my life blood.

"I see you are a purist," says the PM, fixing Mike Duffy as Duffy shakes his head over one of the PM's more stretched excuses of RCMP activity. The PM uses the example of the secret of the bomb in the safe that threatens the city – of course you have a right to break in. But the analogy is a bit of a *reductio ad absurdum* in this case. There is a different *expectation* of morality since Watergate and it cannot be satisfied with stretched analogies.

When the PM and his ministers allow that they don't *want* to know about the "operational" aspects of information gathering, I shudder. This was the whole crux of Watergate. My brother Rick phones today, shaken. It is not good enough to dismiss the press's preoccupation by saying, as Jim Coutts does, that they have "Watergate envy."

We face an inexorable downswing in popularity. The phone rings less; the glare of the spotlight shifts; the RCMP business won't go away. It is an autumn of discontent. Clark is looking good, and the economy is in trouble.

Just to make sure we don't get away with anything, television was launched in the House this week. Show business has now penetrated the sanctum of Canada's most exclusive club. The regime is terrified. They are not performing. In fact, they look indifferent in the face of economic and political turmoil. How flip they seem in front of the "eye" – how mercilessly real.

The PM is woefully unprepared and struggles (but not too much) to put his heart into the instant adversarial politics of Question Period, which provides the only juice that gets the daily attention of television. TV gives us instant winners and losers every day. How wonderful!

I have this image of him, talking on a point of privilege, shuffling papers, looking down, never fixing his tormentor, glasses perched precariously on his nose, making a professorial point, then blowing a good line ("I think that should be sufficient for a spurious point of privilege") by mumbling it as he sits down. Why doesn't he play the game and fling it at the adversary? The demands of the "eye" are set and unswerving. We will have to find a way to teach him how to master this medium.

We are so isolated and wrapped up in the assumption of power. To add to the introversion, Coutts is rumoured to be about to depart – power struggles and rumours of power struggles follow.

A candidate in the PMO for the Coutts succession tells me of his encounter with Liberal MP Jim Fleming: the latter, "Hear you may be principal secretary. . . ." The former, poker-faced, "I'm sorry, can't comment on that!" It is a reflection on the office that we roar with delight at the story while knowing the question was as legitimate as the real ambition barely disguised in the answer.

We are all so cool. We all want so desperately to be in the inner circle, which, in this regime, means having your memos to the PM returned annotated and underlined – the PM's way of letting you know what he has read and finds important.

A Few Successes

November 19, 1977

It's a time to try and be positive. This week, we received a morale booster: the "Romper Room" episode. For months I had been begging the PM to meet a few kids coming to Ottawa with a Kitchener-produced CTV children's program. It was hard for me to keep an optimistic tone on calls from an increasingly discouraged organizer and friend, Janet Nostbakken. Finally they were in town anyway, with no set deal with the PM.

By some finessing, it did come off. I made it so easy that there was no way he could refuse. The PM, a bit dishevelled, on his way back to the Langevin Building after lunch with Coutts, stepped out of his car and into the circle of kids – the camera rolling. I am not sure he knew what it was about, or if he had even read my note.

He was superb for seven or eight minutes, even responding to one tot's question on why the roof of the Parliament Buildings is green with the marvellous "that's the colour of hope!" Not a second was commonplace and, although the shooting left much to be desired, the little sequence took on a life of its own. Miss Diane, the hostess, was helplessly rouged in frozen fear or admiration – who knows which? It was a genuine Trudeau moment.

Well, a month or so passed and this week the show was aired. With the impact of a well-orchestrated PR campaign for both the PM and "Romper Room," every newspaper and TV newscast reported on the PM's appearance on the show. CBC radio, the *Star*, CTV news, all of them. Only Geoff Stevens took a few shots. It was talked about endlessly. Even Bob Murdoch agreed it was a good ten-minute investment! So much for good news!

"I've somehow got to get through to that man. He just has to make some gesture to the civil liberties point of view." So said a rather anguished Dick O'Hagan after a press conference in which the PM delighted some in the office with well-crafted put-downs of the flailing Gallery on the endless issue of RCMP "dirty tricks." But the PM was nevertheless absolutely ineffective in making the slightest inroads on the RCMP issue.

His "high ground," as it is rather self-righteously flogged in the PMO, has little to do with the press or even, perhaps, any public desire to eradicate abuse and bring lawbreakers to justice. The "high ground" means not being involved in, or even knowing about, "operational" RCMP security service matters. What politicians don't know, they cannot be faulted for. "When did you last ask your employees if they have broken the law lately?" the PM flings out to the astonished Gallery.

A valiant Steve Handleman (*Toronto Star*) insists that there is a difference between undercover operations of a "disruptive" nature (the image is the dirty tricks of Watergate, but the PM gives little credence to the fact the game is being played on this field) and plain old surveillance. The PM seems not to hear. As he made clear in an off-the-record session with some local journalists in Fredericton on one of our early stops in the swing to visit premiers, the RCMP's activities have never threatened him, so why should any law-abiding citizen feel uncomfortable? Especially why in Canada, where the RCMP is more of a national myth and symbol than a Canadian FBI.

It should be underlined that on this, as on so many fundamental questions, Trudeau alone seems to be setting the tone and content of responses. It is unlikely his attitude will change. George

Bain passed on his question on the issue at the news conference on Friday, saying the answer probably would not be worth it.

Sagging fortunes bring new scapegoats. CBC and television in the House seem to be serving this purpose with distinction. Nearly a whole session of the Priorities and Planning Committee of Cabinet, chaired by the PM, was devoted to a round-table harangue against the CBC's use of House of Commons material, particularly their gall in using more questions from the Opposition than answers from the Government. There were many threats to privatize the CBC, cut budgets, and lots of self-recrimination about letting the "eye" in in the first place.

Provincial Visits

Meanwhile, and this is the paradox, Trudeau's swing through the premiers' offices seems an original and highly productive exercise. This swing to get the premiers onside for a federal-provincial meeting on the economy has a subplot. The PM is using it to discuss wide-ranging constitutional reform. A remarkably open PM is putting his cards on the table in rare face-to-face sessions with the premiers.

The country is on the brink. All you have to do is appreciate the sea of *fleur de lis* that greeted Lévesque's triumphant return from his visit to France and you know that Trudeau's "reason over passion" quilt, which hangs in the upper hall of 24 Sussex, may have to be reversed. Everything has become symbols, hearts, loyalties, feelings. Is this the end of the Yellow Brick Road? For the moment, perhaps.

The Press Office? We are onlookers, even if we have the best seats. I enjoyed doing the Atlantic provinces' portion of the visit to the premiers. Especially because the bright former New Brunswick civil servant, Marcel Massé, was the Federal Provincial Relations Office's (FPRO) travelling aide on the trip from capital to capital.* He made us feel part of the action.

But as it had been decided that these visits would be done without the normal PMO regional advance help, we had to deal with the basics of setting up for the PM, making sure he has orange

* Not the Marcel Masse who is a Cabinet minister in the Mulroney government.

102

juice and cookies in his room, and other such fundamental details. I found myself in the Lord Beaverbrook Hotel in Fredericton, in the manager's arborite office, reeling off all the PM's personal needs like an old pro. I even had the RCMP check out the noise at a riverside construction site to make sure the PM's morning rest would not be disturbed.

One last note. Again, after endless negotiations, my friend Alain Stanké finally confirmed his photo session with Trudeau for the book he is publishing, which is based on the long interviews for TVA he did ages ago. It, too, is to be called *Portrait Intime*, and needs a lot of pictures. Alain's editor, Jeannine Feral, came up from Montreal with a photographer and was ushered into the PM's office.

The PM looked at an illustrated volume that Jeannine showed him to give him an idea of what she was after. He flashed his "steely blues" and said, acidly, that there was not much sense trying to accomplish that in the two five-minute sessions that had been blocked off!

Bob Murdoch managed to smooth things over. So, I found myself later that day waiting with a shattered Jeannine and her photographer in the hall at 24 Sussex Drive.

He performed well with the kids, but made it clear it would be just that and no more. We were unceremoniously ushered out with hardly a goodbye. I have some pity for this tired man who has to work so hard to protect his children from the inexorable demands of public life.

December 4, 1977

Last week, as part of the visit to the premiers, we witnessed the confrontation between Lévesque and the PM in the "bunker," Lévesque's Quebec City office. The meeting was reported as a failure to bridge their opposing views on unity, when, in fact, it was a minor success in terms of gaining some degree of economic co-operation between the province and Ottawa.

Quebec was, however, only the last of this exhausting round. Fly-ins to Newfoundland, P.E.I., and Ontario preceded it. The Newfoundland experience was perhaps the most revealing. I flew in to make preparations before the PM arrived. A half-dozen RCMP and local constabulary descended on my bleary-eyed breakfast in the Hotel Newfoundland on the morning of the PM's arrival. They told me in hushed tones that a demonstration was expected. Worse, that demonstrators would carry as a symbol a "bucket of blood"! Help!

The day was immediately ruined and I got an instant ulcer. "They are peaceful all right," someone assured me. But the image of blood carried, poured, sloshed, or whatever on his arrival at the legislature building was enough to make even a loutish RCMP brute quiver. And all this to be performed with the press cameras rolling!

We met in Premier Frank Moore's office to consult and to hear more intelligence. I left to meet the PM at the airport with what I believed was a tight plan. Whether we entered the building from the front or rear would depend on hearing a "clear" or "not clear" radio signal from the RCMP on the spot. But Bob Murdoch had other ideas, "Get them off to the side of the steps and the PM will decide if he goes over to meet them or not."

I took my place in the rear of the car with the PM in the front and explained to the back of his motionless head what the situation was. Finally, word came that all was "quiet" at the Legislature. We will go in the front. I assured a worried PM that the demonstrators won't get any extra publicity if he passes them going in. They may get more if the press can say that he avoided them entirely.

We pulled up. Things were not as advertised. We've had the wrong signal. The main group was to the side, but an orderly circle of shouting pickets blocked the PM's way. The result was a tense but controlled nose-to-nose chewing out of our head of government by protest leaders. The PM got off a couple of good lines and moved off – without me – only to get lost trying to find the doors to the Premier's suite. "Don't leave him alone," an annoyed Murdoch snarled. I have to learn. You don't become Prime Minister to have to worry about which door to go in. The "mistake" of the pickets dogged the day. Murdoch reminded me of it a dozen times.

After that, things went fairly smoothly. We were fogged out of Charlottetown, our next stop, and had to stay unexpectedly in St. John's, Newfoundland, occasioning a rush set-up of milk and orange juice and flowers in the Holiday Inn. Oh, the responsibilities of state! I was so relieved to get him settled, that I was noisily yakking with Murdoch in the hall outside his room when a door opened, and Trudeau, in pajamas, told us to be quiet!

P.E.I. was a dream. The whole province has the feel of an overgrown village. The spectacle of the PM and Premier Campbell sauntering across the park for lunch at the hotel virtually alone, except for a couple of TV crews and Murdoch and Massé trailing discreetly, was memorable.

Making all the arrangements was a power trip. I found myself more short and severe than normal – to nice people! My curt orders echoed in my ears as if spoken by someone else. I preceded the PM's steps like some sergeant-major, sweeping all before me, retracing the same steps later with apologies. I even got impatient with press bullshit – but not completely. I tried to charm the visiting press gang from Ottawa from taking over a local press meeting and felt betrayed when they didn't take the hint.

Finally we arrived in Quebec City for the long-awaited face-to-face, eyeball-to-eyeball between the PM and Lévesque. Here, I was more of an observer. This stop in the tour of the provinces was about family rivalry. Rémi Bujold overtly loathes his counterpart in Lévesque's office so the cordiality at the advance meeting is paper thin. But no quarter is yielded.

Claude Morin (Intergovernmental Affairs Minister) came to the airport to meet the "foreign" visitor. It was rumoured that Lévesque wouldn't even come down to meet the PM at the entrance to his office, the "bunker." In matters of strategy and symbols, they had it all over us. Rémi just managed to resist insisting that the PM's car carry a Canadian flag!

It was clear Trudeau was ready for this one. He had done little but prepare for this meeting since seeing Premier Davis last Monday. He was highly tuned up. But Lévesque held the media levers. He decided, after all, to come down to greet the PM (they call him "le PM" too). Lévesque had something to say for reporters, and he captured the early news. We were helpless. I was at the bunker entrance, saw what was up, and told an RCMP officer to radio the PM's car. But my message on what to expect on arrival was not passed to the PM.

The news conference following the meeting was arranged amongst *les attachés de presse* with restrained amiability. There were only glimpses of the intense competitiveness that lies behind every Trudeau-Lévesque event. What do we have to sell that they don't and vice versa? Robert McKay, the unlikely-named press secretary to the Premier, admitted that Alain Stanké's interview on TVA with the PM with his kids gave them a lot of grief. Lévesque hasn't got anything on us on the kid front!

We at least agreed, as rational professionals, that no interest would be served by allowing newsmen or documentary makers to do separate interviews, which are then intercut to create artificially the lusted-after "face-to-face" televised encounter between Canada's two protagonists. In our not so dissimilar operations, that was an advance.

But this minimal congeniality disappeared once Lévesque's people got what they wanted. I stayed back to man the cursed sound distribution box that we lug everywhere so the press can plug in and get the PM's utterances clean for their tape recorders. We set it up for the PM, and everyone used our sound feed for the following performance by Lévesque as well.

I extend a hand to the departing Lévesque as he passed by me on his way out of the room. "Le dernier fédéral." I smile. He doesn't. I am the last federalist on the scene. After an exchange on how futile it is for the two to fight like "tomcats" with the bunker receptionist, I take off into the night – a foreigner.

As I left, the story of Lévesque and Trudeau's deep distaste for each other was already written. It was the *only* story for the press. In fact, they had been courteous, if competitive. But even a hungover, smokey night with French reporter friends of Jean Charpentier's from the Quebec "Tribune" (Gallery), or another with our besotted Ottawa clients, did not change the press's view.

The relentlessly opposing courses of the two makes every reporter dream of a television confrontation. This is longed for, pined for like a man aching to be reunited with his lover. Even Peter Desbarats (Global TV) served up the "clash of personalities" story, preferring to ignore their real economic accommodation in favour of the blatantly obvious – that their constitutional positions have not altered a bit.

It is almost impossible for us in the Press Office to fight what is increasingly seen by most press as the "end of Canada" story. It is certainly the story the U.S. press is writing with glee. *Newsweek* screws us with impunity. They guarantee, as a condition of getting access to the PM, a Trudeau cover and a question and answer with the PM, and then deliver back-to-back, highly conflicting and edited Trudeau and Lévesque interviews. The long article bemoaning the end of Canada is illustrated with a colour picture of Lévesque.

Perhaps the Alain Stanké *Portrait Intime* book with its human side of the PM and his family (even if Margaret, who figures in the year-old interview, is no longer present) may sway a few people – or only fortify militants.

Hate Your Enemies and Solitudes

December 18, 1977

What to say as Christmas approaches? Trudeau himself makes flimsy excuses for not doing a *le Devoir* interview on Friday. "Surely it's an imposition to make them come." I know he is coveting his only free day before Christmas – and why shouldn't he?

Yesterday there was a telling gathering at Mike Duffy's. The jolly P.E.I. native is determined to eclipse Ken Colby as number one CBC TV reporter, and invited a panoply of stars from both political parties to his Arlington Woods mansion for cocktails.

I suppose a nose-to-nose meeting between our chief office militant, Colin Kenny, and Joe Clark was more than Kenny could bear, for he only stayed briefly. Walter Baker's arrival soon tipped the balance of the party decisively in favour of the Opposition.

I am always surprised how black and white politics can be at the top. You must be seen to hate your enemies (certainly not socialize with them) and await the stroke of favourable polls to jump on them when they are down.

Hence, at one of the irregular PMO "Program Committee" meetings the other day, I learn that the Gallup and other "soundings" at the end of January will decide whether there is an April election or not. Everyone is satisfied that the fall got us on the offensive with the economy, provincial visits, and so on, and that the February First Ministers' Conference will clinch that upswing. So here we go again. "In my view" (*the* operative phrase at the PMO), we may be in for it this time.

As for the PM, I am more and more convinced that he is simply being a bad boy – he seems to delight in the discomfiture of his advisers and in hanging them up by sly and ambiguous interventions in the House. The latest had to do with U.S. Ambassador Thomas Enders and his continuing interference in Canadian domestic affairs – a long standing tradition, enhanced in this case by the fact that this is the Ambassador's last chance to make a name for himself as he is not a Carter man, and may soon be replaced.

Having spent two days denying that a sleepy "yes" by the PM in the House meant that a note of protest *had* been sent regarding the latest round of Enders's free trade speeches, we are faced with the PM equivocating in the House once again. Yet he agrees with Eugene Whelan that a lot of people are annoyed by these antics. The misunderstanding now becomes hard to defend. Is he or is he not annoyed? He is playing with us.

On Friday we tape his New Year's message. André Burelle has written a good draft that makes a successful transition from domestic to international "spiritual" disarmament. It is approved and a final draft is prepared. Then Ivan Head, the PM's personal adviser for all matters touching foreign policy, gets into the act. There are indeed paragraphs which touch his area – CANDU, sales of nuclear materials, and so on. Burelle's draft is vetoed and we start over. This time with Ivan's somewhat overwritten draft, full of "fearsome" memories of prairie winters, and the like. This one is going to stick despite Dick's and my efforts.

More solitudes. Westerners write of droughts and hardships, francophones of equally isolated cultural experiences. Nobody writes of what new Canadians experience or tries to bridge the gaps. All that matters is who the PM trusts, and he sure trusts Ivan.

FIVE

ELECTION POLITICS

A *sort of "anything-goes" atmosphere in the PMO is a
sure sign that a propitious moment is again being sought
to call an election. Everyone starts flexing what political mus-
cles he has in anticipation. Seats are opened for friends who look
like winners by kicking the losers into appointments. The PM himself is pushed into the public eye more blatantly both at public
events, where he can be a star, and in very controlled or friendly
interviews. This second round of pre-campaign nonsense pushed
me closer to the press.*

On Being a Groupie

January 25, 1978

Joyce Fairbairn, the PM's loyal legislative assistant, and Ivan Head,
his foreign policy adviser, have the inside track in this PMO, the
one has genuine warmth, the other has cool analysis. A general in
the PCO tells Dick that this isn't the White House. Ivan sometimes acts as if it were.

Last week, for instance, Ivan simply did not inform Defence
Minister Barney Danson of a development directly in his jurisdiction for several critical hours, even though the development was
one of the biggest stories of the season – the Russian satellite crash-
ing down near Fort Reliance.

The Prime Minister was the first to hear. He got the call directly
from President Carter. What a picture! At one end, the whole of

the U.S. political, military, and defence apparatus, at the other the PM's half-asleep executive assistant, Bob Murdoch, at home in New Edinburgh! Secretary of State George Ball's call is checked, then goes through our switchboard and the President is on the line to a sleepy Prime Minister. Yes, the damn thing is going to come down. Wow!

Ivan had been forewarned as it turned out, but the first that we or anyone else at all senior in the government heard about it was from press calls. Dick was advised something might be up by Coutts the night before while rushing for a cab, but he forgot to tell us!

We skulked about the office embarrassed by our lack of information. Then, yesterday, Trudeau announced that space was not part of the Canada-U.S. NORAD agreement, and that the U.S. was under no obligation to inform us about "objects" entering our airspace from the heavens. Ouch! We had been using just the opposite line with the press. In the thunderstorm of calls on this "strange encounter" we failed both ourselves and our clients. So much for polishing up our routines in this election alert!

We are again indeed on a war footing; on twenty-four-hour alert for yet another election decision. Entrails of all kinds are being examined. Jim McDonald, Dick's assistant and the extra body of the Press Office, was named, by Claude Hénault on "As It Happens," as the media groupie who has been assigned to hustle the Gallery and personally soften them up for an election.

It is all hanging out. Seats are being opened up so that more favoured candidates can be run. Joe Guay,* a Manitoba Liberal MP, has a prime seat and is being offered either the bench or the Senate. Tom Axworthy is in charge of revving up the west.

This all is straining my credibility with the press. I am finding that I have to come more than half way to some of their views to convince them that anything positive is going on.

Last night with three senior journalists, Hugh Winsor, Patrick Nagle, and Lise Bissonnette, I almost said too much. I was trying to tell them that it is the PM's real sense of loyalty that is behind Bud Drury's appointment as chairman of the National Capital

---

* Guay was eventually appointed to the Senate in March 1978 along with Manitoba Premier Duff Roblin, Newfoundland Tory MP Jack Marshall, and several others.

Commission while he continues to act as constitutional adviser in the North West Territories. I also tried to tell them that the PM is enormously, even dangerously honest when he is pushed. I reminded them that he admitted legislation was being planned to legalize mail openings, particularly in drug cases, when asked directly about this by Terry Wills (a former aide to the Minister of Finance who had made a successful return to journalism with the Montreal *Gazette*) at a news conference.

I was getting carried away as I needlessly went on about Peter McGuire and Colin Kenny from the office and their strange, sometimes blind, devotion to the man and the job. This was doubly unnecessary since I am becoming friendly with both men. Perhaps it was an admission of admiration for their lack of any doubts about their roles in preparing Ontario for a campaign.

We talked on about the campaign-style Ontario trip Peter and Colin had engineered for the PM last week, aborted when snow stopped us from landing in Windsor and we had to turn the press plane around and spend a night in Toronto. I tried unsuccessfully to explain away a couple of foul-ups that had occurred at the outset at a big rally at the Hamilton Armoury. I was feeling rather bitter about Hugh Winsor's mean piece about that event in the *Globe* the next day, which said it was poorly attended and the audience was unenthusiastic. The *Globe* had even managed to use as a photo a shot of a seemingly deserted hall with a lone figure (me) in the centre! This front page put-down implied a mood of gloom and failure over the whole enterprise.

It is true that the PM seemed to be running out of fresh lines and insights into national problems and was not performing well, either in Hamilton or the next day in Toronto. That's the truth, dammit.

In Toronto, at the PM's final appearance in the Royal York, Terry Wills caught the PM out on a line about continued high unemployment being the best hedge against inflation! The PM even said that the difficulty in finding jobs meant that the "working class" would hang on to the jobs they had and that they now understood restraint! Help! On the long plane ride back to Ottawa at the end of the trip, I recklessly confided my doubts to Terry Wills. He had had the same problems when he worked for a minister and understood.

Later, I sat in the Press Club with my journalist clients munch-

111

ing a bit on the same views. I felt like a groupie – half attracted to my clients, half to my boss and his other followers.

In the meantime, the Liberal political apparatus is again up in arms about what is still seen as the separatist bias of the French CBC – Radio-Canada. Apparently Radio-Canada's systematic news coverage priority list doesn't include every visit the PM makes to the province of Quebec. This enrages the PM and Jean Charpentier.

In the latest incident, Radio-Canada's attractive and professional Ottawa correspondent, Madeleine Poulin, apparently did not do a piece on an English meeting the PM attended in the Eastern Townships of Quebec.

I can see the PM's finger jabbing, "Well Jean, was there coverage? Find out!" We didn't move fast enough, and there was hell to pay. Jean placed rush phonecalls for information to Pierre O'Neill, ironically Jean's predecessor as press secretary to the Prime Minister, now the new head of news at Radio-Canada in Montreal! Nothing had been broadcast. A tearful Poulin told Jean at a dinner this week that she had been temporarily suspended!

More phonecalls are made. The complaint is carried right to CBC President Al Johnson! These are the unrecorded wonders of working at the PMO.

When it comes to promoting our PM with the public, there is a feeling now that anything goes. Two examples stand out. Last year there was no way to get the PM to attend the annual Canadian music industry thrash, the Juno Awards. Now everyone is slavering over three million demographically attractive viewers who might see the PM hob-nobbing with Canadian music lovelies.

Then there is suddenly some sympathy for the unloved *Globe and Mail*'s request for a controlled question and answer session with the PM in which the whole text of the interview would be published. Pretty safe, and an old PMO trick to ensure that the PM's views get out clean and aren't mixed up with the reporter's in the same article! This request comes from Mary Truman in the Ottawa bureau, and has her colleagues deeply divided over the propriety of offering the PM that kind of open platform.

Even the PM is getting caught up in justifying the means by the ends. He more than countenances the activities of Paul Tellier's fifth-column Canadian unity group with its propagandistic overtones. To hear the handsome Paul and his acolytes tell us of their plans to spend ten million next year for the federal cause (on producing Unity TV specials among other things!) is enlightening indeed.

This is war! There is real fervour. There is a meeting to get us onside for an assault on all lazy departmental publicists who are supposed to piggyback unity messages onto existing programs. On the margin of Tellier's year-end report circulated in the PMO is the PM's unmistakable, handwritten "excellent."

Yet, when it comes to cooking his own image, the PM can only be led so far. He won't go all the way in playing the office politics of which we are increasingly a part. He frustrated Michel Roy and Lise Bissonnette of *le Devoir* with laid-back restatements of the obvious in a interview we had endlessly promoted. He would not give them a headline, let alone a decent lead.

But we didn't give up. We decided to try and feed them something that would get the interview on the front page. In a last ditch attempt, Jean called me during the Ontario trip to ask the PM if he was referring to Chrétien when he talked in the interview of federal politicians leaving federal politics to go to Quebec to fight. If the PM said yes, Charpentier would relay the information to Bissonnette and it would goose up the *le Devoir* piece she was then writing.

Trudeau was buoyed by the question when I asked him. But he was not about to help *le Devoir*. He would use it for his own purposes. Later last week he told Chrétien if he made up his mind to stay in no uncertain terms, the discussions referred to vaguely in the *le Devoir* interview would not be confirmed. Unable to get the real reference, *le Devoir* used a more general line. We tried!

One image-polishing exercise is working well. We are finally doing something about the performance of ministers in the House, now that their every finger-up-the-nose is televised for the nation to laugh at. Paddy Sampson, a CBC variety producer and our informal media adviser, and his friend Michael Callaghan, one of Morley Callaghan's tough-minded sons, worked for several weeks with me preparing a videotape that highlighted the most gross behavioural and speech idiosyncrasies of Cabinet ministers in the House. The result was hilarious and devastating. It was a compilation of fast cuts of bad-taste ties, horrible checked jackets (Whelan's the worst), and childish behaviour by ministers as a colleague spoke.

Finally we were invited to do what Paddy and Michael called

their "dog and pony" show before "Political Cabinet." What a day! Ministers were open-mouthed, as was a later session of full Cabinet, as they watched this slick layman's guide to putting your best foot forward for TV in the House. Callaghan and Sampson deserve medals of bravery for showing them on video, their awful outfits, their bobbing and weaving, snickering, and bad posture in Question Period.

Ministers sat stunned. As nearly everyone was hit, there was little laughter. But it was effective. Ottawa tailors started to do a landslide ministerial business. Even the PM stopped leaping up so quickly, and started to give the camera time to find and frame him!

This pre-election mood of bravado is affecting us, and I find myself being more daring. I even managed a breach of a pretty firm Press Office rule.

In literally an eleventh-hour conversation, just before the CBC "National" the night before the recent Cabinet shuffle, Mike Duffy dragged out of me the name of Gilles Lamontagne as the incoming Minister of Defence. Presto! It was on "The National" five minutes later. Jean was furious, and even resorted to dressing down poor old Duff the next morning at the Cabinet swearing-in. Duff protected me, defending me as "secretive." He told Jean he had made a "good guess." Such is protection of sources. But there are rules and I broke them. A small breach, but the office is built on trust, and I am ashamed to have threatened it. I must not get carried away again.

Despite this kind of slip, there is easily more objectivity and perhaps even sanity in the Press Office than elsewhere in the Langevin. For that, much credit to Dick O'Hagan. Dick is sanguine and amazingly candid with the press. He genuinely feels guilty when there is a breach of office information flow, and I really like him for that. He supports us.

Dear old Maple One. He did do a great service for me and the family yesterday. I took my little daughter, Susanne, to the House feeling somewhat apprehensive about a guaranteed friendly welcome from the PM. I need not have worried. He bounded unexpectedly into Joyce's office on his way downstairs to the House and charmed Susanne. He waved at her in the House of Commons as we sat facing him below, and later, upstairs, said affectionate goodbyes as we left. He is wonderful with kids.

114

The sparrows are feeding. It is a beautiful, clear winter after-noon and I wonder if, in the great scale in the sky, this, and the PM's kindness to my daughter, isn't as weighty as much of the rest of what I've been living lately.

Raw Politics

January 30, 1978

Today is Susanne's birthday. Today Francis Fox tear-stains the House by announcing he signed as husband for the abortion of a married woman.* He runs from the Chamber. A flushed Bob Murdoch bows his head – I can imagine what he's been through. A career seems ruined. Such is the brutality of public life. And for a minister I identify with.

February 4, 1978

Yes, the PM did have tears in his eyes the Monday Fox resigned as a minister. The office spent the rest of the week mooning about. Coutts was deeply moved, to the point where he was unable even to confide in his friend Dick. Trudeau remained moody, affected as he hasn't been since the split with Margaret.

Our office starts pondering the why's of this event. Dick wor-ries that a cancer goes deeper. I admire Joyce's judgement in a line penned for the PM, but not used, to the effect that this illus-trates the price individuals who choose public life are sometimes required to pay, and that such incidents must give pause to those who would seek high office. Amen.

This week has felt like a month; like a long fever clutching the throat. Real despair. Bob Murdoch sat, head in his hands, in Cecile's

---

* On January 30, 1978, Solicitor General Francis Fox, the youngest member of the Cabinet, announced that he had resigned his portfolio. Fox told the House of Commons he had had an affair with a married woman some years before joining the Cabinet, and she had become pregnant. When the woman went for an abortion, Fox signed the name of her husband on the admitting document.

It was not, however, the end of Fox's political career. Bright, bilingual, and a Rhodes Scholar, he returned to the Cabinet as Minister of Communications in 1980. He lost his seat in 1984.

115

office. This was a price indeed. The merciless press, "pushed by their editors," keep it alive, trying to discover the identity of the person who wrote the anonymous letter that fingered Fox in the first place. Wednesday was a black day for the *Globe* when it revealed that the author of the "concerned citizen" letter was a woman. All the mean and nasty news that's fit to print.

A bigger worry, shared by Allan Grossman (a PMO policy adviser), is that the PM and his advisers have little to sell at this pivotal point in the life of the government. They have a surfeit of hate, a wartime strategy to conquer, with which to rout Lévesque; but little else.

I balance, trying to stay firmly on the PMO side and not fall victim to the Gallery value system. This is a tough act since naked politics increasingly dominate the office. Joe Guay, a Manitoba MP, is slow in quitting his seat, provoking someone to say, "We've got to get rid of that turkey!"

The next big election-style regional event is a full Cabinet meeting to be held in late March in Regina. Although, as has become the practice, groups of ministers will hear public briefs, this is thinly disguised electioneering. The press will be blasted for saying so. John King did today in the *Globe*, pointing out that the government was paying for the western "campaign style" swing, not the party. How much do we think we can get away with?

February 12, 1978

Fallout from the Fox affair continues. The dreadful feeling persists that the press is closing in on the identity of the wife and the informant, and that "now innocent people will be hurt."

The PM spends a lot of time with party types, almost as if the election decision has already been taken. I squire a reluctant and chippy PM ("Who wrote this junk?") to a Liberal filming for canvassers. He may find these things distasteful, but he does them. He has a new brown suit and haircut. The packaging is ready!

Friday's news conference was a disaster. An ill-tempered PM showed his mistrust of the press in nearly every non-answer. "I love these questions about timing," he snapped at Peter Mansbridge of the CBC who had asked when the PM had first learned of the Fox business, "as if they were relevant at all."

The February 1978 First Ministers' Conference was devoted to economics, and had been elaborately prepared, starting with trips to visit every premier months before. Marcel Massé was head of the Federal Provincial Relations Office in charge of preparations.

PQ and Liberal Militancy

I should note that the exposure I have had over the last few days to our Federal-Provincial "officials" has convinced me there is a serious change of attitude. Normal federal paternalism seems at an all-time low and we can only hope it transposes effectively to the First Ministers' Conference.

Marcel Massé, up from the provinces himself, is a different breed. He understands the psychological matrix that, in so many cases, dooms these exercises before they start. He is enthused by the new attitude of co-operation, but the press aren't buying this new mood. They are so woefully ill-prepared for the start of the Conference tomorrow. Their *cause célèbre*, and the subject of over half the questions at the briefing, is whether the conference will be open or closed to the press, and under what circumstances.

February 25, 1978

First Ministers' footnotes: The real moment of the conference came when a determined wedge of Péquistes left the hall and drove through the Delegate's Lounge for their spoil-sport 3:00 p.m. press conference, a full hour or so before the conference closed. The federal officials blanched. Their months of preparation, of tilling the difficult provincial soil, seemed to evaporate in seconds. Lévesque pulled off the most diabolically effective upstaging of a national forum that could be imagined. It was brilliant.

Everyone watched in agony as Lévesque pronounced what, until that moment in time, was unspeakable. The conference, he said, was only Trudeau's cynical election exercise. He had come in hope, he left in despair. The staged pathos was magnificent. The press bought it – almost.

Does it matter? Lévesque had the first crack at the national TV audience, the first real drama. I have to admit that the first cut *is* the deepest, to rephrase a Gossage maxim for this occasion.

Radio-Canada smugly did its live coverage, but saved its real steam for the evening newscasts, the "Téléjournal," which reported only the Quebec walkout and ignored the positive reaction to the conference from other premiers. Even Premier Hatfield's characterization of Lévesque's actions as "a pre-referendum political strategy of the most cynical kind" was not used.

Because the conference was open and Charles Lynch considered himself victorious over the forces of stonewalling and secrecy at the previous conference, his conference columns dripped with positive sentiment.

This country is fractured by its media. The First Ministers' limited success in forming a consensus on economic strategy, is like the tree in the forest that falls with no witness. As the media preferred to communicate another version of the event entirely – it really didn't happen.

The worst thing was that I had had a premonition. At eleven or so that morning it came to me that this was a likely scenario. I warned Dick and Massé, but no contingency was made.

Is Quebec lost? Is Canada really an English hegemony in which, as today, even the PM delivers his best lines in English only, and forgets to repeat them in French for use on French radio and TV. (This is a constant problem. He is seemingly incapable of knowing or remembering what language he is speaking, or to repeat in the other unless I or someone else frantically cues him!) But, as in many global misfortunes in a pre-campaign period, the genuine partisans are wonderfully optimistic. "Best thing that could have happened," Coutts says, reacting to the Lévesque walkout, "but don't quote me!"

The following weekend there were three days of Liberal militancy at the Liberal Policy Convention at the Château Laurier in Ottawa. It is equally charged with pre-campaign fever, and Bob Murdoch tells me he gives the PM an "85 per cent" overall mark for his performance there.

One journalist describes conventioneers as "smug sycophants." They certainly filled the Château with well-tailored conviction.

A strange blend of compassion and contempt was ladled out by Trudeau in a graceful performance the opening night, Friday. He looked great – young, in control, his steely blues glittering. He was made up by an adoring CBC cosmetician – "He looks so healthy," she purred. Nobody was allowed to mess his makeup by kissing him on the way into the ballroom! There, legs astride, thumbs planted in his belt – the "gunslinger" pose – he delivered one hour of lines whose substance was sometimes lost in style. But, it was a good speech. He hit his political stride. The PM had some knife lines for Joe which overjoyed the best room* I've ever seen for a speaker.

Happily, he was persuaded to reject a killer line directed at the CBC, whose carefully engineered broadcast of the speech became a free-time hour-long political announcement as the PM went forty minutes past the advertised fifteen!

In the clicking press room at the Château, I was one of the terriers yapping and laughing as we watched the man's performance on TV.

On Saturday, I stalked about on my errands. Nobody knew what the "script" was for the closing the next day. We had live CBC TV again from 12:00 to 12:30 on Sunday, and they had to know. Tracking down party president Al Graham or his aide, Sandra Severn, to find out simple things like who closes the plenary session and introduces the PM was like trying to find someone at a midway. For a while there was some doubt whether Trudeau had even agreed to speak! I didn't say anything to my CBC pals about that. Everyone from George James, the CBC executive producer, to the floor director asked me questions, and I paced the corridors looking for crumbs and being gladhanded. ". . . And he's in the PMO" trails all introductions.

Nobody knew, so I waited until Sunday morning to establish from a slightly gray and pasty PM himself before breakfast that he indeed will speak (and more in French, he agrees, than he did on Friday). Finally, Al Graham comes to the press room and we work it out. It flies. I have to talk to twenty people on the platform and in the wings, but it comes off.

At noon precisely the Chairman called for Al Graham who made a snappy introduction to our Liberal leader, the PM. There were three-and-a-half minutes of adoring applause, "For he's a jolly good fellow" and "Il a gagné ses épaulettes" (at which point I got choked up). It was just four minutes past noon. The PM was up and speaking. We were live on national TV. A small victory!

One of the things I noticed while hanging around the press room

* A "good room" is one that has a big crowd who are tuned in to the speaker.

119

during the conference, is how hierarchical the press are; how juniors defer to "stars," and how self-satisfied this latter small group is.

Saturday night in the press room, Mike Duffy gave a hot-stove rendition of his role in the October crisis. It was followed by Jeff Simpson's political analysis of campaign prospects during which he dropped that I, of course, will be the Jody Powell of the campaign (hah!). This made me OK, and suddenly I got the aristocrats' attention right up to Allan Fotheringham.

The press experts were soon making detailed predictions. Ridings I have never heard of were being dissected with insider flare. Dick O'Hagan came in, swept up Fotheringham and the columnist's friend Nancy Southam (bedecked in a wonderful furry sweater), and that's the last I saw of them. The show rolled on on closed-circuit TV in the now quiet press room. It was working, and the press weren't sure they liked that.

March 1, 1978

Everything is politicized. Examples: Israel's prime minister, Menachem Begin, is coming on an official visit to Canada. Where can we get a bigger crowd for a state dinner? Where will it have the most political effect? Toronto or Montreal?

The PM will give an important speech at the Economic Club in New York. How can we use this event politically? How about a Boeing 707 planeload of Liberal candidates to accompany him, at public expense? Ivan Head is appalled.

Some of our equipment is getting run down. We should have better for a campaign. So we order a new portable sound box and speakers. Seven thousand dollars, but nothing compared to the twenty-five thousand's worth of walkie-talkie radio equipment recently pushed through a horrified Privy Council Office financial administration. Our legacy!

Some almost non-political activities chug on – barely. There has been a good deal of work on a constitutional reform package, which is due for publication in the spring. Last week Jean LeMoyne shot down months of work on a draft preamble by rating it "incompréhensible" in any language! In a rare digging-in of his heels, he went via Coutts to the PM with his outrage, and the exercise ground to a halt. Apparently the draft, in attempting to define the nature of the Canadian union, souped us all together as immigrants of one kind or another, obliterating any sense of the contribution of those who first built the nation. It was also untranslatable, and, on the rock of LeMoyne, the project foundered!

One of the lightest moments of my tenure to date came yesterday when a call came from a Roberta someone at CHEZ-FM saying they were having a "Ho-ha-ha" contest, and would it be possible for the PM to give her a laugh for the contest! A request for a prime ministerial guffaw! Well, it is not often he laughs out loud, but we had a great and rare *ho-ha-ha* on tape from the Ontario New Liberal meeting. She was delighted. I did not tell her he was laughing *at* someone!

Politics on Politics

April 8, 1978

Most of the past few weeks have been spent in pre-election frenzy, answering endless calls and queries aimed at helping a Press Gallery in a state of suspended animation fix an election date.

Pre-campaign, in the life of the office, means getting rid of ministers or others who might reduce chances of the party's winning, and, of course, opening safe seats where chosen favourites can run and bolster the image of the party.

Jim Coutts is in his office making the calls, the ultimate power trip. "Would you like to be called to the Senate?" Yes: Jack Marshall, a Newfoundland Tory MP, agrees to clear a seat we might just be able to win.

There was some heavy political action at the recent Cabinet meeting in Regina. The full Cabinet arrived in a squadron of Jetstars and other aircraft. They held a regular meeting, then did some well-photographed visits to local industry in smaller groups, and heard public briefs.

Despite press cynicism about this massive, tax-supported political blitz, the public committee hearings worked well thanks to really impressive interest-group participation. The sea of green caps and windbreakers in the agriculture session was an unforgettable sight – a very serious crowd.

I worked with the Otto Lang people and with Otto's attractive wife and her brother Tony Merchant. They are very partisan, but

I have to admit to the convenience of such beliefs in this world of shades.

But there were few great moments, unless you count Bob Murdoch's horror that demonstrators would be allowed right outside the rather seedy "Cabinet Room" set up on the second floor of the Saskatchewan Hotel. They too were a serious lot, espousing two or three causes. If we kept them forcibly downstairs, they could have captured a story that would completely upstage the meeting, so I arranged for them to come up. Posing as a Cabinet representative, I had a good time officially welcoming them in front of an amused press.

Politics on politics – I spent a great deal of time negotiating Premier Blakeney's visit to the brief pre-meeting coffee to officially welcome federal heavies. The real purpose of the visit, however, was for the Premier's film crew to record every minute for his own electoral use.

I should mention the closing news conference. Under Jean Charpentier's guidance, French questions dominated, to the horror of the phalanx of uncomprehending western Cabinet ministers flanking the PM on either side!

Another sidelight. One of the many unforgotten and now gently aging young Trudeauites from 1968, Don Peacock, had been hired to produce a document justifying federal prairie policies. This was to be fed to public and reporters during the Regina Cabinet session. The Privy Council Office refused to bless it as a government document, which would have given it official status and importance. But a determined Tom Axworthy brought it to Regina in quantities, regardless. Only two copies were taken from the press room table!

Soon, to my delight, we were off home, assigned to a distinctly wet Jetstar (prime ministerial Jetstars were dry, except for wine at meals). Judd Buchanan provided the forty ounces of scotch.

Trudeau later complained that they had put him in a plane with no time to prepare the four or five speeches he had to deliver. As things heat up, his mood darkens. He takes a tremendous load and maintains a monastic routine, while his aides drink up the glamour of the greatest show in Canada.

Last night Rémi Bujold persuaded a reluctant PM to fly in and out of Quebec City the same evening, to attend a reception honouring Raynald Guay's fifteen years as a Liberal MP. Our line to the press about the PM's personal delight in doing such things is a bit thin. Oh well, he performed well anyhow, and reduced a grateful Guay to choking and sobbing in a display of public emotion that would be hard to match.

The large, amiable Quebec City press contingent could not believe there was no hidden agenda in the evening. Later, in the Jetstar, an amused PM asked what headline the folksy event and his professorial talk would produce. I told him the press was utterly confounded, and so was I!

This has been a week of other barely explicable happenings. On Monday I administered a rare and elaborate CTV television filming at 24 Sussex. This exceptional access had been gained, not by the Press Office, but by the sophisticated and seductive work of Stephanie McLuhan, one of the beautiful, impressive, and, one must assume, persuasive daughters of Canada's most famous communications theorist.

Although the interview was agreed to over dinner between Stephanie and the PM, it fell to me to turn sweet *yeses* into some sort of reality with a grumpy PM whose kids had chickenpox! He set out strict interdictions for the filming. The unrequited lady was in a fit when her Toronto network bosses threatened to pull out of the project.

Finally I worked out a mutually acceptable filming sequence, and the professional crew, under producer Lionel Lumb, went to work turning the pool and the living and dining rooms of the "residence" into full-scale sets.

Stephanie preened in the downstairs bathroom while we awaited the PM's return from the office. All went remarkably well. The calm producer, Lionel Lumb, controlled Stephanie's more outrageous ideas.

Justin, the only healthy child, performed beautifully, and I was moved by the intensity of father-son rapport – especially so when the two played piano. The matched profiles in concentration showed a quality of life you seldom see, let alone capture on film. The PM agreeably did a superb dive for the pool sequence.

The filming, of course, was only Chapter One of this saga. CTV, or, as I taunted network executive Tim Kotcheff, "Canadian Trudeau Vision," had a major soul-searching on whether to grant airtime to such a palpably positive document. They swallowed hard and decided to put it on.

We fussed over the future use of this intimate cameo footage. "I can't guarantee what will happen to it once it's on the shelf" the producer assured me. Trudeau himself is delighted with the session.

Another Non-Election

April 24, 1978

As the decision day for an election nears, the office and its work, my life in fact, become more and more politicized. Confidences, insights, and chance exposure to the inner workings of getting a government re-elected are as dangerous to think about as they are to write about. They are like the secret battle plans of a desperate military campaign to repel an invader. The pressure from a bored and tired press to give some indication of how and when their lives (and mine!) will be blown away, mounts to absurd proportions.

The PM seems faintly out of control. He is more and more the star of an unruled and uncontrolled machine that runs ever faster and in ever-multiplying directions. His face was a study of elegant resignation while he did his duty at a Toronto Maple Leafs game this week. There he was, between the first and second periods, with two candidates, men he barely knew, waiting patiently to be crowded by fans, autograph seekers – anyone to validate his being there. But, when the time came, only three bosomy women appeared. They gushed up to plant their kisses and brought the dimples to his face.

Today he was pensive while Paddy Sampson, Michael Callaghan, and I gave him some specific advice on his performance for television in the House. We have been waiting a long time for this appointment. Apparently so has he! "First advice of this kind I've had in ten years!" he tells us.

He was angry that he had to argue with his staff against using the Jetstar for a purely political two days in Toronto. They should know better than to expose him to criticism over the political use of a convenience paid for by taxpayers.

On Thursday, after a successful meeting in Trudeau's riding of Mount Royal, we flew to Toronto for a couple of events. Thursday night, one of the office's political experts strutted into my room in the Royal York. "I have told the PM we are using the following lines with the press," he intoned, sipping courtesy booze meant for the absent Bob Murdoch. Then followed the unlikely reasons we are supposed to pump out to the press to explain the PM's unlikely Toronto program. This is the lineup: "Government work in his room" – hah! – then, "meetings to inform himself on civic issues with civic leaders" (read candidates) – double hah hah! I am not ready for this hype. (This aide paid for his too-clever approach by the PM's morose and silent manner at the first photo-lunch-visibility session with a candidate.) I am to use the above explanations to explain this "soft" visit. The word is to stay in the shadows for the next couple of days.

I did, but accompanied him to Exhibition Stadium Saturday afternoon, and it was there things started to fall apart. Real boos greeted his entrance and his throwing of the first ball. "This is swing country," I joked, and every reporter within earshot used this quip as a lead.

Hindsight, like moonlight, becomes the office. Today, I heard over and over that the guy who throws the first ball is always booed. I even heard a Pearson anecdote from Axworthy, our resident historian, to this effect. Great. But prime ministers are not booed, and an eager press spread the word of this grand hitch to a waiting Canada. Only the sports pages, bless them, quote players from both teams laying a few laurels at Trudeau's feet.

Trudeau is not amused.

Planning, savvy, leadership – finally I am exposed to it. I am invited to a meeting of "Red Leaf," the infamous interagency group responsible for Liberal party advertising during a campaign. There I am, with the boys, in Jerry Grafstein's Toronto boardroom, having hustled all the colour shots of Trudeau I can for a campaign-poster selection.

We choose. Jerry Goodis fingers a toothy one by Mike Evans (a *Time* photographer who had a few sessions with the PM) and all agree vocally. Later, when it is too late, Coutts dissents. They know the "Least Objectionable" theory, so Montgomery's macho pose of the man standing behind his desk in his shirtsleeves will not line every Liberal hall from St. John's to Victoria.

The rest of the time is spent being generally brilliant and intuitive-guys trying to pull "issues" out of the air when they barely know what the pipeline deal is about. The gurus strut their stuff. Goodis stabs the air with a marker and argues the need for "good news" economic material if he is going to come up with catchy lines. He needs these to insert, underlined, into Trudeau campaign speeches, so the agency film crew can tell they are coming and can capture them and cut them into campaign commercials.

Gerry Robinson, the executive director of the party, promises to get some happy facts. I know of at least four different groups digging up this stuff, each unaware of the other.

May 8, 1978

The press has all but buried the PM. Having defeated him, retired him, and replaced him earlier last week when polls showed him neck and neck with Clark at 41 per cent!

Lately the job has consisted mostly of garbling, bluffing, and laughing my way, often hysterically, through a maze of press attempts to prod, poke, and pressure out of me any indication of a possible election date.

"Can I go to Montreal this Friday?" asks Lise Bissonnette.

"Can I go to the Socred Convention?" asks Jeff Simpson.

"I'm putting together some files. Only for use after an election. What's the date of preparedness?" This is from Terry Wills.

"What's the PM's schedule for the week? Who is he seeing? For personal planning purposes only, of course." This from just about everyone.

I was always a June 10 man, mainly because I know that it is the date Colin Kenny is pushing for and I admire his dogged tenacity. Gallery people have lost lots of money on earlier dates. They might have called!

Meanwhile the machine took me in. We had a monster election-planning meeting ten days ago. All the regional guys and the PMO attended. Colin Kenny pronounced his strategy of going where the well-planned event was. This would guarantee success.

As for press strategy, I am working on a packaging document for press advance – a manipulator's manual. It will be the first detailed, professional compendium of everything you need to know about PMO press operations and tactics. Everything, from setting

126

up news conferences and press rooms, as well as all sorts of advice on how to facilitate the press's job and make sure the PM looks and sounds great. It is a highly sensitive political document, which could be fun to quote selectively. Copies are numbered and we warn recipients of the dangers of their circulating.*

We talk about a press strategy during the campaign and agree unanimously that the weekly press-conference routine should continue. Dick sagely allows that he will "reserve judgement."

We are a gung-ho gang. In our minds, at least, the campaign charter aircraft has virtually taken off. All that remains is some wrangling over who will occupy the two Press Office seats at the front! Tom Axworthy wonders whether his idea of a train for part of the national tour, as was used in Diefenbaker days, will be shot down. Advances are being done for certain predictable events. Anne Jamieson flits about the office talking about manifests, baggage tags, and expense accounts.

Then, like a call from purgatory, last Tuesday Dan Pottier of the Montreal *Star* phoned me out of bed to get a reaction to disastrous Gallup results. Their implication doesn't sink in immediately; my enthusiasm to hit the trail lingers a few more moments. "Man does not live by polls alone," is Jim Macdonald's clever line, but the office does, and there is a truth session with Trudeau Thursday to prove it.

At once, the knives are out. Bill Fox lets me in on his notion that the PM might retire. I admit "the thought crossed my mind." It had that morning, but I call Fox back to reassure myself that he won't use it. He doesn't.

There have been more frequent staff bitch sessions about the press than I can remember. These are exacerbated by a nasty little note from the Press Gallery executive noting press-conference "abuses" (meaning that we aren't doing them in Ottawa each week anymore). We spend hours honing a reply. Is this the real business of the office? A bunker mentality has taken hold, and I catch Ralph doing his CV. We make a joke of it at the Press

---

* Ralph Coleman updated this seminal work (!) after our 1980 election win, and sent me a numbered copy as a memento when I was working at the Embassy in Washington. It contained much the same material as our first effort, but was slicker and better presented. I sent my copy to Bill Fox, who had recently been appointed Mulroney's press secretary. Honour amongst thieves, I suppose!

Club, and it goes over well. The Second Floor goes to ground.

Meanwhile, Claude Ryan (the newish Quebec Liberal leader) comes to town. We call a White House-type press debriefing on the lawn for the two leaders at Sussex at 2:00 p.m. By 3:30 we are still waiting and I am running out of small, let alone big, talk for the first time. Finally they emerge. Ralph and I notice a prime ministerial serenity we have not seen for weeks and conclude he has made up his mind.

He is marvellous that day; patient, even when our sound system goes down and a forest of mikes appears, gracious with the pack during the first scrum in over a year. What's happened? But few notice the rare warmth or explore the meaning of two towering men of words and intellect perhaps deciding the country's future.

Nevertheless, as the wait for the decision drags on, the press peck away at what they consider exposed flesh. Mary Janigan of the *Star* picks up some Rockcliffe gossip about reconciliation with Margaret. I try to kill the rumour to anyone who will listen by a logical argument in ordinary people terms – Margaret is around because who else is going to look after the kids while he is on campaign? But they would rather speculate on the PM giving up politics as the price of reconciliation! This is a sentiment worthy of Harlequin, not of national political reporting.

May 17, 1978

Last Thursday the PM announced that he and the Canadian public did not want an election this spring. We have called the days since "The calm before the calm." It's a time for feet up. The PM is undaunted in his good humour. Guess who won this lengthy debate? Perhaps there is no link, but on May 2, Natasha, our venerable Afghan, is put down – a heartbreaker for Helga; a necessary act I would not face up to.

As in all truly great PMO machinations, the visible signs of activity virtually disappeared behind one, even two, closed doors during "decision time." "You could have taken bets on the possibility of an election at 1:30" (the announcement was at 2:00), a Gallery member told me later. You would have found many takers in our office too! That's how much we live in the dark at these really critical moments.

Even Dick wasn't invited to the morning staff meeting that fateful day. Coutts alone was consulted, then the PM went to Cabinet. I ventured over before he got out, and I and a jittery Bob Murdoch were soon joined by party president Al Graham, more flushed than normal. After a brief meeting, the PM and Graham emerged together into a mob of sweaty cameramen and perspiring paparazzi.

There would be no election call this spring.

I played the only role possible in such situations, that of a trusted aide who appears to have a big secret (when he doesn't). The press wanted to believe I knew!

The ill humour of the Opposition benches contrasted with the forced gaiety of the government benches. Later, a jaunty PM waltzed into a nice shadow-boxing session with the press. He explained to the incredulous Hugh Winsor that politicians had a "second sense" about what the public wanted, and that these intuitions were not to be questioned by the likes of the critical press! As is now increasingly the case, the news conference was more like Question Period than the venerable institution itself!

There was not a single question outside the theme of the election and leadership. Before the decision to delay an election was taken, the press had buried the PM, assuming he would be defeated in a campaign. Now the press assumed he would resign and be replaced by John Turner in a leadership convention before the next election. I am assured that the likes of Francis Fox are surreptitiously getting their leadership campaigns ready, including hiring staff.

I do not foresee any such radical turn of events, any more than I subscribe to the Gallery cant of Margaret returning and forcing the PM to retire. He will go when he is ready, and we and the Gallery will be the last to be forewarned.

The press's tendency to try to predict what the PM will do by making analogies to their own lives or the lives of those they know was indulged in with tiresome frequency this week. These analogies simply don't apply. Trudeau has very different standards, that's all. Few of the press appreciate what a disciplined life the PM leads, and how little he leaves to whim or emotion.

Slowly, slowly this week the PMO hawks have come back to roost–Axworthy, Coutts, and Kenny. They are grumpy but regroup nonetheless. There is a lot of griping about hierarchical problems.

Some claim that Coutts is acting as if the campaign was on and he was pulling all the strings.

The press is in disarray. The story of Trudeau's defeat at the polls is on hold. How dare the PM force them to revert to real coverage of real events in Ottawa! They would much prefer the pseudo events of a campaign. Making "gut" judgements on the campaign's outcome is much more fun than covering the economy, not to mention drinking time on the endless flights about the country, nor to overlook the huge amounts of campaign overtime so cruelly denied. Ninety per cent of all the calls since the second election that never was, deal with the PM's non-election travel plans – a sure sign of priorities.

SIX

MAL DE PMO

*T*he decision to defer going to the polls until the fall of
1978, perhaps even until early 1979, left the office adrift.
*This was partly because PMO staffers tend to work one term, then
move on. Many in this PMO came after the 1974 election, and had
been waiting patiently until after the expected 1978 election to
leave and return to normal life. Their plans were now thrown for
a loop, and they had to decide if they would wait another year.
Many key players decided not to. Their confusion was reflected
in a confusion of policy direction. What do we do now?*

*But, nature abhors a vacuum. The turning down of the politi-
cal heat to simmer gave External Affairs a chance to crank up
the PM for a major peace speech. It was delivered to the UN
Special Session on Disarmament, and unveiled the interesting
idea of "suffocating" nuclear development and research as one
way to slow down the buildup of nuclear weapons.*

June 4, 1978

New York. The UN Disarmament Speech. That this was a solid
effort was attested to by no less than Hugh Winsor and Marjorie
Nichols, both of whom wrote favourably about the PM's ideas. I
enjoyed the pleasant, even sane press companionship at the St.
Moritz Hotel.

Klaus Goldschlag (the real operator from External Affairs on the disarmanent dossier) and I rode out to the airport together to meet the PM. Michael Pitfield and Allan Gotlieb, undersecretary of state at External, went ahead of us in another car. "Why they would want to ride out to the airport together is beyond me," Goldschlag said mischievously. "They talk to each other endlessly every day."

While Jean Charpentier, Pitfield, Gotlieb, Goldschlag *et al.* lounged in the $120 a night Pierre Hotel, I got drunk with the press, and listened to a rather sad and bitter rant from CBC radio's Terry Hargreaves about Trudeau's refusal to use the press to communicate with the public, instead feeling he had to best them in debate. Not a bad point.

I missed the extraordinary little drama of Bob Murdoch pushing a desk into position in the PM's suite so he could rehearse, in his bathrobe, his General Assembly speech before Jean and Goldschlag. But I didn't miss going to the UN in the Secret Service cavalcade with hidden loudspeakers blaring at cars that threatened to disrupt progress – "Plymouth, keep back!"

I did make one distinctive contribution for our press corps. French President Giscard d'Estaing's reception in the stuffy Pierre ballroom was closed to all press save a pool of reporters from France. The PM was already inside, and I wanted to get at least one Canadian photographer in. "Absolument pas moyen . . ." was the repeated answer to repeated attempts by Bob Fowler (an official from the Canadian UN Mission) to break this prohibition. We decided to beard French officials during the reception itself. We tried everything. Then Giscard's press officer hove to, and we escalated our lies and demands in earnest. Finally, he consented to one stills man (a still photographer). Canadian Press's Freddy Chartrand was ushered in wearing his best safari suit.

I decided to try one final pitch for the CBC, who, after all, are our "réseau d'état." (The term is used in Quebec to describe the CBC. It means, literally, the "state network," making it sound like official state TV, something the French from France understand.) I eventually hit the right note by mentioning that a piece would go on that night throughout Quebec (Lévesque was the darling of Giscard's France). "Ah . . . un moment," intoned my Lanvin-soaked French press officer who returned shortly with a nod.

Regrouping

June 6, 1978

The polls started to turn favourable today, like a good PMO weather forecast. Our two-point gain and the PC's two-point loss is psychological dynamite for PMO partisans and Liberal MPs alike.

The Gallery is a bit much. Mark Phillips, CBC TV's rising star, is particularly provoking, demanding at the United Jewish Appeal dinner on Monday night, "When the hell is your fucker [the PM!] going to be on?" I told him that if he was trying to get me angry he would not succeed. He retorted that sometimes he felt he had to use a sledgehammer.

What's going on? Does our legendary cool drive them nuts? Would they rather we bitch at them, carp openly about their work when they are too critical, like so many ministerial aides? They will wait a long time to get that satisfaction from me. Or, are they just tired of the Trudeau saga that even they have not been able to end?

A few weeks ago we got an acid letter from Christine Hearn, the new president of the Press Gallery ("that idiotic little girl" is how Jean describes her!), complaining, amongst other things, of the number of PMO types sitting in the press theatre at *their* news conferences, and the treatment Ottawa press travelling with the PM get compared with local press at news conferences on the road. They do not, apparently, like the fact we give local reporters a chance to ask questions too.

The office buckled under to the first complaint. Dick, however, showed a real desire to get these news conferences "on our turf," since, as long as they are held in the press theatre, they are chaired and controlled by the Gallery itself. A reply to the letter was laboriously drafted, redrafted, and dispatched. It was moderate, on the whole, and ended with the memorable line that their needs on the road would be kept in mind "animated with a sense of equity. . . ."

The pique of the Gallery was not long in showing. It was the gossip of the Press Club. How dare he! How arrogant! What does he mean? Another memo was circulated, more drafts were circulated. So go our perverse relationships with the press.

Today we hear for the first time that Robert Murdoch, chief aide and lieutenant to our Praetorian Guard, will leave August 1 after five long, aging, grinding years in the office next to the PM's. This event calls for reflection. He is a man of considerable talents, of wit and imagination, who has been stifled and suffocated to some degree by his life of "second guessing" a hard-driving but lonely leader.

The PM could be touchingly human and compassionate with Bob. I saw this side of their relationship one Friday when Bob and I shared the limousine with the PM to New Edinburgh. Bob said his relatives were coming to visit. Trudeau said, "Oh don't bother . . ." making the call or whatever Bob had said he would do, "You work hard enough. Be with your family, it can wait."

Murdoch's rewards for countless hours of patient protection of the boss are few. He goes to private, not public reward, back to Lafarge Cement and to James Sinclair (Margaret's father) who connected him with Trudeau in the first place. His only fault was his habit of transmitting the PM's anger to the nearest office associate. In that sense, he sometimes added to the strains of the office, strains which he, of course, felt most severely. But we easily forgive this. What now will he do with all he knows, has seen, has laughed or grieved over? He takes away an iron stomach and a trove of memories that perhaps he will never share. I'll miss him, and I'll even miss his ill-mannered cut-off of a legitimate question on the intercom!

A Great Leak

June 14, 1978

Last week was the week of the "Great Leak." Monday was the target date release of the "long awaited" White Paper on Constitutional Proposals. We had anxious meetings with sweaty staffers from the Canadian Unity Information Office who described their monster organization for distributing six hundred thousand copies to all Post Offices in time for the release day. Well, press officers do think the same thing at the same time – namely, that, in such cases, the more copies that are out in the field before being made public, the greater the chance of one falling into the hands of the dreaded press.

The Friday before the Monday release day, Standard News's

Jim Munson was on the phone. "Could I order an English copy of a book? Supply and Services number such and such entitled, *A Time For Action*." Yikes – *it's out*! I heard great guffaws at the other end. He told me *la Presse* had a leak of it.

I slammed down the phone and rushed into the hall. *It's out*! Jean Charpentier had just received a similarly gloating call. We moved quickly. Jean got Paul Tellier at the Queen Elizabeth in Montreal who bought an early edition of *la Presse* and confirmed that they have the "faits saillants," the summary pamphlet, not the whole thing. He was delighted, especially as it is a positive story. With his consent, we then "authenticate" the leak to all comers.

I phoned Joyce Fairbairn to have her inform the PM and Marc Lalonde of the leak and our response. Madeleine Poulin of Radio-Canada called to say she has a copy and will confront Lalonde with it when he comes out of the House. Two hours later we are informed by Joyce and by Michel Rochon (a new addition to the PMO Second Floor) in no uncertain terms that our line is foolish and we should make no further comment! Dick had even talked to Ray Heard at the Montreal *Star* and told him his story sounded OK. Would he be quoted too? "Not me, baby" was Dick's reply. He wasn't!

"Marc Lalonde is furious," Michel Rochon tells us. "We'll have to look into how you guys in the Press Office work out your press lines."

Our theory was that if we confirmed the leak and got it out of the way, the story would then be on the document's content, not on how the document was leaked.

Nevertheless, when the full document was finally distributed, it slowly seeped into the gallery's consciousness as an "historic" reform (although no scribe in his right mind would have used that word the day it officially came out). Miracle of miracles, that day there was no leak. The full document was new, hence "news" in the Gallery's logic. But there were incredible morning screw-ups. Two mistakes in the summary were thrown at me. We cranked out a corrected version while thousands of uncorrected copies were being delivered all over Canada.

It is this lack of professionalism, plus the navel-gazing propensities of our press clients, that nearly drove me out screaming.

Mal de PMO

June 25, 1978

Last week, CJOH's Jack Fleishmann showed up for an appointment with the frequently absent Jim McDonald to film a story on "Mediaday," the PMO's daily press summary I had initiated. The Gallery was suspicious that we were using this detailed news analysis to construct lists of reporters who were friendly or unfriendly to us – which, of course, we weren't.

I had to be the stand-in for the media summary story. I was furious, of course, and even more so when Fleishmann confronted me with allegations from "two good sources" that we were doing "further analysis" on the news! "Mediaday" is seen as the source and basis for a Machiavellian "friends" list. The press are convinced we only talk to those who, statistically in our media summary, write good things about us! What garbage! My view of the Gallery and my job both suffer a setback.

Then Claude Hénault of the *Gazette*, from whom I expect better, did a paranoid little take-out on how we were supposedly using our news monitoring service. I had the misfortune to see him at the following Tuesday news conference and expressed my displeasure. "Manipulation" was the key word in his piece and it animated our argument. Manipulation, according to pure press doctrine, means that I talk more openly with those I trust than with those I have good reason not to. Futilely, I tried to explain that I tried to answer all questions from all comers.

On Wednesday night, the PMO hosted "Wonderful Wednesday," a very Liberal weekly institution that brings together ministerial, PMO, and even Liberal MPs' political aides for an after-work cocktail party thrash, usually in a lush reception room in the Centre Block. It was hosted on a rotational basis by ministers' offices. This week was the PMO's once-a-year turn.

This meat market (even the press admitted that Liberals have the best-looking females!) on political lines dragged along and finally at 7:30 PMO bossman Jim Coutts arrived and told Marie-Hélène Fox and I that he would like to have dinner with us. Amazed, we trotted over to the Rideau Club and there, in solitary splendour, got a glimpse of the refreshing human side of Canada's most powerful backroomer.

But, as soon as the imported white asparagus of the main course was consumed, Coutts suddenly rose, and out we went as peremptorily as we had been invited in. We walked with Coutts to the Langevin, where, as in a dance, he went up the centre staircase to his office while Marie-Hélène and I went to the washrooms at either side of the landing. Rejoining minutes later, we hustled out into the street and both exploded simultaneously with "What was that all about?"

We spent a long time over drinks trying to untangle the Byzantine maze of influence and personalities which forms the office. She confirmed something I had read into an earlier Coutts comment that there are plans for me in a revamped PMO. That's all I needed, strangely enough, to keep me on board and more content than I had been for months.

July 9, 1978

Today I really feel alone inside my own skin. It is part of the job in a prime minister's or president's office, I'm sure. Call it the "mal de PMO," but it could as well be the "mal de Maison Blanche," or the "mal de 10 Downing Street" – it's all the same.

For a few moments yesterday, while talking about the surface of the day's obvious political events, I felt like Murdoch – unable to voice my real knowledge or fears because of my "position," or from fear of saying what I really know. I feel isolated in my own real interests and relegated to the most banal exchanges with outsiders. Since I have some distrust for the "insiders" too (and I am sure I am not alone in this) the problem is compounded. With whom can you share your real concerns?

But I have learned much from this job nevertheless. It is, as was my experience of trying to be a priest, of much more use to the inner than the outer man, and has little relevance to relating with people in a normal way.

Jim McDonald suffers no such split life. He merrily, and with some panache, uses all he knows, feels, and is as a PMO staffer with both the women and the journalists of his life. He also knows how to plug in, at a verbal level at least, to new, rising influences in the office. Michel Rochon is the latest of these, now second-in-command to Coutts. Jim has mounted a considerable campaign to impress him. Some on the Second Floor find it "disgusting."

I find myself dreaming questionable dreams, and surprise myself. Marie-Hélène Fox and I like each other. I trust and respect her. I wonder, when my mind should be on other things, whether such a friendship might translate into frontline service should her brother Francis make a bid for the leadership. Help! What has this job done to me?

Magical Mystery Tours

In the summer of 1978, the Summit Conference of the Industrialized Nations was held in Bonn, West Germany. Because of the PM's real friendship with the host, Chancellor Helmut Schmidt, this was a very special occasion. For the PM, the summit was followed by what was billed as a "private" holiday with Schmidt, which included a visit to Schmidt's home in Hamburg, then a sailing excursion from Kiel to Denmark. Little thought was given to whether or how the press would cover this part of the German visit.

For trips of this kind, a full "advance" is done by someone from the PMO, the RCMP, and External Affairs. So, eventually, I made two trips to Bonn, Hamburg, and points distant, one in preparation, and one the real thing.

As it turned out, by some sleight of hand, on the real trip I became tour guide for a band of press tagging along after Pierre and Helmut as they toured Germany and Denmark in just about every conveyance possible. This trip, more than any other event, cemented my relationships with the press.

July 9, 1978

My first major trip to prepare a foreign visit by the PM, the advance for the Bonn Summit and later Trudeau-Schmidt holiday, did a lot for my ego. RCMP Inspector Guy d'Avignon, the PM's personal bodyguard while he is out of the country, accompanied Vaughan Johnston from External and me as we went over every predictable footstep the PM would take during that week. Guy assures me all details of our adventure are filed with the Force.

We were treated royally. We were swept about in fleets of black

138

Mercedes, entertained, and even, to our surprise, made guests of honour at a splendid protocol banquet at le Redoute in Bonn, a wonderful little baroque residence used by the government for state occasions.

Guy deserves his own note, for, as the PM's latest RCMP companion, he is one of the finest individuals I have ever met, period. Perennially sucking on a comforting pipe, Guy exudes a competence and confidence and a serenity which truly impress me.

Vaughan Johnston's attempts to represent External's ever-changing demands for representation on the delegation were frustrating for all of us. So too were our endless long-distance conversations with the outgoing Bob Murdoch in Ottawa (his successor Allan Lutfy listening in) on every detail of the itinerary's progress, the PM's accommodation, and what would be expected of him.

We had one strange evening in Hamburg. On a night off, we took in an explicit sex show in the best possible company, that of the Hamburg police, friends of Inspector d'Avignon. We were treated with great dignity under the circumstances, and received only *courteous* attention from the female staff!

On my return to Ottawa, only the "holiday" portion of the trip still remained an unknown. I tried to get Dick to pry a decision on what we would do with the press for this period out of the Second Floor. But even he could not comprehend or unravel the web of influences that permit the PM to take off to an undisclosed secret holiday destination following two secret days with Schmidt. The "optics" as we say, of such secrecy are awful. I can only assume that Dick suffers more than we think.

September 6, 1978

The Bonn summit, and the adventures that followed, are still fresh in my mind, even though holidays intervened between my return from Europe and getting back to work at the Langevin. The German escapade forced me to use every skill, every ounce of invention and personality I possessed. And it forced me to face whose side I was really on, the PMO's or the press's. For that period in July, it was the press that commanded, not just my every waking ounce of energy, but my affections as well.

Despite the advance work we had done, the whole trip had to be made up virtually as we went along - at least the press's itinerary did. And, of course, since no real thought had been given to how we would stick with the PM and Schmidt on their "holiday," that portion of the trip was a barely controlled madness.

At the first press briefing after our arrival in Bonn on Saturday, a pompous nerd from our Bonn Embassy announced that the arrangements would not be as foreseen, and then, with wrenching formality, read his own self-serving press release on the summit. I was appalled. I knew this meant that I would be virtually alone in making sure the press could cover this event.

When presidents and prime ministers meet at summits, the press are at the mercy of aides and officials for information. The media cannot see or experience the private discussions amongst the mighty, so they rely on briefings, glimpses of the leaders at photo opportunities, and their own instincts. On the whole, our press has relatively poor background and underdeveloped instincts to deal with international stories and events, and these weaknesses are not helped by traditionally poor Canadian briefings.

We press officers herded our guys and girls twice or three times a day into our press-briefing room just off the bar of the nearby Hotel Tulpenfeld, praying that Bob Fowler, Trudeau's foreign affairs expert in the Privy Council Office would be able to tell them clearly what Trudeau's contribution had been in the discussions just completed. Whether because of Bob's modesty or anxiety or both (certainly not due to any lack of knowledge or wit, Bob has both in plentiful supply) this seldom happened.

There is a lack of will to get the message out through the press in Canada, a lack of this tradition in our officials, and hence a lack of skill. It is simply not a priority as it is with the Americans and British (to name two countries who out-briefed, out-photo-opportunied, out-everythinged us at Bonn). What a lesson! Had our media had the wit or the time to attend the U.S. briefings, they would soon have deserted ours!

We were outdone on the visual side as well as the substance side. Numerous White House press aides staked out and held the best positions for their cameramen and photographers for the "family photo" of the leaders the first day. And there, illegally stationed as "written press" right alongside the entrance route where the Heads had to pass, was CBS's lovely Leslie Stahl with a wireless mike stopping President Carter and getting an on-camera comment for U.S. TV! We managed no such clever extra access for our people.

Trudeau made news in these picture sessions nevertheless, but not quite as we might have liked.

On Monday morning, the second day, our Canadian Press photographer, Freddie Chartrand, told me we had no decent shots of the PM and Schmidt together, and, after all, they were to have an extended bilateral "holiday" together after the summit. I launched a furiously complicated operation to get the two aside from the other leaders on the lawn at the residence of the German president just before lunch. This operation involved sending notes into the meeting, trying to persuade Schmidt's aides, and finessing the PM, Murdoch, and O'Hagan – everyone had a role, not the least "Ziggy," the locally engaged German press officer from our Embassy.

Finally, following the group photo, at the other side of President Scheel's residence, we breached nightmare security and got our cameramen past the dogs. Ziggy virtually ordered Schmidt and Trudeau away from the others. Carter thought something special was going on and, well trained as he is, moved in. But not before our photographers had the friendly shot of the Chancellor and the PM.

Later I saw Freddie. How was the shot? "Oh, I think I missed it." "What?" We were talking of different shots. The one Freddie thought he had missed became the centrepiece of the day.

During the group photo on the other side of the German president's mansion just before our "exclusive," Trudeau, fed up with yet another photo session, playfully gave the press the finger just as the group withdrew into the building. Freddie had the shot of this "vulgar gesture" from the side, Associated Press from the front. Neither still photograph lent itself to as fully insulting an interpretation as the U.S. network pool TV shot!

The ABC people, lodged across the hall from our press centre in the Tulpenfeld, were only too happy to show me the sequence backwards, forwards, and in slow motion. Great stuff! My heart sank, and I had to be the messenger of bad tidings to O'Hagan and Murdock at headquarters.

There emerged what Bob Murdoch assured me was a scene of some ferocity on his part. It was his last trip, his last few days

141

with Trudeau, and the boss was not going to get away with this. Murdoch confronted Trudeau with this "foolishness" later that day. Trudeau insisted that he didn't know what the gesture meant, and the exchange apparently became quite heated. Oh to have been the rose in the PM's lapel for that one!

Happily, there was some real news from this summit and we recovered. Although the PM's "vulgar gesture" ran worldwide, it was a wonder for only a few hours. Moreover, the key item of general public interest coming out of the summit, an agreement on highjacking, had all the marks of a Trudeau idea stamped on it, and that helped immensely.

The formal summit finished, the stage was set for our magical mystery tour with Pierre and Helmut.

The first day or so of meeting businessmen and touring industrial facilities was more or less routine. Things started to become insane only when we straggled after Trudeau and Schmidt en route for Hamburg.

The two friends got ahead of us almost immediately. The press plane was a Canadian Armed Forces Cosmo, a revered turbo-prop veteran. It would not start. The obliging West German air force even rolled up a small jet and cranked it up, hoping its jet blast might turn the propellers of the Cosmo into life. It didn't. How humiliating! Well, the two leaders boarded the Chancellor's jet and soon got impatient waiting for the press plane.

Vaughan Johnston, trying to mastermind this logistics disaster, and running from plane to plane, got the various permissions necessary for press personnel to fill up the few vacant seats on the Chancellor's plane. It would go to Hamburg and return for the balance. This was a "you, you, you, and you, *run!*" operation. The chosen few did, trailing bags, cameras, and curses, and I stayed back with the rest.

There was a death-watch atmosphere in the cold, deserted military waiting room as we stomped about, tried to place long-distance calls through the German military switchboard, and told jokes. The camaraderie that marked the rest of the trip started during this other-worldly late-night wait.

We had all had a few drinks on the stalled Cosmo, and one inebriated scribe from a Maritime paper cuddled up to the forbidding Anne MacMillan of CTV, London. A look of horror crossed her face as (name withheld!) tried to put his hand on her knee!

Finally we were picked up by the Chancellor's jet and brought to Hamburg where the fun really began. Then, in a German luxury bus, we followed a sleek motorcade of bulletproof Mercedes 500s carrying the PM and Schmidt to the northern port of Kiel. From there, while the PM and Schmidt sailed to Fåborg in Denmark, we were to go overland.

We made the Kiel stop purely to see them off, right at dockside. The press wanted to be reassured with their own eyes that the PM actually boarded with Schmidt. We were all draped around the jetty when Trudeau wheeled, just as he was about to go down the gangplank, and gave the nearest woman, this time the *Star*'s Mary Janigan, his rose. Of course, back home that was the photo of the day and poor Mary, who puts immense effort and nervous energy into being a serious journalist, was nearly in tears when she heard.

The bus became a travelling circus. It was well stocked with alcohol, and the group was in a holiday mood. Since the story of "killer rabbits" attacking President Carter's raft during a trip down some western U.S. river was still fresh, Peter Lloyd started to claim that he had sighted several outside the hotel. They were becoming, in fact, a little-known threat to world security. A "sighting" of a real bunny in a field during the early part of our bus jaunt launched an increasingly hilarious theme for the trip.

The press, as always, were superbright in fast creation – it's their trade. Given the killer-rabbit plot line, they developed it *ad infinitum*, even *ad absurdum*! Screams of mock terror greeted any "sighting" of a rabbit. After Freddie Chartrand bought a furry hand rabbit at a gas stop, and someone in the CBC entourage bought a toy, wheeled rabbit that rolled down the aisle of the bus, everyone lifting their legs in fear, we knew we could laugh through just about anything.

The rabbit number enlivened hours and hours of bus tedium. When we finally arrived dockside at the little Danish port of Fåborg, the grim Mercedes cavalcade was there too, and so was the ketch, the *Atlanta*. In full view of everyone, Trudeau and Schmidt were leisurely having tea and cakes in the deckhouse.

For once, things went from better to better, thanks to the kind of relaxed holiday humour infecting the two friends, Trudeau and Schmidt. The two of them went alone into a tiny church while we lounged below in the courtyard of the rectory listening to a muffled rendition of Bach played by Schmidt on the church organ for Trudeau's enjoyment. They came down to our little group and Anne MacMillan asked a question. Trudeau: "Hey Helmut, come over and tell them what we've been doing," and, of course, he did.

Then a news conference was set out in a tent in the lush garden of the old resort hotel where the two were staying. The Danish press and our people munched a hurried lunch while I urged Trudeau, and then Schmidt who walked up, to meet with the press quickly since we had to leave to get the last ferry. "Sure," said Trudeau, "OK with you, Helmut?"

This was the real Trudeau, relaxed in a way possible only when you are with a friend who stimulates and respects you, who wants nothing, and with whom you know you are accepted.

It takes a trip like this to underline the paradoxes of power, Canadian style. In some ways, the PM is more like the mayor of Canada than its president. We rattle along after him like a rag-tag gang from local newspapers and radio stations.

The White House runs a grand moving palace. One almost expects steamer trunks! During the summit, Jody Powell, Carter's press secretary, was in the bar of the Tulpenfeld saying *"we've dropped human rights . . ."* while I tried to soothe a slightly intoxicated and emotional Don McNeil from the CBC, whose interview (read baby) with the PM had been cancelled.

Nevertheless, our press, for their own reasons, more often than not play along with the idea that Trudeau, and hence Canada, is important internationally. Their seeing the obvious rapport between him and Schmidt helped consolidate this impression. After all, they are a self-interested part of this evaluation. They like these trips.

144

The CBC's Mike Duffy (centre), Gossage's long-time Press Gallery sparring partner and the butt of much PMO humour, shares a joke with Gossage at a late-night restaurant outing with Gossage and Canadian Press's energetic and gentlemanly John Ferguson. (Page 193) (*Fred Chartrand*)

During the 1980 campaign, Gossage developed a system of hand cues to let Trudeau know how long he had to finish his speech. Here, at a 1980 staff party at which Gossage spoke, Trudeau cues him right back. (Page 214) (*Robert Cooper*)

TOP: When the Prime Minister was snowbound while skiing in Lech, Austria, at the start of a North-South trip, Gossage tried to keep the press fed by organizing his first and last telephone news conference. (Page 208) (*Canapress Photo Service*)

RIGHT: After a delightful ramble in the jungle near Manaus, Brazil, a relaxed PM found a native canoe a pleasant way to put some distance between himself and the travelling press corps. (Page 211) (*Robert Cooper*)

FAR RIGHT: Allan Gotlieb (centre) and Marcel Massé (right) try desperately to catch up to the PM's boat on a trip up the Amazon River during a 1981 visit to Brazil. They had been delayed when their boat ran aground on a sand bar. (Page 211) (*Robert Cooper*)

On long foreign trips, the Armed Forces Boeing 707, which ferried the PM, his staff, and the press in first-class comfort, became a second home as countries and cultures flashed by. Here, Gossage and his colleague and friend Ralph Coleman are somewhere over the Atlantic during a three-continent tour in 1981. (Page 212) (*Robert Cooper*)

A happy PM leads the thumbs up for a successful visit to three continents in 1981 on arriving at the final stop in Mexico City. (Page 212) (*Robert Cooper*)

President Reagan's visit to Ottawa in the spring of 1981 was planned with awesome attention to the kind of detail that would impress the White House couple. An enormous RCMP officer was provided who towered over the President on cue for this highly successful photo opportunity at the National Arts Centre gala. (Page 227) (*Official photograph of the White House, Washington*)

Dick O'Hagan, Gossage's former PMO boss, came to his going-away party to deliver some sage advice to his former Press Office colleague. Ironically, Gossage was going to Washington to fill the Embassy public affairs' position Pearson had appointed O'Hagan to more than fifteen years before. (Page 246) (*Robert Cooper*)

Trudeau applauds one of the ribald speeches at the going-away party for Gossage, seen here with his wife, Helga (on Trudeau's left). Tom and Roberta Axworthy complete the table. (Page 246) (*Robert Cooper*)

The Press Office slogan on a T-shirt was one of the most appropriate gifts given to Gossage at his farewell party. Ralph Coleman, who organized the party, beams from the podium. (Page 246) (*Robert Cooper*)

When Kate and Anna McGarrigle and their band visited Washington in 1983, Gossage arranged American press coverage of their performances and placed this photo in *Billboard*.

TOP: Gossage and a willing guest do the Charleston to enliven a too-quiet party at the residence of the Canadian Ambassador in Washington. John Kenneth Galbraith (seated on left) ignores their antics. (Page 249) (*Robert Cooper*)

RIGHT: Margot Kidder and Pierre Trudeau were first seen in Washington together at a reception at the Canadian Ambassador's residence. Paul Robinson, the American Ambassador to Canada, and Ben Bradlee, Executive Editor of the *Washington Post*, look on. (Page 268) (*Robert Cooper*)

SEVEN

THE PHONY WAR

*T**he PM returned to Canada greatly impressed by his conversations with Schmidt. He decided to "reorder priorities" personally and went directly to the public in a nationally televised address to announce $1.5 billion in spending cuts. He said he was calling ministers back from their holidays to plan how to cut their budgets and stimulate the economy.***

September 6, 1978

I saw the insides of the August expenditure-cutting announcement, or "exercise" as it was called. All the institutional checks and balances, concerns, apparatus, the party, Cabinet–all were ignored in a bid for the PM's personal credibility.

A dramatic restraint program was pulled together to be delivered by the PM as a TV pitch to the nation. It was drafted in hours by Coutts and Axworthy, polished by the PM himself writing directly on to the teleprompter script in the CBC TV studios, and delivered by the PM with really remarkable professionalism in one English take and one French. The English taping was completed only two minutes before air time. The whole operation didn't deserve to come off, but it did.

I rode back in the limousine with a delighted PM to the Langevin. Dick told him it had been cut too fine. Trudeau obviously didn't care. A tiny group had got his very own message directly to the public for once.

This act turned out to be just the start of three weeks of more ill-prepared economic policy initiatives by the Second Floor. All were greeted with deserved cynicism, and our credibility suffered in the process. Each new late-night operation provided fresh evidence to the press that the country was being manipulated by a few Machiavellian politicos in the PMO.

Chrétien suffered the most. As Minister of Finance, the fact he was deliberately not contacted about the August 1 announcement shattered his ego. He got the "good team player" epitaph for not exploding publicly.

But we are all good team players. Ralph and I bounced increasingly nasty bunches of calls. Our "deception index," as we call it, rose to unprecedented eights and nines!

Pitfield had told us that there had been no appreciable results from springtime warnings to all ministers about restraint, and that this draconian act was the only way to prove to them that the PM meant business. But it was a hard line to sell.

I hate being deceptive, and to this journal I admit I have been so these past weeks. I've lied abut simple things, like reporting Coutts on holiday when he was in town. I've resorted to more intricate web-spinning like maintaining there had been ministerial consultation before August 1 when there had been virtually none.

Now I'm involved in another kind of magical mystery tour. The PM has put himself at the service of reluctant candidate John Evans in his bid to be elected as MP from Rosedale in a by-election, no doubt on the way to a Cabinet post prior to the next election.* Dr. Evans, the lanky and somewhat academic ex-president of the University of Toronto, may seem an unlikely grassroots politician, but the PMO dreams of the effect such a star will have on flagging Liberal fortunes in Metro Toronto.

* Evans was a prominent member of the Task Force on Canadian Unity. His work impressed Trudeau, who wanted him in the Cabinet. Others saw Evans as the next leader of the Liberal party. When Finance Minister Donald Macdonald quit politics and vacated the riding of Rosedale in Toronto, Evans announced his candidacy. His opponent was David Crombie, the city's popular former mayor. Evans campaigned hard but was beaten soundly.

We spent two days trying to convince Evans's riding staff to produce something of an event or program for the PM that would "fly." We were doublecrossed. Someone told Evans he could do any event he wanted with the PM, and that if he didn't want press along, that would be just fine! We faced this *fait accompli* on arriving a few hours before the PM at Evans's committee rooms.

We tried to convince Evans that some media coverage of the planned canvass with the PM would help the cause. "A media publicity stunt," Evans shouted out at us. "No way." Well, Colin Kenny, the old pro, brought it off somehow. Trudeau will do a door-to-door canvass with Evans, there will be press, but there has to be some secrecy. We won't tell the media where the canvass is going to take place until the last possible moment, so there will be no crowds, and Evans won't get a "circus."

But, of course, you can't win. Instead of reporting on Trudeau listening to voter concerns at their doorsteps (and Dr. Evans incidentally dispensing a good deal of free medical advice!), the press highlighted the lack of crowds, the absence of Trudeaumania! The PM was very patient while he was led by the ear from one nose to another to another. He put up with running reporters, camera crews, wires, mikes, and the media's intrusions into normal discourse.

Then we were off to the Global Television studios for a lengthy and rare interview with Peter Desbarats. Just to warm the PM up on the way, I told him a bit about Desbarats's all-too-public marriage difficulties.

In the studio, the interview wound its predictable way until, towards the end, despite my warnings, and doubtless on the urging of his bosses, Desbarats asked *the* question: Didn't Trudeau think his marriage difficulties affected his role as PM?

Without taking a breath, the PM remembered our conversation in the car and shot back, "What about you, Peter, do you think your marriage troubles affect your performance?"

Desbarats was stunned. His companion, the show's producer, who was beside me in the control room nearly fell off her chair! Trudeau and Desbarats argued for a minute about who was or was not a public figure. But was Trudeau's question legitimate? I think so.

October 7, 1978

The office is relatively quiet. Imperceptibly, the press is shifting its most intense scrutiny to other places. The Gallery no longer finds it an absolute necessity to shadow every movement of the Prime Minister – to keep the "death watch" as it is called. Their focus on the PMO softens, and there is growing mystery about where the power centres are developing.

John Turner is somewhere in the wings, a sort of ghost-like image. We don't talk about his assumed ambitions in the office, although the press increasingly does. But the PM is noticeably relaxed in a Jack Webster interview when the question about Turner as a successor is squarely put.

"No, Turner told me he was quitting for family reasons – I take him at his word," Trudeau tells Webster. Perhaps that last fateful resignation meeting was the only time Trudeau bothered to give some consideration to that man.

There is a feeling that we are at the end of something. The feeling is palpable. Bill Teshke, one of the most deservedly senior economics advisers in the Privy Council Office, is leaving. We are losing one of the PCO's soundest minds. Another very senior PCO type wondered in an aside if he would be kept on in a Clark government. There are more and more leaks. "Aides" are being quoted every day, and they aren't us. The defeat of Gerry Regan's Liberal government in Nova Scotia hasn't helped. "Can't stop a tidal wave!" There have been polite indications from candidates and their workers in some ridings that perhaps they don't need Trudeau to come and help.

Meanwhile, an amazingly rejuvenated PM is tirelessly campaigning for the by-elections.* In a by-election swing through the west coast of Newfoundland, he waded through hysterical schoolchildren in Stephenville. He was bulldozed by a mass of humanity in Ste.-Hyacinthe and had to climb on an apple box to deliver some real "teachings," as he calls them, to the crowd.

---

* Having decided against a general election in 1978, Trudeau called fifteen by-elections for October 16. The results were a disaster for the government. The Tories took five Liberal seats in Ontario and one in Manitoba, and held four others. The Liberals won only two, both in Quebec. The NDP won two and the Social Credit one. Among the elected were David Crombie, Bob Rae, and Donald Johnston.

This week the Governor General, Jules Léger, reminded me that Trudeau "needs smiling faces" and that he had been getting them on the road at least. "He's a good campaigner," David Halton admits. But this observation goes unreported. My own silent frustration boiled yesterday over a very negative George Oake piece in the Ottawa *Citizen* written from the just completed Newfoundland by-election trip. It so bitterly set on end my own, albeit emotionally tinged view of that day's success that I felt robbed of my own perspective. Was I on the same trip as Oake?

October 11, 1978

Speech from the Throne today. As André Burelle, the new Jean LeMoyne of the office, says, the real speech was on August 1 when the PM announced his restraint program. A few paragraphs are read by Governor General Léger, then his dear Gaby takes over. What a sad sight. Already, the race to replace Léger is on.

The PM sees more and more of Philip Gigantes, a journalist with Liberal sympathies who has been brought in to work up some good econimic news. "Can anyone tell the PM this is bullshit?" an angry PMO type asks me in some anger.

On October 16, the Liberals suffered the worst by-election defeats that any government has since Confederation. Of the fifteen seats up for grabs, opposition parties won all but two in Quebec. This setback was widely interpreted as marking the end of the PM's political career.

October 17, 1978

The mood last night reminded me of the gloom over the PQ victory in Quebec I noted when I first started working here. The committed militants were glued to the TV in the Press Office watching the election results, incredulous as seat after seat fell.

We called the PM, who was working at home – not even watching the disaster unfold! Finally he was on his way to face the press and make a statement. Clark was already in the basement "scrum" room, 130S. I rushed to prevent a meeting between the two in the corridor – an encounter the cameras would enjoy all too much.

The reporters waiting in the crowded little wedge were all hyped by this "stunning" by-election upset. The PM strode down the corridor to the scrum room, indifferent to their mood. I take much courage from the PM's stoicism. It is remarkable. Since he has been removed from our backroom mania, he can honestly shrug it off.

"The first day of the rest of the mandate," someone intoned tonight over a glass of wine in my office. We were living the hangover of the day after. The morning PCO meeting rang with talk of preparing CVs. Last night Mike Duffy suggested that Coutts was in his last days. Certainly the vast majority of the press thinks Trudeau is finished. "Don't count him out so easily," is our rather weak line to all comers.

The facts of the by-election results from last night are otherwise. All day they ripple through the office. As Marie-Hélène tells me, the results didn't hit home so much last night as they did this morning. The mood is nasty. Colin Kenny, especially, is the brunt of the most vicious comments. But I saw him a day before the election looking pensively out his window over the hill, predicting we would be lucky to win three seats, and saying that he would advise the PM to be "humble." "We've been too clever by half, that's the problem," he said prophetically.

Dick is almost inert. At a Press Office staff meeting today in a lively discussion of whether to hold a press conference, his contribution was glaringly honest, "I'm ambivalent, as usual!" This could well be the epitaph for our whole operation!

Last night, with results final, four of us from the Press Office, Dick included, went to face the music at the Press Cub after Trudeau's statement. We were soon joined by our Press Office equivalents from the two opposition parties, Tim Ralfe and Don Doyle from the Tories, and Malcolm Wippler from the NDP. It was their night, not ours, however good our working reputation. We are now no longer *the* news, automatically, by virtue of the office. We will have to claw with the others for media attention. The phones barely rang today – only one aggressive call from "As It Happens."

So, a new era begins – the crawl back to credibility as a government, perhaps with some substance, not just politics. We wait for Michael Pitfield's prediction that the government will recover on the basis of its program.

As if a sign, Pitfield himself exchanged concerns with Ralph and me on Monday in an unprecedented personal visit to the Press Office. The new initiatives will be good, he assured us, only there is this lag between action and the public's perception. To attack this we have to improve our "information" efforts, he told us as we listened open-mouthed. We have never heard anything like this from the top of the heap. "Anything I can do?" he offered. "Declassify documents? Just let me know!"

Yet, aside from such well-meaning outbursts of concern, there are no meetings to discuss ideas or policies or approaches that might put a new face on new activities. There is no real exchange between the different levels of the PMO staff – the Achilles' heel of this PMO. We will all leave it, clutching privately to our hearts those of our memos that made it into the PM's nightly "bag" for his perusal. But the ideas we try out on the PM we may never have taken the trouble to bounce off our colleagues. Heaven forbid!

There are two theories in vogue to explain the by-election disaster. They are probably used every time a party in power loses by-elections. One is the "the knives are out" theory, which focuses all blame on the leader and his weaknesses, and predicts reduced life expectancy since these defeats will bring out his political enemies. This theory is popular in the press and in the middle echelons of the PMO. Certainly the fact that Trudeau is a rare and legitimate Canadian "star" focuses discontent with the government on him in a dramatic way. So, the easy thing is to blame him.

The other, the "slap on the face" theory, would have us believe that the voters were trying to "teach Trudeau a lesson," and send him a message not to take them for granted. But, at least in my view, it is as much his advisers who should be taught a lesson. It was, after all, their tricks he so faithfully performed during by-election campaigning. The press know this, but the more conventional wisdom sees the results as a massive rejection of Trudeau himself!

October 24, 1978

The Second Floor, together with Senator Davey and others, are to decide this Wednesday whether to go ahead with the idea of buying time for "fireside" TV chats by the PM. This is a big event in Press-Office land. We working stiffs are incredulous.

It has been a really bad, horrible week. Principally the family

151

suffers, especially Helga. In an intemperate rage I broke her glasses, convinced she had no sympathy for a plight that seems so clear and compelling to me!

Today it's better, but a bitterness lingers. I always seem to reach situations that have peaked and are sliding to inglorious conclusions. And, as can be read in nearly every face in the office, it's too late to leave now.

At lunchtime at the Press Club I am hailed by, "All I am interested in is the date of Trudeau's retirement." I talk myself blue with the *Star's* Peter Lloyd about the unlikelihood of this happening. He is not convinced.

The phone is deathly silent. Logistics questions, that's all I get. Jean Charpentier wears a grey smile-mask. He no longer intones disaster: we are living it. Marie-Hélène rants about what a closed shop we work in, nobody is really telling anybody else the truth. She wants a Cabinet shuffle before she goes off to Europe. Perhaps there will be something for Francis.

My friend Alain Stanké phones from Paris where he is attending a book fair to tell me the German rights for Margaret's book fetched $100,000 and the Canadian rights are up for the same in hardback! It is to be published April 2, and will likely be syndicated by the *Star*. That's something to look forward to.

Distancing The Press

October 28, 1978

"I guess we are too closely identified with the press, and he just isn't in the mood to listen to our advice," Dick told us as he announced that, again, the PM won't see the press this week. Apparently there had been a quite nasty argument with Trudeau, and only Dick held up our side, with some support from Pitfield. But this was a small event in a week during which the PM consulted widely on strategy for next week's First Ministers' Conference.* Nevertheless, his refusal to see the press presages for

* A three-day federal-provincial conference on the constitution was held in early November. The premiers agreed only to continue the search for ways to patriate the constitution. Predictably, however, René Lévesque said he wanted no part of making the British North America Act a Canadian law.

me a growing mutual hostility between the PMO and the press which has the earmarks of a typical end-of-regime routine.

It took Jean two days to persuade PCO "officials" to give the press a basic briefing before the most important Federal-Provincial meeting in a decade.

Worse, the Liberal party agency takes up more and more of the time normally devoted to routine press matters. They met twice this week with Joe Koenig, a former NFB producer now in charge of our image-making. This group even has a private soirée at 24 Sussex. The "packaging" of the PM, as Marie-Hélène Fox puts it, is overriding good basic communications. Evidently the content will remain the same, only the "image" will change. As I exhorted in a memo that will go no further than Dick's desk, this PM cannot stand any more tampering with his persona.

Margaret is in town, proofing a ghost-written manuscript that will be published in early April. Alain Stanké has been offered French rights for the book. He won't take it, of course, but tells me the publication timing is "calculated" for maximum political impact as the government's term will be up in the spring, and an election is inevitable. "She is being used," he tells me.

The book will be the most cutting intrusion into his personal life that any prime minister has had to face. In the next couple of days I have to decide how to approach him with all this information.

This week the general edginess of the office escalated into a real witch hunt. Canadian Press's Doug Small, with some inadvertent help from me, wrote a make-believe Cabinet shuffle. It was embarrassing. It suggested who would go, who remain, who the PMO liked, and so on. It was malicious in the extreme, strewn with PMO "informants," "sources," and "aides" as his sources. Coutts finally became thoroughly upset and flung rare accusations at the Press Office. Dick fronted bravely for his staff in a recrimination-filled meeting. I am suspect, but strangely feel less than contrite about the piece. It at least suggested a radical renewal of Cabinet.

But these unsettled times benefit Joyce Fairbairn and the Centre Block gang. She now chairs a daily House strategy meeting in which I participate. "Top Secret," of course. But, it is typical of the deep desire we all have to serve the PM that even Joyce, who sees lots of him, was really thrilled at the PM's positive reaction to the use of her first "report." It was quite moving.

*In the winter months that followed, there was little to unify or
inspire our activities in the PMO, except the determination of the
PM himself. Power in the office was shifting and unfocusing.*

*Press relations became increasingly irritated as the PM strained
to get out of routine press contacts, and even directly attacked the
Gallery. As for the media, their interest concentrated more and
more on the man who they were sure would be the next prime
minister, Joe Clark.*

November 7, 1978

There is no doubt now that the media-relations heyday of last
spring – interview on interview, regular news conferences, easy
openness – is over.

"He is overexposed," Joyce states flatly. This is the commonly
held theory. In an elaborate speech arranged for a group of foreign Embassy press attachés by the Belgian diplomat Paul
Ponjaert, Dick argues that our "success" in giving the press regular exposure to the PM is now widely perceived to be a factor in
the focus of discontent on Trudeau.

During the past weeks the PM has gone out of his way to provoke the press. There is even the beginning of an unstated assumption in the Press Office that the media can be kicked around
with impunity, and perhaps even with advantage to "our side."

Jean particularly seems enamoured of this theory, detecting a
"softening" of media comment since the latest round of our "aggressive" PMO acts. This was the "unilateral" moving of the PM's
weekly press conference from the National Press Theatre where
the Press Gallery itself is in charge, to the Conference Centre
where the PMO chairs and controls the action. There was such
outrage over this break with tradition that we quickly dropped
the "experiment."

The next provocative act occurred at the Liberal Party of
Canada (Ont.) convention at the Hotel Toronto, where an admittedly reluctant PM had to turn on some heat hastily in the keynote
address, and did so by blasting his critics. This included a calculated swipe at the press. The PM clearly declared the press among
his, even the country's "enemies," and used the Coutts axiom
"Watergate Envy" to describe their behaviour.

Never have I felt so tense facing my media clients after the partisan cheers died down. Even the presence of the sparkling

Patricia Poirier from *le Droit* didn't help. The London *Free Press*'s fairminded John McHugh, and a lot of the gallery types I liked most, were hoisting the PM, me, and a drink together. The Nixon analogies were unavoidable. It wasn't wonderful.

In the Jetstar the next morning coming back to Ottawa, the PM was less than contrite about his attack on the press. I flattered him, saying I was sure he had more developed views on the role of the press than those expressed in his speech. He allowed that he did, but did not elaborate.

I at least got a laugh out of him over the headline of a party tabloid that appeared at the convention, "Buchanan fully supports Trudeau." I told Trudeau it was like the headline, "Pope believes Christ died for our sins." He cackled.

He only obliquely apologized to Jean for the incident a few days later after reading a rather touching, if inaccurate, note from Jean on some "onside" indications amongst certain media commentators. Perhaps this suits a man who is no longer being pressed to treat regularly and generously with an "estate" he feels is only out to gain more power for itself.

The PM's concerns about the Ottawa-Paris-Quebec triangle may seem arcane, but the fawning relationship between Lévesque and Giscard d'Estaing caused the French Canadians in Ottawa acute annoyance, the same anger felt when De Gaulle delivered his famous "Vive le Québec libre!", treated Canada with disdain, and played our internal politics. This time it was a behind-the-scenes war between Ottawa and Quebec for the French government's recognition as the primary representative of the French fact in North America. Its weapons were the symbols and the abstractions of formal diplomacy.

With political advisers in the PMO gone to ground in the by-election aftermath, the bureaucrats are having a field day. De Montigny Marchand, Pitfield's number two or so, is central to a clever plan to get the PM and French President Giscard together in Paris where they can thrash out their differences over Quebec independence once and for all.

Great secrecy attends this planning. In the days of Ivan Head (now departed, and not replaced – Jacques Roy, a PCO official on loan from External, fills his role) and Bob Murdoch (now replaced by Allan Lutfy as the PM's Executive Assistant) all this kind of planning was done by phone and personal contact. These days it takes mountains of paper as it passes through the External Affairs bureaucracy. Of course, the more who know about such plans, the more likely there would be a leak to the press. We have one by Monday – great consternation. Jean, Ralph, and I smugly say we warned them.

The visit of Israeli PM Menachem Begin showed the PM's new-found testiness. He refused to speak at the airport arrival of the Israeli PM, throwing the advice of Coutts, O'Hagan, *et al.* back in their faces. His rationale was that we can't be seen to yield to Israeli pressure. The lost political opportunity will not soon return.

Then our elaborately arranged joint news conference was alleg-edly misunderstood by the wily PM as being for Begin alone. Ralph had to keep him on the platform almost physically. Later he chewed out Lutfy when he discovered the length of time he was expected to spend at the evening reception. He cut it back by a half hour, considerably embarrassing his hosts.

December 3, 1978

Snow is swirling through and around the backyard of our home at 84 Union Street, powdering and masking the harsh fact that Ottawa's brutal winter is well installed. Winter here produces its own longings for escape. While the past weeks have seen matters of some note, the real agenda, hidden under successive dulling blankets of white, relates to flight and escape from Novgorod on the Rideau.

Finally the PM's Paris trip is announced. This will be a final assault of the most personal nature on the dangerous Ottawa-Paris-Quebec triangle. Nobody talks openly about this aspect of the trip.

The warm-up act for this strange confrontation will be an offi-cial visit to Canada by the French prime minister, Raymond Barre. Our Ambassador in Paris, Gérard Pelletier, has finessed the most elaborate arrangements for the visit.

Difficulties over finalizing arrangements for Barre's trip risked compromising Trudeau's visit to President Giscard because of *césure*. I assumed this word to be some sort of code until I discov-ered that the central irritant for the federal government was the horrendous possibility that Barre would break his visit between its Quebec and English Canada components. We feared this would somehow show the world that France recognized Quebec's separateness from Canada! This was clearly what Lévesque wanted.

Such a break, or *césure*, was to be a trip to New York after Barre's visit to Quebec. The French were firm: no *césure*, no trip for Trudeau to see Giscard. Accepting this would be admitting a victory for nasty French diplomacy. *Quel horreur!* The Byzantine compromise we negotiated, which saved the PM's four days with Giscard, involves an incognito "break" in Barre's trip to be spent in the Laurentians!

Meanwhile, the idiot fringe keeps cranking out rumours of the PM's impending retirement. Marjorie Nichols, in an otherwise informed piece from Washington for "As It Happens," announces that Pelletier is in Ottawa from Paris to consult on retirement with pal Trudeau. This, the week before the trip to Paris that Pelletier has spent months finessing!

Well, Dick is less sanguine about these really groundless speculations. His nose tells him there is something more, but the PM tells him straight out that the subject did not come up and that he has made his statement about running again. Period.

A more delicate problem. I had finally decided that the best way for the PM to be fully informed about what Alain Stanké knew of Margaret's book and her plans for its release was for Alain to write the PM a personal note I would deliver. This week Stanké told me that his letter occasioned a half-hour call from the PM, who was most touched and appreciative. Amazingly, the PM had had no details on the book. He thought that Margaret was probably trying to help him by writing it.

Schreyer In, Dick Out

December 10, 1978

A sparkling day. From where I sit, I can appreciate the first frenetic visit of the grosbeaks. Berlioz's *Childe Harolde in Italy* wings my thoughts to more timeless preoccupations. In France, Childe Pierre is no doubt cleansing his mind of the second-by-second piercings of Canadian parliamentary reality.

It's been a long, tough week. Tuesday brought the Gallup, forty-three to thirty-five for Joe Clark. As the poll was taken just after the First Ministers' Conference, the naive were not only ready to conclude that Clark would inevitably be the next PM, but that the public was decisively against constitutional change. People apparently change their political views instantly on the basis of one event. I spent much of Tuesday trying to heap abuse on this approach.

My own feeling is that the poll reflects attitudes from the late fall – feelings of being cheated out of a general election, the lousy PR of the August announcement, the "teach Trudeau a lesson" mood so evident in the by-election disaster in Ontario. "We got this message in October" was my line.

There is a better feeling now. The "old" Trudeau has reappeared in this week's real bombshell, the appointment of Ed Schreyer as Governor General.

The Schreyer appointment came out of the blue. I was glad to have suggested to Mike Duffy that the old Ontario fix (in which case it would have been George Ignatieff) was not on, and that a real effort was being made to get someone from outside central Canada. Nobody, of course, wanted to believe me. Too bad! But what I like is that the appointment seems to represent a victory for Trudeau over some of his closest political advisers.

The announcement was actually made by the PM to the Queen in a courtesy call during a brief stopover in London on the way to his famous meeting with Giscard. Jean was with the PM, and we who were left behind were somehow to co-ordinate the release despite the barest advance warning. But, in the end, it was poor Jean Charpentier who was left in the lurch, not us. We had wind of the announcement at 9:30 a.m. or so. In London, Jean was given no warning and blithely sent his travelling Canadian press corps off to drinks and the cinema with promises that there would be no further news that day!

Thus, our Ottawa clients got the news before the gang on the spot! Poor, poor Jean. As for us, Dick dictated a point-form biography of Schreyer, and our announcement exploded at 11:40 a.m.

My only inside information relates to Trudeau hinting mischievously at Schreyer's name in front of Keith Davey a few weeks ago, and the latter, of course, not taking it seriously.

At the Thursday Cabinet meeting, by all accounts, MacEachen's announcement of Trudeau's choice was greeted with silence until

Monique Bégin saved the day by saying, "At last, a contemporary man!" much to Pitfield's relief. He, I gather, played a not insignificant role in the whole affair.

One can take some delight in the potential discomfiture of the entrenched Rideau Hall retinue, who may, as someone said, get some "peanut butter on their pinstripes" as a result of the appointment of a G.G. who has young children!

Last night a Who's Who of middle-Ottawa society gathered at the house of the socially adept David and Stevie Cameron. My sole use, it appeared, was to provide dialogue on the family fortunes of my boss. It was a resounding bore which has affected the good humour I feel may be my most important contribution to the next few months. Everyone has privileged information, conjecture really, on the state of one man's mind. Presumption on presumption feeds the opinion machine in this small capital.

I have been saddened by our last contacts with the Légers. I have met them several times in the grounds of Government House. He is drawn and can articulate little. Few will credit the changes he brought to the office. For instance, he traced the institution of the G.G. back to Samuel de Champlain, not with fanfare, but by installing a couple of engraved panels in the reception hall. This was typical of his underground activity – an intellectual rather than physical effort which surely will mark the history of this nation.

January 21, 1979

We found out this week (we were not told, of course) that Dick O'Hagan is leaving. I feel real physical and emotional discomfort. The years with Dick have been endlessly exhilarating. Perhaps he leaves discouraged that his sage media advice did not compete on a par with Pitfield's or Coutts's advice in other fields. Perhaps we could have had a stronger advocate. Dick's great strength, however, was that his very presence and the vibrancy of his personality established the credibility of the Press Office in the eyes of the outside world. We all fear his departure will compromise this.

In typical PMO management chaos, his successor, Arnie Patterson, was ballading about the office as early as Thursday, well before Dick's announcement, telling everyone we would be working together. Ralph finally cornered Coutts on Friday and demanded to know what was going on after even my face-to-face encounter with Dick at a party the night before failed to produce more than sheepish laughter.

Coutts's response was "I didn't have the heart to say no to Dick . . . didn't he tell you guys?" I should have known something was up a couple of days earlier, when, mysteriously, Dick had a fresh carton of cigarettes placed on my desk without comment – sort of a final clearing of accounts that, given the months of purloined smokes, was definitely in my favour. So, the end of an era. Dick is making a clean break and going to the private sector. He will not take a Senate seat or any other partisan reward. Typical of the man. I admire him for that; and much else.

We who are left behind look like hangers-on, facing a spring that will surely raise the most important issues since Confederation. The PM is increasingly pugnacious about the unity battle – and becoming more and more certain how to join it.

Clark's and his entourages' ineptitude in the unity and international arenas heightens Trudeau's appearance of maturity and competence. This is an unexpected and welcome gift. Even Broadbent can't resist exploiting Clark's shakey views on Quebec.

The Trudeau Ideological Phase

So, with or without Dick's dream of a "Communications Strategy," with or without Axworthy's policy initiatives, with or without relief from falling dollars and rising unemployment, Trudeau will make his views of Canada and Quebec the great issue to which all Canadians will have to react. The government ceases what could be called an anecdotal phase (Trudeau's personal future, cabinet shuffles, and such gossip) and enters the Trudeau ideological phase.

For us, this means he will be increasingly impatient with "detail." His reaction to a strong memo from Dick via Coutts on media "necessities" was sharp. When a highly critical *Globe and Mail* piece by its publisher, Brigadier Malone, landed on his desk, he wondered aloud whether such activities were useful at all.

With the departure of strong voices like Ivan Head to the International Development Research Centre and Dick to the Bank of Montreal, we perceive a fragmentation of advice. De Montigny

Marchand is strangely influential in the London-Paris trip, as well as in the French PM Barre's visit next month, right down to press strategy.

We go to Jamaica for the Jamaica North-South Summit at Runaway Bay for what could have been a fairly positive political exercise. There, Jacques Roy from the PCO and Bob Johnston from External are chief advisers.

But the PM alone puts his mark on this event. He has an impatient, almost a "let's get on with my holiday" attitude, which is not lost on the press (many of whom feel the same way!). At a lunch break at his rented villa overlooking Runaway Bay, about all he communicated was his frustration at not being able to take advantage of the splendid pool.

Yet I am convinced of one thing that is absolutely predictable. Between now and July, nearly everything of significance will change except Trudeau and his basic beliefs.

In this context it seems absurd to mention polls, but a few days ago the December results showed a more normal spread. Keith Davey's earlier prediction that we had "bottomed out" comes true.

One footnote to the last months: as things heat up politically, and perceptions of political change become more fashionable, bureaucrats start behaving in flagrantly self-protective ways.

At Dick's New Year's Day party, a polite Richard Gwyn finally introduced me to the lovely Sondra Gotlieb, wife of the Undersecretary of State for External Affairs, Allan Gotlieb. She was holding forth in a group that included the *Globe's* influential columnist, Geoff Stevens. "I always read your columns," she said. Turning to acknowledge her introduction to me, she snapped, "Oh, I don't talk to Liberals!" and studiously avoided further contact with me.

I might have considered this a simple attack of bad manners if I hadn't detected a definite "us" and "you guys" attitude growing in the normally friendly and politically helpful (in the small "p" sense, of course) Privy Council Office.

February 16, 1979

I don't want to overdramatize too much, but there is a pall over the office this week. Dick has gone. His office door is ajar, and what was once a beehive of fretting and concern lies vacant and

161

still. His mark is still everywhere. The huge corner office has been refurbished, impressive new photos decorate the wall, courtesy of the National Film Board and Lorraine Monk. There is a look of order and efficiency.

Dick worked tirelessly for improvements, for reforms. There was a feeling that, while he was here, media affairs were taken a bit more seriously by Coutts and the PM than they would have been otherwise. But that passed in one second on Wednesday as Dick left the office. The last memo has gone, the last letter has been signed.

Dick was a true personality. He led not so much by honed skills, but by pace and endless caring. It was his Press Office. He was the animator. We now float. There is nobody left to turn to, not so much for decisions – we often have to make decisions on our own and on the fly – but for validation. He gave us that in abundance.

We have to adjust now to a new press officer as well as to a new boss. Both are feared and dissected before their arrival. Our gang, the "A" team, as we now call it, has to absorb Suzanne Perry, a long-time candidate of Dick's. Arnie Patterson is to replace Dick. He is a loud, energetic radio-station owner and long-time Liberal from Halifax. He has a bull-in-a-china-shop quality that makes us worry for the fragile dealings he will have with the PM.

"Disoriented" best describes the last two weeks. There has been too much after-work drinking and futile speculation. The opening of the Winter Games in Brandon came and went – an amazing interlude in which the PM was accepted as the huge star he is, apparently divorced from his role of prime minister and leader of the Liberal party. We even managed a productive prime ministerial meeting with the Brandon *Sun*'s editorial board.

The visit last week of Raymond Barre, the French PM, was in a class by itself. To focus real ideological divisions over Quebec between Ottawa and Paris so acutely, without straying one syllable from correct attitudes, was a feat that could be accomplished only by a French head of government.

Who actually won this long, engaged struggle, or who, if anyone, cares, is a moot point. We were all made losers by playing it. All we did was to try to score baby debating points with a man who enjoyed making us nervous by cruising close to sympathy for Quebec aspirations.

Trudeau was nervous at the press conference with Barre. We

emerge convinced of a Federal victory! The sleigh ride on the canal is wonderful. Barre likes the gift of Eskimo parkas!

Does the world care? Can they take this side show seriously? The family quarrel I took part in when Trudeau visited Lévesque now seems a quarrel in the extended family of French speakers. Can Lévesque really shatter the generous dream of his old debating partner, Trudeau?

As for the role of the press, I've seen some really amazing dishonesty from some of the francophones. They are simply not reporting some of Lévesque's blatant gaffes. The English media are just as biased the other way. Ouch!

Yet the day before, in Brandon, at the opening ceremonies for the Winter Games, Premier Sterling Lyon spoke in French before an amazed Prime Minister – signs of understanding after all, except that the Quebec athletes milled about unimpressed. The PM's sense of a pan-Canadian francophonie is happily fed at these events, which is just fine for him!

His and Lévesque's opposing views of *la réalité canadienne* are like the two pieces of some shattered crystal object, beautiful but sharp and dangerous. From my privileged point of view, I will be seeing which will be the one that is recut and kept.

March 17, 1979

We are in the Jetstar, just starting our approach over the white ocean of the prairies into Winnipeg for a refuelling stop. Flaps and undercarriage shudder, but Simma Holt's (a Liberal MP from Vancouver) high-pitched argument with the PM rises above the clunks and hisses. I move. "Simma, the Prime Minister wants to do his interview now . . . " She is up before I can finish the sentence.

"Sorry, perhaps I should have come earlier?" I say quickly as Terry Wills shuffles up for his interview from the rear of the tiny aircraft. "Yes, you should have," Trudeau replies dryly. I feel like a faceless servant.

We are in the last pre-election hold. We are a new team, our inexperience showing all around, particularly in the Vancouver swing just ended.

Arnie Patterson, forever florid, is a tactile kind of instant friend who wants to push the PM out toward the press. He blithely inserts "add-ons" – PMO lingo for surprise interviews or whatever that are not on the schedule agreed to in advance. Allan Lutfy, our new executive assistant to the PM, is dismayed, particularly when one such add-on allegedly produces a "bad mood" at the next event.

The headthrashing amongst the keen rule-book puritans is something to behold. Arnie is obviously a spoiler who will drive them crazy. "Damn it," Lutfy says. "It's in the book that he should have an hour alone before an event."

What is Arnie's judgement, his sense of political strategy? We will see. It will be an unforgettable campaign with this topper, that's for sure.

There's Bill de Laat – a more attractive and solid young man I can't imagine. A pacifier, but as clean and reliable as a young Guards officer. He's not quite the detail man we might want as the enormously complex campaign unfolds, but when he's teamed up with the equally charming Ted Johnson we'll be fine in the West. Both have good senses of humour, and that's a relief.

The PM's mood, as usual, is at the heart of everyone's concern. He calls a creep a creep at a rather wild session at the University of British Columbia and it seems like the old arrogance, foot in mouth, and so on. Then he reads flawlessly a Jim Moore text at the fundraising dinner which follows and it's tough, witty Trudeau. There is no mood really, just a series of different responses to different situations. For B.C., "two out of three ain't bad."

As a footnote, it struck me this trip that we all spend so much time with "cops," the ubiquitous RCMP security guys, drivers, and others, that it is easy to begin to think a bit like them. They form, after all, the controllable part of the whole travelling PMO operation.

EIGHT

CAMPAIGN TO DISASTER

*O*n March 26, 1979, the PM finally dissolved Parliament and called an election. The Liberals were neck and neck in the polls with the Progressive Conservatives.

I set out with spirit and hope on this great adventure, taking my assigned seat next to Marie-Hélène Fox on the chartered Air Canada DC-9. Physically, I was in the position I wanted, right on the border between the PM and the press where I belonged – I sat in the last aisle seat between the press in the back of the plane, and the ever more senior prime ministerial staff and the PM himself at the front.

This was my first election campaign, and was to be only the first of two in the amazing twelve months that followed.

The immediate challenge of the 1979 campaign was somehow to make a liveable situation out of almost eight weeks, six days and nights out of seven, criss-crossing the nation in terrifying proximity to danger at both the front and back of the plane! On the border between the press and the PMO heavies, I was constantly scrutinized by both camps, and I felt it!

I soon found that to survive a campaign with humour requires a kind of partisan commitment I did not know I had. It requires a belief in the justice of one's cause and a blind faith in the victory at the end. So, I quickly settled in my mind that it was inconceivable that the awkward and wimpish Clark could seriously challenge my smooth and sophisticated boss, and set out hap-

pily to use everything I had ever learned to impress our fifty or so travelling journalists and photographers with the confidence and optimism of the PM's entourage.

I did not have to be told that one break in our wall-to-wall grins at the front of the plane would be a dead giveaway for the press that things were indeed going as badly as they thought they were.

So determined was I to convey this mood of confidence that I missed what soon became obvious to everyone else – ours was, in fact, the losing plane. My tenacious, if unfounded optimism made the final defeat even harder to take. I systematically ignored early signs that things were going awry, which were perfectly obvious to just about everyone else.

This is what it is like to lose a political campaign. The signs of defeat were there early if I had cared to notice.

What follows was written at varying degrees of distance from the events they describe, which culminated on election night, May 22.

June 15, 1979

Only a week into the 1979 campaign, on Wednesday, April 4, 1979, I made a note to myself. The tour had hit the Admiral Beatty Hotel in Saint John, N.B., known to us, not without affection, as the "Admiral Bedbug." I wrote, "PM saying, '*If* we win election.' This noted by press." I should have listened to myself that night. Instead, in my tiny room, I boozed with the boys, thought Andy Moir from CBC's "Sunday morning" was an intelligent reporter, and collapsed in bed. I forgot the note in my CBC reporter's pad.

There were other signs. A couple of days before the end of the campaign, somewhere in Southwestern Ontario, Ian Urquart, a *Maclean's* Ottawa writer whose wry ways mask the seriousness of his journalistic output, organized a pool amongst the gang on the plane. Nobody in the media predicted a Liberal win. Urquart poked away at the staff. "Afraid to get in on the pool?" Finally I threw in my money and wrote Liberals 135, PC's 125 on a scrap of paper. I honestly still believed we would at least get a minority!

But that week was ominous even from my limited point of view as a frenzied flack. The Liberal tour had been deserted by all the senior columnists and commentators. We were left with the "B" group of media. No immaculate Geoff Stevens from the *Globe*, no florid Fotheringham, even the razor-eyed Christina Newman, soon to be a sort of semi-official Liberal party chronicler, apparently saw little interest in auditing our death rasps.

I still thought it would be close. I believed that an unexpected Trudeau victory would be twice the story of a Clark win. And even if (the absolutely unthinkable) these were the last days, what wonderful material! What history!

Years ago, as a local television producer in Toronto, I had picked wrong in devoting two full days of *cinéma vérité* filming to who turned out to be the losing Toronto mayoral candidate. But it was a great document, moving in a way the story of victory could never have been.

Could nobody in the press understand this? Only the *Toronto Star's* modest and somewhat bookish Andrew Szende actually covered what the man was saying those last days, and what he was saying increasingly was what was in his heart about Canada. Szende did justice to Trudeau's last speech in Guelph, which many partisans thought his finest. It had all the earmarks of the farewell wrap-up of an outgoing PM. Szende did not miss the import of the PM's sermon-like intoning of "Love ye one another" at that moving performance.

Other faithful journalists stayed on, including the *Toronto Sun's* wonderful Claire Hoy. But the majority of those "heavy hitters" we had tried so hard to cultivate shook the dust off their Guccis and went off to cover the "real story," the now obvious victory of young Clark from High River.

On "Black Tuesday" (as we called it) May 22, 1979, as CBC results flashed on the huge TV screens in the ballroom of the Château Laurier hotel made it impossible to avoid the horrible truth of defeat, I ran into Richard Gwyn lolling confidently at the edge of the bandstand in that sweaty scene. "Well," I surmised, "at least Trudeau lost for the right reasons." I believed that during the last part of the campaign he generally spoke from deep conviction about unity and constitutional reform.

"On the contrary, Gossage . . ." Gwyn came right back. And Gwyn listed for me our campaign mistakes and cynical appeals to the electorate. "But you weren't along at the last when he really took off." No, he wasn't.

Gwyn had been working on and off on a Trudeau book that assumed the defeat we were experiencing. He was the first to predict it. Why wasn't he there at the end to taste it? He should have been there, at least in the interests of literary accuracy.

The conversation unsettled me. Perhaps I had been totally naive in clinging to hope. The "history" our journalists were writing had unceremoniously dumped a central player even before the results were counted. I guess it is their job to act on informed prognosis, and this time they were right.

This, however, is at the heart of what it is like to lose, at least from my vantage point. The adrenalin is still pumping in your veins, and you discover others have already picked your side as the losing one. You really were only occasionally in the spotlight, only sporadically taken seriously. You thought you were riding in on a tide, but everyone else knew it had already turned!

The May night when we actually lost hammered me again and again with lasting images. I was dazed and shocked, accepting condolences as my self-promoted myth took its short, hard fall. It was agony to go through the motions of keeping the press informed of where the PM was and when he was coming from Sussex to deliver his "last" as PM.

One of the evening's long-term effects was the politicization of my wife Helga. She lived it as an outsider suddenly drawn into an intimate hysteric/historic scene. She suffered with us all, whether in the suite where staff consoled each other privately or downstairs in the Château Laurier ballroom where the drama unfolded.

Arnie Patterson and Jim Coutts put insanely brave faces on for live TV interviews. Later a Montreal RCMP officer who had long escorted Trudeau and probably knew more about him than any of us, openly wept.

I heard Marie-Hélène Fox, the literal and figurative heart of the travelling circus, intoning in the ruins of the larger defeat her brother Francis's almost obscene twenty-seven thousand vote plurality.

Jean Charpentier's face was an immobile mask as he awaited, on his last night as the PM's press secretary, the call from 24 Sussex that the boss was on his way to the Château.

Later, there was a final push and shove after Trudeau delivered his parting lines to a swelling chorus of "No! No! No!" Nothing befitted that campaign more than this final bull-headed reminder of dozens of cooked, forced Ontario events. The "blitz" team, with its heavy-handed tactics, acted out their last Trudeau exit with a flying wedge of movement out of the hall and into "transition."

July 24, 1979

Campaign, defeat, and our own version of transition are now well behind me. I have had over three weeks away from the office. I have read Haldeman's and Dean's Watergate apologies. I know I have weathered my own version of what they saw politics as – namely everything to do with tactics, little to do with morality.

I know there was a lot more to those eight weeks than losing. The tour was a living experience, a living thing. One of those "how can you possibly understand, if you haven't been on one?" kind of things you become impatient over with wives, sweethearts, children, and parents. But now, in the hot remove of summer, trying to achieve some possible understanding may be worth the effort.

The campaign's mood and inner life are as important as what happens on individual days. For the tour does have a life of its own, and a controllable one at that.

The leased Air Canada DC-9 itself, the basic motive power and only real "home" of the constantly moving tour, contained carefully controlled physical boundaries and social structures. There were the unmarked borders between the PM and senior staff, between staff and photographers and cameramen, between English and French.

Since we had the same aircraft throughout, the bulkheads and areas around the windows soon started to ressemble the inside of high school lockers with clippings, cutouts, collages, and slogans taped everywhere, much to the horror of Ray, Air Canada's permanently assigned steward. He soon became inured not only to the media's aptitude for interior decoration, but also to their taste for particular beverages like the "Mimosa" (champagne and orange juice) that the francophone reporters demanded on early morning flights.

The press broke into other subgroups, especially self-appointed groups like the "grunts," a trio (Derik Hodgson of the London *Free Press*, Jim Travers of Southam, and Jim Maclean of Newsradio) who made it a point of being as disgustingly amusing as possible – all this in a stretch DC-9!

The flying PMO Press Office included reliable Ralph Coleman, my fellow assistant press secretary, and the "Count," Press Secretary Jean Charpentier, who managed to be fastidious even after the most disastrous late-night encounters with drunk Quebec reporters.

We were more or less led by Arnie Patterson. As well as glad-handing everything that moved, he carried around a portable polling machine in his briefcase. Patterson would plug in this machine in his hotel room, and the automatic device would merrily start calling people at random asking them to state their electoral preference at the sound of the tone. Clearly ahead of its time, this high-tech gimmickry impressed nobody.

Tom Axworthy was the opposite of Patterson. A somewhat academic member of the team, on this tour he provided the PM with ideas and quotes, and because of his populist leanings he was known as keeper of the liberal flame. There was a late, late night ritual in any one of dozens of messy hotel rooms which would find the "Ax," as he was affectionately known, in his rumpled pajamas squirrelling through his overstuffed briefcase in search of to-morrow's "quote."

Then there was Suzanne Perry, a more recent recruit to press relations duties at the PMO. On the surface an immensely appealing, tall and somewhat dishevelled young woman, she had a carefully disguised but cutting intellect which served us well in our psychological warfare with the drooping press.

By the end of the tour, she and I were pretty deeply and consciously into some sort of mood-control exercise. We had to be! In a situation of sliding fortunes and expectations, some enforced, engineered silliness was required.

On one particularly glum morning out west, Suzanne and I decided to issue all the press with crayons and colouring books. We stood at the plane at the bottom of the ramp that morning and handed out materials to each, welcoming them as "boys and girls." We told the "class" that they each had to draw a picture of their beloved teacher (the PM) and that the best drawing would get a prize. Well, all but a couple of those hard-bitten scribes and reporters got right to work, producing horrendous renderings of the PM, all in the required child-like style.

Trudeau himself got into the act and presented the prize for the best work to Iain Hunter, a bit of a Gallery wag who had the habit of appearing at formal and not-so-formal occasions in a kilt. I have never met Hunter since without remembering this idiotic gimmick and how it raised our spirits that day. It even created a brief bridge between the PM and the media.

But from a substantive, if not personal perspective we lost the press. We looked after them well; we were the best. But given Trudeau's deeply held convictions about them and their role, and the actual content of the campaign, we couldn't hold them.

Alas, the often delightful Arnie Patterson alienated the anglophone press as surely as he won the francophones with an overwhelming display of patient affection. The unilingual Arnie could be found in the middle of the night listening to French songs with the knot of Quebecers who felt like expatriates on a tourist excursion into anglophone Canada.

He was less than professional with the English reporters, misleading them on silly things. This was typified by his banal and ill-prepared attempt in Edmonton to explain to the press an important speech on energy policy. His exaggerated *bonhomie* and optimism simply didn't wash with a younger, harder generation of newsmen. Too bad. His fierce friendliness was well meant. I will long remember his assurances about getting the "heavy hitters" – the big columnists and commentators – onside. Poor Arnie. I harboured no such illusions. They not only systematically predicted our defeat, but worse, they completely deserted the plane for the last week.

I concentrated on keeping the Frisbee in the air, to coin an expression that was more than appropriate for this tour. Frisbee-playing filled nearly all of the tedious periods of waiting that are features of national campaign tours. Even the PM got in the act a few times as we waited for the aircraft to be loaded on one runway or another.

On April 25, a casual game while waiting for the PM's arrival outside a modest hall near Nanaimo nearly ended my campaign. My belief in "going the second mile" for my media charges had me climbing up on top of the tour bus to retrieve the campaign Frisbee. Suddenly I slithered off the rounded aluminum roof and landed hard on the parking lot below. I dusted myself off, and saw the PM's event through. But on the long bus ride to Comox airport, with Standard Radio News's Jim Munson gyrating at the front of the bus beside me in his sexy and raucous imitation of Rod Stewart,

I discovered that I could barely move my arm without feeling the most devastating pain.

I started to perspire in some dread. This could be the end of the campaign for me. This was a PMO staffer's nightmare horror – the fast-moving campaign cavalcade from bus to plane to bus leaving without me! Even the chorus from the back of the bus of "Oh Joseph Clark, boring as a fart" found me unusually limp and unresponsive. This was a personal disaster!

Back in Vancouver that evening, I called my doctor brother and I was soon being operated on at the Royal Victoria in New Westminister. I returned to the hotel in a cast and sling. My "broken wing" became a trademark and a source of some amazement and comment. The PM expressed curt, if unusual sympathy as we filed on the plane the next morning. *Maclean's* did a little piece on the incident the next week. "More than one way to become famous" was my line.

Becoming a bit of a personality helped me keep my spirits up. I was one of the more unlikely looking press aides ever on a national campaign. With the cast over my elbow there was little I could wear beyond a loose, sloppy bush jacket and short-sleeved shirts. It was difficult to wash my hair as often as I would have liked, so it became a bit of a thicket. I hardly looked authoritative. So, I made up for this and bolstered my own optimism by being outrageous.

I shouted at the press and called them "scum" a couple of days later and got away with it! I teased and made fun of individuals over the public address systems of the buses we rode on. I did other mock announcements, "This is the captain . . ." on the plane's intercom. I jumped into the arms of Luc Lavoie, a television reporter from TVA whose taste for and amusement with the exaggerated matched mine. I kept putting on the show that was supposed to communicate our winning self-confidence.

At the time, I even tolerated the excesses of the Ontario PMO crews who prepared elaborate "spontaneous" welcomes at every stop, ensured that "hand painted" signs were pumped on cue, bused in hordes of young "supporters," and then retired for endless parties. As long as I was still healthy and could still convince myself of a minority government, these manipulations went with the territory.

The adrenalin, which keeps the front line fighting in any campaign, just kept pumping. But this positive attitude was not just a product of my self-imposed optimism. It was also the result of mood control in reverse – in this case designed to work on foot-soldiers like myself.

Every Sunday, our one day off the road each week, there was a carefully managed morning meeting for campaign staff in the second-floor boardroom of the Langevin Building. There, from Davey, Coutts, and others we would hear only the good news, almost until the end of the campaign. It was admittedly manipulative, but absolutely necessary. By the last meeting only Keith Davey showed some residual pep, the indefatigable Coutts was subdued, and nobody else even opened his mouth.

What of the PM himself? He was frustrated, I would say. Frustrated by his assistants' attempts to sell him speech ideas he often did not believe in. Alone on so many platforms, thumbs in his pants in the famous "gunslinger" stance, when the spirit or the crowd so moved him, he developed his own material that grew out of his real convictions. Perhaps he did this also to assert his authority against the advice of his staff. Then we would hear about patriation, constitutional reform, and the need for a strong central government. But he seemed to sense it wasn't going down, that he was casting pearls before swine.

The media could distinguish between the "script" and the real thing, but preferred to write little about this. No, what made news and stuck were not such subtleties, but his "arrogant" treatment, early in the campaign, of drunks, unemployed, and other assorted sad cases, his "cynical" vote-buying programs, and increasing "signs" of a losing campaign.

We ran a relatively open campaign, and what hype there was managed to be masterfully inappropriate. Our advertising, for instance, emphasized the "leader" and "leadership" quality in grand images that only further distanced the already distant Trudeau.

In one piece of packaging and manipulation, we not only succeeded, but we had a lot of fun doing it. A few days before the televised "leaders' debate," I was pulled off the campaign and sent to Ottawa to work on preparations. I was soon joined by the PM, ready to study, and to be trained and directed. The first thing

I had to do was to "dress" Trudeau for the debate. The ubiquitous and elf-like Paddy Sampson, on secret assignment as he was a CBC producer at the time, was in Ottawa to help prepare the PM. This was part of the assignment.

During a briefing session with the PM on the elegant little glassed-veranda at the back of 24 Sussex, the question of what he would wear finally came up.

"What have you got?" piped up the totally unintimidated Sampson. "Why don't you and Patrick come up and have a look," answered the equally informal PM.

So this unlikely crew trotted off to the dressing room of the leader of all Canada. The room was as ascetic as I expected. What came as a complete surprise was the unbelievably small choice of suits. We had seen most of them a hundred times. Paddy tossed a couple out, felt them, checked the colour at the window, and chose a pale beige number. Trudeau was pretty well tanned, and we hoped that Clark wouldn't dare wear a light colour. Trudeau tried on the jacket. It looked fine.

Now we had to find a shirt. What a spectacle we made – Sampson rummaging through the Prime Minister's bureau drawers. "Is this all you have?" he asked, amazed. Well, yes. It was.

We chose a silk shirt he had never worn. Then we went through the same procedure to find a tie. Finally, we had a wardrobe, a fine one, and one the PM had never before been seen in!

The coaching of the PM for debate theatrics was a more serious business, one we honed to a fine art. We decided early on to make use of the PM's natural talent for movement against Clark's stiffness and awkwardness. For instance, we found a predictable point where Trudeau could "make a move" on Clark that would be both natural and intimidating. The image lingered long after everyone forgot what they were arguing about. Clark cowered physically as the PM, in his choreographed ballet, moved from behind the little plexiglass podium and around to make his telling point of the "you don't know what you are talking about" kind.

We may have made a good showing in the debate with Clark and Broadbent, but we lost the election. There was general agreement at the sombre meeting after the defeat at which Tom Axworthy advanced his theory that we started losing about the time of the PMO's unilateral restraint announcement of August 1978. This infamous August "exercise," when the PM went over the heads of his Cabinet and announced a radical program on television, undercut two of the Liberal regime's most positive traits – teamwork and competence.

The dissolution of this sense of team was evident months before the election. A tired and disillusioned Michael Pitfield, hanging on in his last days as Clerk of the Privy Council, told me a few weeks after the defeat that Cabinet-making had become "impossible"; too many egos who had been around too long all had wanted the too few senior posts.

So, the Liberal "team" demonstrated little cohesion and few new ideas. The campaign showed only Trudeau tilting at windmills. Clark looked like a credible change almost despite himself.

Perhaps, too, the Canadian public neither wanted nor needed to have its fundamental divisions and weaknesses so exposed by one man's thinking. I have lots of evidence of Trudeau's anger at Canadians' lack of care for their country; a lack of care as he understood it.

Francophone reporters in the plane loved to throw back at Trudeau over and over again in the most mocking tone the PM's phrase that summed up his challenge to francophones to love and preserve their stake in Canada: "On va lâcher ça? Mais, voyons donc!" He used this with varying success to provoke a proud sense of proprietary affection for the whole country, for all its beauty, for all its opportunities, and so on, in audiences where many were ready to separate. Roughly translated, it means, "Are you going to throw all that away? Come on, now!"

Pierre Trudeau, the man, was simply seldom able to communicate his feeling of communion with Canada. He had come close in the "Portrait Intime" interview when Alain Stanké asked what the PM would like to accomplish on retirement, and the PM answered that he would like to know by name every tree in the woods! But, this feeling of communion with the physical Canada was not an easy concept with which to move people. Trudeau also rightly despised the divisions between French and English because he considered his exposure to both great cultures a privilege.

Ideological and cultural divisions between French and English reporters on the campaign plane were a microcosm of the larger problem, and deeply troubled us all. Even simple things like different approaches to news were little understood or appreciated by the other side. Radio-Canada's debonair TV reporter, François

175

Perrault, revealed this to me a few weeks after the end of the campaign when Susanne, my daughter, I, and the wonderful Luc Lavoie of TVA were guests on Perrault's sailboat on Lake Champlain.

A chasm between the two camps had been opened by anglo reporters' remarks about the francophones' "barbarian" singing and their vociferous high spirits.

Then, late in the campaign, Mark Phillips, Perrault's CBC English TV counterpart, caused a minor sensation when he ran a story that Trudeau would "hang on to power" even if defeated. This story came out of remarks Trudeau made at an informal lunch between the PM and a few reporters. There had been arguments amongst reporters over whether he was serious and what he really meant. Phillips and a couple of others decided to make the most of it.

Perrault simply felt the story was not clearly enough substantiated and ignored it. He received a severe reprimand from Pierre O'Neill, then head of news at Radio-Canada. He was accused of being a Trudeau patsy, and was taken off the plane, bitter and angry. He was a popular francophone, and most of his colleagues supported him. The incident only worsened relations between the two solitudes.

Thus the national malaise flourished in the flying inner sanctum of the campaign plane itself. Trudeau tried to diagnose the malaise. Clark ignored it and won.

PART TWO

NINE

RESIGNATION AND REBIRTH

*I*n the weeks following our defeat, there was a kind of numbness as we packed up our lives. Suddenly we were the untouchables in the Langevin Building, which was now awaiting the arrival of the young PM and his new staff. Of all the Privy Council Office officers with whom we had worked so closely, only foreign policy adviser Jacques Roy and David Ablett, a former *Vancouver Sun* reporter from Priorities and Planning, still talked to us.

There was much early afternoon boozing in the Dick O'Hagan memorial office where, so recently, communications plans worthy of the eighties had been hatched. Arnie Patterson had taken his suitcase polling machine with him and disappeared with hardly a goodbye.

We barely survived Keith Davey's courageous attempt at assembling the campaign team at a dinner at the Four Seasons. Trudeau spent much of the evening bitching about the speechwriting and media and policy advice he'd been given. Suzanne Perry and I made a lame attempt at humour.

In a reverse power trip, Coutts chose who were out (about 85 percent of the staff) and who would stay on to work in the greatly reduced circumstances of Opposition. He "did" about a dozen a day. Everyone waited for the phone call to summon him. At this stage these were the only calls that we got. We waited.

"How would you like to be Press Secretary to the Leader of the Opposition?" Coutts asked me. CTV's Craig Oliver encouraged me, saying that he had told Mr. Trudeau that the press liked me. I've been told that the former minister Judd Buchanan also put a word in for me with Trudeau. Pitfield said it was a great opportunity. I accepted, and Suzanne Perry stayed on as my assistant. Louise Webb, O'Hagan's former secretary, and a rock of steady support during the campaign as a general helpmate, completed our new Press Office.

In a final childish act of defiance, just as our files were being loaded for the ultimate trip down the street to the Office of the Leader of the Opposition (OLO), the Press Office girls scrawled "we'll be back!" in lipstick on all the mirrors on our end of the first floor.

The media spotlight quickly moved off us, leaving no afterglow. The only story the press was interested in now from the OLO was the redecoration of Stornoway, the official residence of the Leader of the Opposition and soon to be Trudeau's new home.

The last "photo opportunity" with the boys at 24 Sussex provided one warm interlude in those unhappy days. We had long promised United Press and Canadian Press an opportunity to shoot Trudeau at play with his three sons. It was hardly a priority for a man who made a strict distinction between his public and private life. Nevertheless, he now agreed.

For him, it was not a time to pose for photographers (who he generally liked), but an opportunity to steal a few unplanned moments of fun with his kids. They played marbles on the terrace overlooking the river completely unaware of the clanking of motor-drive cameras, Trudeau utterly engaged in the game.

There was one final reception at 24 Sussex before it was relinquished to the Clarks – an outside garden party for all the dispirited staff. Trudeau was difficult about the arrangements and wanted nobody inside the house. But he was civil. He moved about charming the women and then disappeared inside.

A flushed switchboard lady arrived late. She desperately wanted to see her old boss and say goodbye. The switchboard people, who knew all our secrets, were part of the permanent staff that Clark would inherit in the Langevin. But the normally courteous ex-PM had had enough and would not come out.

I wrote the following passage well into Opposition days. I tried to put the best light on living with lack of power.

November 1979

As I write this, there has been another major rotation in the world for those very few who are still tuned into the capacious mind of Pierre Trudeau. We are adjusting to power loss. It is a different, in some ways more satisfying life with him in Opposition. But the changes are enormous.

It is a grey Ottawa afternoon. A clammy November wind blows over the bare Gatineau hills, across the confluence of the Rideau, Gatineau, and Ottawa rivers, the geographic reason for this community's existence. It brushes 24 Sussex perched high above the wide Ottawa River, and laces through the few blocks which separate our small New Edinburgh home from what we used to call the "residence."

In a few weeks, on November 22, it will be six months since the defeat. There will be snow on the ground then. National Capital Commission workmen will start putting up dozens of strings of blue lights on the huge balsam at 24 Sussex. When I walk the dog, I will admire the effect as I have for the last five years.

But there will be a profound difference. Three years ago when I joined the PMO, 24 Sussex was part of our neighbourhood. Helga and I had visited there socially, and we had met Trudeau and the "boys" several times in the parks that frame this little annex to Ottawa. I had been at the residence countless times on official business, bicycling there many times in the fine weather. The last time, on a glorious sun-drenched afternoon in early June, I had arrived early to help set up tables of wine and cheese for the final reception for PMO staff.

We have new neighbours at 24 Sussex – Joe and Maureen. I know they are warm individuals. We have met them several times at parties at our former next-door neighbours, David and Cecilia Humphreys. Joe, I recall, was once particularly charming with my ailing father, here for a Christmas visit.

But the other day, I actually had a legitimate reason to go to 24 Sussex to deliver copies of the little community newspaper I now co-edit. I could not bring myself to do it. I would have liked to say

181

hello again to the patient and pleasing Heidi Bennett (I always thought she looked a bit like Margaret!), who is still there running the household staff. She was always so helpful when I arrived at the kitchen door with a score or so of motley reporters to disrupt an official dinner or reception for a photograph.

By now, I suppose I show every sign of being drenched in self-pity and regret. Not quite. When there is a hierarchy as strict as that which works down from a head of government to his immediate staff, one gets in the habit of taking cues from the apex. Trudeau was delighted to have a summer free to do things that were impossible under the strictures of office, such as a wilderness canoe trip with two reporters, Craig Oliver of CTV and Jean Pelletier of *la Presse*. This would have been impossible as prime minister, the pursuing helicopters notwithstanding.

Trudeau is clearly happier. He has found that his convictions about the nature of Canadian federalism are topical, even arresting, for a growing number of Canadians. His optimism spreads.

Although I may miss him as a neighbour (he now sort of camps in the amazingly barren "Stornoway" a mile or so away from where we live), and I may even regret the glamorous self-importance which mantled even the lowliest messenger in the PMO, the new tight "OLO" setup gives me something I did not have in the PMO – a closer working relationship with Pierre Elliott Trudeau.

Trudeau is now more adaptable, but his convictions have not changed. He is asking as much as answering questions now, and he enjoys the turnabout. He is closer and more open with those around him, with the press and with those he meets in his travels. This is why I really have few regrets.

Perhaps the difference for Trudeau is simply the disappearance of the "bags," those omnipresent reminders of a life nailed to the needs and timetables of the state. Margaret rightly hated them! The enormous and efficient briefing machine that is the Privy Council Office blows its tempest of paper under Joe Clark's door now.

The former prime minister moves about Canada as Pierre Elliott Trudeau, citizen. He likes it, and his delight is infectious. A couple of weeks ago, after a party function, Trudeau and I left the Four Seasons in Calgary in a cab together for the trip to the airport and the flight home. Trudeau sat in the front seat as usual. We chatted, but the stiffness and silence of the driver was obvious. Finally he blurted out how honoured he was – that this was one of the most important things that had ever happened to him.

Trudeau, although not his best in the morning, thanked him, then proceeded to draw him out in the most charming way. The driver was Turkish, and Trudeau, who had travelled there, with his photographic memory asked the amazed man precise questions about his homeland. The driver refused to accept the fare, and bowed, scraped, and carried on in a way Trudeau didn't know how to deal with. But he was warmed by this encounter, and by the constant attention he got on the Air Canada flight.

His new role finally allows him to react, or not, with the man on the street. Now there are no phalanxes of security or overprotective staff to make this difficult. Although the night before at the Liberal dinner and dance in Calgary, caught in the ample arms of a huge blonde, he made it crystal clear as he swirled by me that he wanted to be "saved," and thanked me when I cut in!

At any rate, we who are still with him are the beneficiaries of this new man. I miss the invitations to Government House to receptions on state occasions. But I do not miss the PM who had to ration his time and emotions so severely in order to run this fractious nation. Perhaps I cannot say I know him better, but I have seen a broader personality.

The following piece was written as an attempt to summarize my feelings about Trudeau after what seemed to be his final resignation as Leader of the Liberal Party on November 22nd, 1979. I later read portions of it aloud to the first meeting of the "Glorious 13th" Society, a group of those of us still in the Office of the Leader of the Opposition when the Clark government was unexpectedly defeated on December 13, 1979, an event which led to Trudeau's return to fight the 1980 federal election.

December 5, 1980

If I were asked to do a summary of what I think about Pierre Elliott Trudeau, I would have to say that he never struck me so much as a man of a certain age, but as a man who occupied a certain space. A certain removed space that neither his staff, nor often the people of Canada, could easily penetrate.

This remove enabled him to disguise his intention to resign for weeks, as we found out later. A very lonely, personal, and pragmatic decision was made during the very weeks he appeared more ready than ever to challenge Clark decisively in the House.

He says now, of course, that he had to keep giving his job all he had until the two federal by-elections were over. But, in retrospect, it must have been an act of sheer will to go on performing, militating, and responding to the demands of press and party alike when, emotionally, he already has severed himself from the job.

I vividly remember his long, patient address to Ontario Young Liberals during the Liberal Party of Canada (Ontario) Convention the weekend before he resigned.

The session was supposed to be a question-and-answer format – very informal. I had set up a small meeting room in the Harbour Castle Convention Centre in Toronto with a circle of chairs and padded benches. The idea was for him to move around the room and meet as many young Liberals as possible, then field a few questions.

Even before his arrival, the room had become unbearably crowded. Pressing the flesh would be impossible. The gaggle of TV crews, radio reporters, and other media who were poking equipment around to try and get some "actuality" from this rare appearance, didn't help. After Trudeau arrived, they jammed what little aisle space remained. As the flesh closed in around him, there was nothing I could do but quickly get him on a chair so the whole room could see him over the heads of the TV crews.

I found the public address mike and pushed it into his hand, then poked up three or four other microphones for radio reporters who, by this time, were crouched below the chair. One girl, whose microphone cable was too short to allow her to sit on the floor, was forced to remain half kneeling for the whole thirty minutes. The crush was quite frightening.

Trudeau was not expected to speak at length but the group was obviously ready to listen, rather than question. So, modestly and quietly, he began a freewheeling discussion of Liberalism.

The combination of TV lights and bad ventilation soon turned the room into a danger to health. The press and the party alike melted attentively. The PM was rolling, picking up cues from the entranced young audience. To their delight, he mocked himself when he lost the thread of his thoughts while juggling four microphones and a water glass I had proffered, yet maintaining absolute composure.

Somehow he was not in that sweaty room; he was not being fried by four TV lights right under his nose; he was not barely balanced on a rickety chair; he had not just had oral surgery that left one side of his face swollen. He was as if in a big hall; cool, rested, and preoccupied solely with what he was saying.

He spoke feelingly for half an hour, spent another twenty minutes meeting people and signing autographs, including the inevitable couple of casts on broken arms and legs. Nobody could have guessed he had already decided to remove himself from these activities. In fact, this performance convinced several journalists, including Mike Duffy, that he was in for the distance. As usual, he had taken his own space with him, and it had served him well.

So, we were as stunned as everyone else when it became clear a few days later that he was, in fact, resigning. Even that day, there was little hint of anything untoward, only a rare call for senior staff to assemble in the Leader's Centre Block office at 9:00 a.m. When I arrived, I realized the morning had been set up with protocol precision.

Others were told while we waited. It was not difficult to guess what the word was from the solemn faces and red eyes of the small groups that emerged through his door into Cecile Viau's small secreterial office. I barely remember when my turn came, except that Trudeau showed that inner calm that always nourishes him in adversity. His thanks were sincere, if brief, and we left.

I called the Press Gallery at the last possible moment to gather the gang, and then took a long, silent walk with him to the West Block and the waiting caucus. The announcement there was short. I waited outside to accompany him on the familiar walk to the press theatre across the street on the other side of Wellington Street.

He emerged from Caucus clearly shaken. He waved off Jack, his chauffeur, who was waiting in the car at the back of the building, and we hoofed it at his normal clip behind the building, around to the front, and to the top of the stairs leading down to the light on Wellington.

There he paused. I looked over. Tears were welling up in his eyes. I stopped and shielded him as he regained his composure. It only lasted a few seconds. It was a very private glimpse of the emotion he was feeling.

The news conference, where he read out his resignation statement, was *pro forma* – for him. The faces of the press showed their genuine emotion, but not his. By the time he had crossed Wellington, Trudeau had put the mask back on. His wit returned as he ended his statement with this nice twist: "And if I can be permitted to turn around a phrase, I would say that I'm kind of sorry I won't have you to kick around any more."

Pierre Trudeau started really to detach and unwind when he spoke to members of his riding association in Mount Royal, November 27, 1979, shortly after his resignation. There he told his followers, "Most people said, 'Welcome home'; that pleased me more than those of you who said 'You look so well.' When I was thirty or forty people didn't say that. So don't say now that I'm looking so well, because then I'll detect a little surprise in your voice. Why shouldn't I look well, I'm only sixty!"

It was a bittersweet moment; a flash of self-deprecating humour that lit the familiar Town Hall in Mount Royal with laughter and applause. Trudeau had come home to the community that first permitted him to take his ideas to Ottawa fourteen years before.

I stood below the stage, as I had done countless times in the past, trying to unmask the words, to see into the unpredictable. It became obvious to me that if his political leadership was to be lost to Canada, his intellect was not. He used this Mount Royal "family occasion" to launch the powerful idea of proportional representation, describing it urgently as one of the most effective remaining ways for the federal government to remain relevant to the whole country. Only six days after the painful announcement of his resignation, he was bringing fresh commitment to solving the problems he had wrestled with for two decades!

On the same Montreal excursion, I sat amazed in the living room of Michel Roy, the brilliant editor of *le Devoir*, listening to Trudeau deliver precise, fine-tuned ideas about the Quebec referendum. His already formulated project was to explain to Quebecers that a "no" vote would be interpreted not as a vote for the *status quo* but as a "yes," a positive vote for a new kind of federalism.

What amazed me most, however, was not that he still had ideas of how to wage the war of his life, but his diffidence in answering Roy's last question in the long, probing interview. Roy asked him to review his performance against goals he and the other two "wise men," Jean Marchand and Gérard Pelletier, set for themselves when they joined the federal Liberals in 1965.

Trudeau paused: "I guess that's a question I am going to have to answer many times . . . I guess. . . ." Pause. The answer itself was short and tangential. He talked of electoral reform, listed a few other changes, then finished by saying "I guess I will have to make a list. . . ."

I was overwhelmed, not just by this modesty, but by the fact he really is set four square to the future. A man who keeps no diary, he is like a thirty-year-old whose past weighs little against the challenge of the present. He was writing, with his ideas and actions, a new chapter in his life. His age meant nothing. He was taking his space with him.

Within weeks of my last diary entry, an extraordinary turn of events would propel us back into another election campaign, and the man, about whom all the rather unflattering political obituaries had been written in November, took a few of us back into power.

Before this future unfolded, the office busied itself for a fortnight in sniffing out who to support in what was obviously going to be an early Liberal leadership contest. I discussed how we would handle the press at a convention, and there were long meetings on which city to choose as a site. There was enough time.

We clung to our senses of humour. Herb Metcalfe, the eternally ebullient husband of long-time Trudeau office devotee Isabel Metcalfe, and their fine friend, Doug Kirkpatrick, cooked up a "Go with Gossage" leadership campaign for me! It came complete with a T-shirt and button, and the campaign slogan "Have a sausage with Gossage!"

In the corner offices of Tom Axworthy and Jim Coutts, deciding which real candidate to work for was more serious business. They showed, externally at least, astonishing resilience. Trudeau had resigned. Who was next?

There was the implicit message that Don Macdonald was Trudeau's choice, and that he would be the choice of office loyalists. But we were never directly asked to do anything. Tom Axworthy, who with his brother Lloyd had worked for Turner years ago, was widely expected to side with the handsome and evasive Toronto lawyer, but we were not certain. Tom himself kept mum.

For me, the exercise was academic. Trudeau's resignation had given me a clean opportunity to move on. My family were more than ready to resume a more normal life. We made plans for Christmas, and I started coming in late to the office.

The Liberal Caucus Christmas party was a warm family affair

187

that year. Helga and I lounged with Marc Lalonde in someone's sumptuous office, feeling relaxed and unpressured. The party talk of bringing the government down seemed of the remotest reality.

But a few days later, on December 13, the bells were ringing for a critical vote in the young Clark government.

I was in the Opposition lobby, just behind the curtains listening to a couple of hawkish Liberal MPs physically threatening a wavering colleague who didn't believe we had the numbers to tumble the government and couldn't face the prospect of an election. There was rough language as members were almost pushed into their seats.

In the corridor outside, I collared Mike Duffy and told him that we were geared to defeat the government and had the will, and probably the numbers, to do it. There was only Duff and a few other press about, when, for once, I had what I increasingly felt certain was a hot story!

The government did come down. We cracked, almost in disbelief, hastily purchased champagne in the Centre Block offices. Here we were with an election to fight, no leader, and only a skeleton staff in the office and in the party. Slowly it dawned on a few that it would be suicide to have a divisive leadership campaign, then run with an untried winner in a federal election. Perhaps, someone should try to persuade Trudeau to come back!

The intrigues of the next few days included hasty polls, and train-loads of MPs and staff streaming to Stornoway where the tired and somewhat confused former leader, Trudeau, was now living on borrowed time. But most of all, the period was marked by Jim Coutts's singleminded determination to persuade the man he could run again and win.

Trying to get a "line" on what was going on, I visited Coutts one evening at his Ottawa apartment that looked, as always, unlived in. He had kept his Toronto house and had never really psychologically moved to Ottawa during all those years. I believe he gained great strength from that. Coutts offered me a glass of champagne, and answered one of a huge number of calls that came in that evening. I heard him saying, "We've got the numbers, I can tell you, Jean, we can win . . . ." Chrétien was being "networked" for the cause.

On Monday, December 16, there was still such uncertainty about what Trudeau would do that I held two contradictory speeches by Coutts for Trudeau's use at a news conference we were convinced would be called the next day. One announced his decision to run again, the other his decision to stay out of the running. It was extremely difficult to assess his state of mind. He was distracted in a way I had never seen before. It was clear he was going through a dark night of the soul, and what he had told his children and planned for them in retirement weighed heavily on him.

Nobody knew what his decision would be. I was outside his Centre Block office after he consulted with two solid MPs, Don Johnston and Ed Lumley. Their encouraging middle-of-the-road advice to Trudeau to stay buoyed me.

The next day we called a news conference for 11:00 a.m. Coutts went alone to Stornoway, and I waited in agony at the office. At about ten to the hour, I went down to the corner of Wellington and O'Connor and lounged about outside the press conference theatre with the waiting cameramen. At about five after the hour, Jack, the driver, wheeled the car up, and Trudeau bounced out. A dark-haired, middle-aged Italian woman almost grabbed him as he stepped on to the sidewalk. "Please Mr. Trudeau, will you run again?" she begged as the cameras ran ahead for the shot. "Si," I could barely hear Trudeau confiding.

With this decision, Trudeau fired the starter's pistol for the beginning of another marathon. For the second time in one twelve-month period, I would be with Trudeau at the front of the plane in the thick of another election.

Those days were unbelievably congested. Lives were wrenched about brutally half a dozen times in as many weeks. I went from the half life of having no prospects and no leader into another election campaign where everything pointed me towards the coveted corner office on the ground floor of the Langevin Building.

We were soon in the air in a new DC-9. Many of us were the same team, given a chance to turn around the failure of the last campaign. We felt like a hockey team called back for a second try at winning the cup after they thought the season was over. These things just don't happen. But, in 1980, they did.

We had a new and simple strategy. We campaigned not to get more support but to keep the winning margin we had. The sole objective in this campaign was not to make any mistake that would reduce our lead. Keep Trudeau on a "short leash," tacticians told us – hang on; don't say too much. If he got "loose" and said what he wanted to, he might alienate some group or other, so no regular news conferences and no unplanned scrums. This is the classic contemporary ploy.

This time we knew we were winning. I wasn't running on adrenalin and self-delusion as I had in the 1979 tour, but on knowledge and information. The Sunday meetings in Ottawa, chaired by Coutts, were not brainwashing sessions, but serious discussions of how to "fine tune" Trudeau's carefully scripted message to pull in an ounce more support from the public, whose mood was scrupulously polled every day of the campaign.

The dishevelled Toronto guru, Martin Goldfarb, constantly pulled polling results scribbled on scraps of paper from the pockets of his baggy trousers. He used his figures to try and push the group towards more radical policy initiatives. "I tell you, the support is there," he would say. But, for the most part, Coutts, Jack Austin, and the others played it safe.

As my job as master of the press was to keep them happy and away from direct contact with the PM (the press called it a "peek-aboo" campaign), my role at these meetings was to report on the media's increasingly bored and sullen mood.

I lived a permanent paradox. I knew the strategy was working. Scripted words were being spoken, however unenthusiastically, by a leader ready this time to do what had to be done to become prime minister again. We had even had a portable podium built, knowing that we had to make it comfortable and dependable if Trudeau was to follow the "script." It was at the right height, had the right light, and the microphones were just at the right level. It was designed so Trudeau knew even where his water was, in its own hidden compartment! It fitted into two large boxes, and we recreated our very own Calvary as we hoisted it from hall to hall.

Trudeau was both predictable and looking good. His words got out to the public, because, most days, there was just enough substance in his speeches to provide a television or radio clip, or a Canadian Press "lead." This substance was rationed out bit by bit by our tireless travelling speech and policy maker, Tom Axworthy. We called the solid meaty material "Gainesburgers." Working through the night in his pajamas, Axworthy also crafted into his speeches irresistible short snappy lines (often poking fun at Clark) for TV and radio clips. Sure enough, they would be picked up and used.

All this slowly convinced me that however much TV reporters talked over a Trudeau clip, however they served it up and carved it up, and however the pundits (many of whom had become entranced with Clark and his Cabinet) ranted, Trudeau's words, and the carefully nuanced nationalist Liberal program, got out to the public.

I adapted my principles to the unreal war game of campaigns. In "peacetime," between elections, I believed that providing the media with real information and real access to political leaders in the long run was the fairest, surest way to serve the democratic debate. With this position, I came close to endorsing the Canadian media's often-claimed "right" to know, a right exercised by journalists as surrogates or advocates for the public, who cannot ask questions or ferret out information for themselves. But the tight and deliberate media control we exercised during the 1980 campaign forced me to confront this argument directly, and publicly.

I sat before the cameras at least twice, once when questioned in Halifax by an ever-polite but quite perturbed David Halton of CBC-TV, and again later in Toronto when confronted more gruffly by my old pal Bruce Garvey, now a Global TV reporter. In both cases, believe it or not, I defended our right to control access to the leader and to direct the flow of information in "wartime," as it were (during a campaign), as distinct from "peacetime" (during a period of government or opposition)! I argued that the public's rights, as represented by the media, were in suspension; that the public was not being tricked or cheated, because it understood the hype and exaggeration of these occasional contests for their hearts and minds. Finally, I argued that campaigns should be judged more as promotion exercises than as the normal exercise of political responsibility in our parliamentary system!

I can hear myself telling Halton with a straight face that the media had no right to set the agenda for a campaign by asking Trudeau questions when they pleased and thereby sidetracking our strategy. We had every right to set our own agenda and get our message out as clearly as possible. The media were to be neutral vehicles, imposing no judgement on what they heard or saw!

Despite this argument, I used to tell the strategy meetings on

Sunday mornings in Ottawa regularly that I didn't think it would be such a dramatic break with the closed campaign strategy to have a couple of news conferences. After all, Trudeau was grown up and could handle himself – especially in such a well-scripted campaign.

The "back of the plane," as we called the press, was getting restless. I was running out of reasons why Trudeau should not submit to an hour's media questioning. At one point in one of the endless discussions on this subject, I said to a group of reporters, "Well, I've asked him and had no luck. Why don't you people try?"

I forgot about this stalling exercise until, somewhere in the air out of St. John's, Newfoundland, I received two pages, which remain the epitaph for this winter wonder tour. A neatly typed headline announced "Petition to the Right Hon. Pierre Trudeau." It was followed in both official languages by a formal and polite request for a news conference "in view of the fact that Mr. Trudeau has not held [one] since December 18th"! Members of the travelling press corps had all signed neatly underneath. There were twenty-nine of them, thereafter known as the St. John's Twenty-Nine!

I took it up to the front of the plane right away, and, with barely a word, gave it to the former PM. He put on his half glasses, studied it for a moment, looked at the names, and then wrote "*fiat medial conferenciam* – P." This was probably as correct Latin as exists to permit a news conference to go ahead!

The resulting session in a provincial Quebec motel brought to our tour a gaggle of media heavies. But the little information Trudeau cared to pass in his long rambling answers was easily overshadowed by the escapades that morning of a young female reporter from a local newspaper.

The enterprising lass had decided that the only way to get an "exclusive" with Trudeau would be to get into her bathing suit and swim and sauna with him! Luckily our press officer, Suzanne Perry, was also doing morning exercises in the pool and was able to rescue him. Nevertheless, "I had a sauna with PET" made a wonderful little piece of first-person journalism, which was reprinted in several metropolitan newspapers!

Trudeau clearly won the news conference round with the press. They virtually gave up fussing over getting real access to him or real answers out of him. Even Jeff Simpson of the *Globe and Mail* swallowed his pride and allowed himself to be the vehicle for a formal question and answer session with the PM towards the end of the campaign, all of which his paper dutifully printed.

The campaign crew's attitude to the press produced one evening of low comedy. It was shortly after the now-famous energy speech in Halifax, in which Trudeau sketched the outlines of the National Energy Program. This was late in the campaign and we were all a bit worn, particularly Axworthy, who had been cranking out pretty solid speech material at a fantastic rate, and had been acting as go-between with the strong-willed Liberal platform committee at the same time.

A good deal of scotch flowed that night in Halifax, poured enthusiastically by Don Jamieson and our travelling Liberal president and general gentleman about the plane, Senator Al Graham. A few press came and went, and we discussed the low credibility the press had given the energy speech, particularly CBC TV's Mike Duffy. Axworthy thought his coverage insulting. Suddenly, in an inspired outburst, Axworthy shouted, "Get me Duffy, that porker! Get me the porker!" Sensing some good fun to be had at the expense of Duffy, usually the best of sports, a couple of us volunteered to drag him from his room for the dressing down he deserved!

But we overplayed it. It was about 2:00 a.m. and The Duff was asleep. We shouted at the door, "OK Duffy, open up! Axworthy wants your hide. He's furious about your item. Come out and face the music!" Well, the rudely awakened Duff took us a bit too seriously. He became even more apprehensive when Axworthy himself appeared and started banging on the door (that Duffy had by now put furniture against), demanding to see the "porker."

Mike felt his physical safety endangered, and called his Toronto desk to report the threats! We all laughed for days over the incident. For months thereafter, poor Duffy seldom saw Axworthy without being reminded of the "porker" affair!

Some of the travelling pack found highly original ways of embroidering this campaign to victory. Late in the campaign in Levis, Quebec, Trudeau quoted a French poet, Léon Bloy, and some of the press enquired about the author's identity. That evening, Jim Maclean, a radio reporter with an English literature degree, came on the DC-9's PA system, thanked the Leader for "raising the level" of the campaign, and challenged him to identify a parody he then read. In Winnipeg the next evening, during his speech, Trudeau rattled off an equally good parody of *The Tempest* and, to the amazement of the audience, finished by saying, "That's to get even with the press who suspected I didn't even know some parody from *The Merchant of Venice.*"

He had thrown down the gauntlet to Maclean, who announced on the next flight the start of "Poetry Wars," in which Trudeau used parodies of poems in his speeches and Maclean identified them.

The evening we found out we had a twenty-point Gallup lead, Trudeau inserted into a speech, "Things fall apart, the center cannot hold, and mere anarchy is loosed upon the Tory party."

Maclean correctly identified it as from Yeats's appropriately named work, "The Second Coming."

This parlour game set the tone for our final wrap-up party in Toronto. It was a rare production of song, parody, poetry, and mock newscasts – a sort of grown-up fraternity night. An amused Trudeau, surrounded by the press, ended the evening with a dramatic recitation of a long French poem, *Les Conquérants de L'Or* by José-Maria de Heredia (1842–1905), an epic describing Pizarro's conquest of Peru.

I seated Trudeau near his biographer, George Radwanski, by then a *Toronto Star* editorial page editor, and across from Bill Fox, Southam News's brash and uncompromising political writer and an old colleague of George's, and Patrick Nagel, a witty observer of the media scene. Radwanski, who had spent more time interviewing Trudeau for his book than any other journalist, had the humiliating experience of hearing Trudeau repeatedly call him "Peter"!* As Trudeau early on had often called me Peter as well, Fox, Nagel, and I had to exercise a lot of self-control to avoid bursting out in laughter!

Finally the life in a thousand and one hotel rooms was over; we were back in the Château Laurier ballroom in Ottawa for election results. There was little of the apprehension of the year before.

---

* Radwanski had Dick O'Hagan arrange eight hour-long interviews. The material was used in his biography, *Trudeau*, published by Macmillan in 1978.

The suite was alive with laughter and confidence. Trudeau delivered his memorable line, "Welcome to the eighties!"

The day dawned when the Clark troops were out of the Langevin Building and we could move back in. It was somewhat of a reunion with the two Suzannes at the PMO switchboard, and with Ernie and the other guards. I poked my head into Dick's old office. The old leather sofa set originally from the East Block that Dick had used since he was Pearson's press secretary was still there. The building was a mess and looked as if it had been quickly vacated. There were no "we'll be back" lipsticked messages on the mirrors. I pinched myself. We had come back.

TEN

TRAVAILS AND TRAVELS

The Referendum

With the Quebec referendum on sovereignty-association set for late May, the reborn Prime Minister immediately geared up for his role in the campaign. Jean Chrétien was assigned to the campaign on permanent point duty, and André Burelle, an intense intellectual who worked down the hall from me in the Langevin Building, was assigned the task of finding the tactics and words for Trudeau's interventions.

Given Chrétien's front line position, Trudeau's role was to be limited, but meticulously planned and scripted. There had to be a theme that developed to a conclusion through a few key speeches. Only huge turning-point events, which would make for maximum impact, were to be considered for the PM, who steadfastly refused to play number two to Claude Ryan. Ryan, now leader of the "no" campaign in Quebec, was Trudeau's old intellectual enemy from the 1970 October crisis when Ryan was editor of *le Devoir* and did not support the PM's imposition of the War Measures Act.

In a sustained exchange of ever-more-honed texts, the Prime Minister and André Burelle created in their minds and crafted with their pens words that still sing today. These words rang particularly on May 14, 1980, in the electric atmosphere of the Paul Sauvé arena in Montreal.

I drove with the PM in the RCMP motorcade to a darkened side entrance of the huge sports facility which, less than four years before, had shaken with the wild celebration of Lévesque's provincial election conquest. Now we hurried through concrete passages to a holding room just below and to the side of the front of the arena. I went out into the arena and was met by a stir and urgency and closeness in the audience such as I had never experienced before. It was not just the number of people packed into that space that made the atmosphere so charged, there was also a special intensity. As I checked microphones at the PM's podium and looked out over the mass of expectation, I knew this was the turning point of the campaign.

I saw the string of speakers onto the stage and moved down in front of the huge platform to join the media. First Chrétien and then Ryan spoke, and finally Trudeau moved gracefully to the podium in his "aw gee" humble pose as the crowd hooted, yelled, cheered, and shouted their approval, on their feet, waving banners, chanting – a deafening, overwhelming demonstration. This passionate ovation went on for five, six, seven minutes. Trudeau grasped the podium, and for once was at a loss, overwhelmed by the emotion of that mass of friends and, for that evening, family members.

I stood with reporters in the huge roped-off "pen," which had been set aside for the forest of cameras below the stage. Most reporters were, frankly, awe-struck. Particularly so was L. Ian MacDonald, the political writer from the *Gazette* who later, in his book *From Bourassa to Bourassa*, invested this evening with almost mythical importance.

Trudeau spoke as if to family or close relatives: "Bien sûr, mon nom est Pierre Elliott Trudeau. Oui, Elliott, c'était le nom de ma mère. . . . Et puis mon nom est québécois, mon nom est canadien aussi, et, oui, c'est ça, mon nom."

With this single phrase, he took on the whole PQ referendum subplot of racial purity, flinging his bi-racial background back at them, personifying and embodying Canada and accusing the PQ of trying to destroy, not just the country, but his own personal birthright and that of many Quebecers.

The promise he hammered home was equally daring. It had been developed when he was in Opposition, but delivered to that crowd, it set the PQ campaign on end. A "no" to sovereignty-association would be, he swore on his Commons seat, a "yes" to a renewed federalism. Constitutional reform was joined with a fervour we had never heard from him before.

For the press, the referendum was a big, passionate story, filled with strong personalities and conflict. With the Prime Minister performing at the peak of his energy and intellect, the media simply watched and wrote. They needed no help, no promoting, leaking, stroking, or whatever from the likes of press secretaries. The "story" took over, and ideology found less place in the reports than we had expected. PQ sympathizers in the press wrote and spoke of Trudeau's and the "no" efforts with clarity and objectivity. The stories almost wrote themselves.

Later, watching the results of the referendum pour in on TV in my office I was reminded of a very different experience watching results of the Quebec provincial election in November 1976. Then, in the same setting, we had watched the PQ victory make expatriates out of our tough little gang of federalist francophones. Three-and-a-half years later, this gang had helped engineer the defeat of a now confused idea. There was a great sense of satisfaction.

In a sense, the voyage of these French intellectuals through Ottawa was nearly over. The family quarrel had been settled with their own intellect and logic – with the assist, of course, of a good dose of emotion from Jean Chrétien, Monique Bégin, and others who spoke from the heart.

That night, I felt, was really the end of Trudeau's singleminded crusade for Canada. The constitutional battles to come, however much tenacity they required, could only ever be the legal ribbons on a package that had been delivered with all his mind and heart to waiting Quebecers in his remarkable referendum interventions.

Death in Venice

The referendum campaign over, we took off on a series of travels with the Prime Minister which amounted to a full-scale travelling classroom on international issues for both the press, the Press Office, and not a few other aides and officials. The PM became an increasingly tolerant and lucid tour guide and professor as we wound our way around the world from summit to summit, from North to South for in-person examination of the problems between rich and poor countries, and, later, from East to West on the PM's personal crusade to lessen tensions, his peace initiative.

Our first big organized overseas trip with the PM was to Venice for the Summit of the Seven Industrialized Nations in the spring of 1980.

Trudeau, despite his year's absence in opposition, was still the longest-serving leader in the western world. The Venice summit, attended by the leaders of the United States, Italy, West Germany, Britain, France, Japan, and Canada, was preoccupied by the OPEC oil shock and its revelation of the western world's dependence on foreign oil. At the previous summit, Joe Clark had promised to raise Canadian oil prices to world levels; Trudeau retreated from this commitment. Calling the push to world prices "wrong and unjustified," he nevertheless agreed to a joint communiqué that urged a reduction in the use of imported oil through conservation and higher prices. Canada, however, was not specifically asked to adopt the world price.

Two years before, at the Bonn summit, I had been somewhat wet behind the ears in coping with the fierce international press competition. This time, at Venice, I was at least keenly aware of how difficult it was going to be to attract attention for the PM's positions in the media circus that summits had become.

The Americans had such superior logistics that we regularly lost our own press to their briefings during the summit. At one point they briefed on a summit communiqué a good hour or so before it was released generally, and piped the briefing to non-American journalists grouped around a loudspeaker they had strung out into the common press area. The U.S. version was the only one sent home that day.

We did, however, have a secret weapon to impress our journalists in the person of one Gilbert Reid, an immensely worldly staffer from our Embassy in Rome. Gilbert was assigned to help with the Canadian press. He spoke flawless Italian and knew every superb eatery in Venice. We took to gathering small groups of journalists together at ungodly hours and spoiling their palates rotten with the best Venice had to offer. Reid was a tireless promoter of Italy, and was full of advice for our press during the brief trip to Rome which followed.

The night before our departure from Rome, Gilbert told Suzanne Perry and me that he had arranged for us to have dinner with the famous Canadian photographer Roloff Beny at his lush penthouse in the most desirable *quartiere* of Rome. We agreed and, after some soul searching, decided to invite Allan Fotheringham along.

The "Foth," as he is known, does not travel well, and, in all honesty, we felt he needed a lift. The early part of the evening provided the kind of intelligent relaxation we all needed. The physical setting of hanging gardens and a magnificent view of Rome was spectacular. Beny was generous and expansive, and his German assistant cooked up an instant feast. Fotheringham, too, was at his best, charming Suzanne and telling evil jokes on Ottawa. Beny had mentioned that he had asked Trudeau to drop by, and near midnight there was a knock, knock and who should appear at the door but the PM himself saying how relieved he was to get away from a stuffy diplomatic dinner with our ambassador. As we walked out to the terrace, I told him that Fotheringham was there and he seemed amused, apparently mishearing the name as Father Ingham and assuming he was going to meet a priest.

This misapprehension corrected once he was settled facing the Foth. Trudeau easily engaged him with mock-serious questions on how Fotheringham found subject matter for his daily pieces, and where he got such endless inspiration for wicked satire. Foth, by contrast, was ill at ease. He made some oblique references to how long it had been since he had interviewed Trudeau, and then retired to the background, returning later to overhear an interesting exchange between Beny and the PM.

Beny was explaining in detail that he had offered his enormous photo collection to his native province, Alberta, without success. Would Trudeau intervene? The PM made encouraging noises, and gracefully changed the subject, becoming entangled instead in a long conversation with Beny's aged father, who was also present. After about an hour at this agreeable, if incongruous, gathering, the PM excused himself and departed.

I was delighted that the Foth, the acerbic genius of Canadian political letters, had effected a modest exchange with the PM. Wasn't this the way things were in Washington – media heavies rubbing shoulders with the President? On social occasions like this, it being understood, of course, that conversations were off the record.

Exhilarated by the evening, Suzanne and I stayed on for some time, saw an exhausted and, by now, somewhat the worse for wear Gilbert safely to his room and then retired only a few hours before the early morning departure for the airport.

That morning, Gilbert Reid was supposed to organize a complicated pickup by bus of the Canadian press who were staying at two different hotels. Unfortunately, dinner on the balcony had done him in, and he overslept. We were left stranded on the sidewalk watching helplessly as the PM's motorcade pulled off for the airport. Finally a sheepish Reid appeared with a commandeered bus, and we struggled unescorted through the traffic as I urged ever greater exhibitions of illegal and maniacal driving from the terrified chauffeur. I flashed my diplomatic passport at the shocked guards as we rolled through the gate on to the tarmac, only to see the Canadian 707 slowly taxiing off. I waved and shouted out of the window of the careening bus and, to my relief, the huge plane stopped and the crew put the ramp down. They had been perfectly prepared to leave without us!

This was not the only fallout from that late dinner. A couple of weeks later back in Ottawa, I read Fotheringham's column and found, to my horror, that he recounted the major events of our evening on Beny's terrace, including Beny's plea to Trudeau about his photo archive! I wrote him in some dismay a "Dear Allan" letter explaining that, after all, we had invited him out of the goodness of our hearts to give him a lift. Then "more out of regret than anger," I said how let down I was, and that his actions made it hard to think of having that kind of fun again. How naive I had been. Fun with Fotheringham nearly always has a price. Happily, this was about the only letter of that nature I ever wrote.

Our press is different from most in the world. They are more independent, less regimented, and certainly less part of the system than the Washington corps, for instance. Nothing is really off the record with Canadian media, and social occasions are (and probably should be) sources for material like any other.

If I had thought that having the big Press Secretary title was going to mean that I could chum around any more easily with our media heavies and let my guard down with any more hope of protection, I had learned my lesson.

A Night in the Desert

The first major trip in support of the PM's ideas about trying to get rich countries more involved in the real economic problems of the poor was scheduled for November 1980. It was designed to impose Canada and the Prime Minister on the North-South dialogue in a dramatic way, by visiting one of the richest nations (Saudi Arabia) and one of the poorest nations (North Yemen). This was planned as the first in a series of visits to world leaders leading up to the next summit in 1981, which was to be hosted by Canada. Trudeau was determined to have North-South issues discussed fully on that occasion. Trudeau had returned to power determined to make the North-South dialogue the focus of his foreign policy. He felt particularly strongly that Canada, with wealth, skills, and strong links to the Third World, had a special responsibility to advocate more assistance, more trade, and more investment for underdeveloped nations.

It should be admitted at the outset that, while Trudeau's intentions were serious and honourable, there was an element of tourism in these international jaunts. The PM *enjoyed* putting Canada on the map again internationally, and he was very good at it. But he equally enjoyed the kind of sightseeing open only to heads of government – the most exotic displays of native or tribal rituals, scuba-diving in inaccessible waters, or being guided around ancient ruins by a world expert.

In his new, youthful executive assistant, Ted Johnson, Trudeau had the perfect juggler of these two aspects of any trip. Johnson was athletic, a pilot and canoeist, and an inveterate traveller and tourist as well as a perceptive and diplomatic political animal. Ted had the challenge of planning trips that maintained a balance between public and private time for a man who, in even the most exotic locales, knew *exactly* what he wanted to see and do when he had a free moment.

Poor Ted. The Press Office tweaked his conscience whenever possible, probing the "softer" side of his plans, and causing him no little concern that the media should find out! Also, we added to his conflicting priorities by demanding as much press access to the PM throughout his trips as we could get. This, of course, required considerable logistical help from the military, from the External Affairs' world-wide network of staff, and, as well, local assistance.

In the case of the Saudi Arabia/North Yemen/Egypt/Germany/France tour being planned, there was hushed talk of scuba-diving in Saudi, of a visit to the Valley of the Kings in Egypt, and of the fact that the PM's second son, little Sacha, would be accompanying him. All these interesting diversions competed with the frenzied preparation of official agendas and discussion points.

Then came a tough surprise. Trudeau announced at a staff meeting that, on the forthcoming trip, he planned to ditch the Boeing 707, and with it the press entourage, and fly with only a few aides in the small Jetstar, which would have to be laboriously ferried to the Middle East!

I was flabbergasted and tried to make cogent, practical arguments to keep the usual configuration. But Trudeau was not impressed by any inconvenience the press might experience in trailing after him on commercial flights. He was determined to travel free of encumbrance, just as his friend Helmut Schmidt managed to do.

His decision stuck. Consequently, an amazingly courageous twenty or so aides and press were booked on commercial flights to London, then via Saudi Airlines to Riyadh. For the first time in years, we were bound on an international trip with the PM, but had to check our own bags and worry about tickets!

One of the rationales for separating the PM and the press was to avoid all the annoying "process" questions and stories about gifts exchanged, and what it was all costing. But on this trip, a supposed secret got out of the bag, so to speak, more easily than if we had been travelling normally.

The gift for the Crown Prince of Saudi Arabia was to be a Canadian gyrfalcon, a very hush-hush fact as the gyrfalcon is an endangered species. (This one had been raised in captivity.) At breakfast at the press hotel the morning after our arrival in Riyadh, there was the falcon on the arm of his young Canadian Wildlife Service keeper who had also come by commercial airliner and was now mingling with the reporters and happily telling his story.

This incident turned out to be just the first strand of a general unravelling of the blanket of secrecy and isolation so carefully wrapped about the PM and his immediate party. The Saudis saw the Canadian press as a legitimate part of the official delegation. They were invited to official functions and treated with great respect. Press buses careened along behind the open red convertibles and the black Mercedes limos of the official motorcade as they purred through the cleared sandy streets of the desert capital.

The PM's immediate staff stayed in a palace of the utmost garish luxury. The PM would pull up for a meeting to the sound of squealing from the limo's spotless Pirelli tires on the immaculately polished marble of the entrance drive. But the press was never far behind. They poked about the railway-station-scale halls drinking juices as the PM met a string of ruling family members and their friends.

The biggest disappointment for a PM who wanted to have a private visit came just after his first tête à tête with Sheikh Yamani in the guest palace. I had heard that Yamani had offered Trudeau a "night in the desert" to see the fabled medieval ruins at Madain Salih, a national shrine an hour's flight north of Jiddah. Knowing that the PM had difficulty saying "no" to my media requests in front of other leaders lest he appear anti-press (I had used this technique when he was with Helmut Schmidt), I intercepted the two chatting after the meeting and inquired innocently if there had been any thought of bringing the press along.

"How many have you?" Yamani asked. I told him. "We can accommodate that many," he said. Here was a man who obviously did not have to prove he was powerful. He asked Trudeau if he agreed. How could the PM say no to this generosity? He would have sounded undemocratic! And what generosity! It turned out that expanding the group from twenty or so to fifty or so took a whole fleet of aircraft. Tons more supplies had to be flown into the desert campsite the very next day.

Yamani put his own plush jet at our disposal for the first leg of the trip, and then we all piled into a fleet of five or six STOL aircraft for the flight up the coast. Awaiting us on arrival at the desert strip were dozens of Jeeps, Land Rovers, and Toyota wagons for the bone-rattling final leg to the "camp" site in the shadow of the ruins.

Everybody mingled about as we toured the burial places carved in the red rock bluffs and bounced across the desert in another cavalcade of Jeeps and Toyotas to walk the site of the town. The PM, press, and handlers were down to shirtsleeves, while Yamani and his aides strode gracefully in their flowing robes. Reporters forsook tape recorders and notepads for their own cameras. A kind of peace, a truce, captured us all as we let ourselves be taken up by the expanse of the timeless desert stretching before us. Little was reported of that excursion – everyone was too busy experiencing it.

Only Brian Kelleher, the tireless CBC radio journalist whose gruffness was easily punctured by a good joke, chased after Yamani with his tape recorder for a comment on an oil deal. Yamani, striding across the little compound after his sundown prayer, was polite. The rest of us "mellowed out," picked tent partners, and wandered about the campsite.

A long narrow tent, open on one side, its floor simply oriental carpets rolled out on the sand, had been set up for the evening banquet. Sheep were being killed and bled. I caught Sacha Trudeau looking awed at one hanging upside down from a truck. They were cooked whole over open fires.

Called to eat, we all squatted on the carpets in no particular order; there was no head table. Cans of pop were passed around, and plates were soon loaded with mutton roughly carved off the whole cooked animals and heaped on several gigantic platters. The carving was done by Bedouins who stood astride the animals and sliced them expertly with wicked-looking hunting knives.

The PM, with his impeccable sense of occasion, appeared in a close-fitting brown caftan. Sacha was suitably Arab-looking in a little beige one. The press were very decorous and well behaved.

The only incongruous note was struck by the wives of our ambassador and senior trade officer who, one could feel, were only just tolerated in this all-male gathering. They had been provided with American-style trailers that they were locked into at the end of the evening while their husbands slept in small tents with the rest of us!

As dinner wound down, the plates were removed from the middle of the tent, and a rather rag-tag group of musicians assembled. Not long after, rhythmic wailing desert music filled the tent and pierced the moonlit silence beyond.

The first men up to dance were a couple of elegant, if somewhat androgynous, Yamani aides in the most luxurious robes traced with gold threads. Their flowing and languorous movements had a somewhat ethereal quality. There was nothing ethereal about the two Canadian women, who decided to do a mercifully short exhibition of a bad counterfeit of the dance the men had been performing.

Then the Prime Minister decided to dance, and Sacha joined him. They were good, and a credit rather than an embarrassment to the rest of us. The pace picked up, and Trudeau whirled and dipped in a perfect compliment to the music. He was joined by

Yamani, and the two men danced in absolute control of themselves, both stunningly unselfconscious. The dance in the desert.

Later, after the banquet finally wound up, Ted Johnson and I went for a long quiet walk in the silver desert. The liquid stars hanging above, and that awesomely silent place, affected us both greatly.

The remainder of the trip was memorable for other reasons. Yamani's generosity even extended to lending us one of his marble-lined private jets for the next leg of the trip to North Yemen. But the moment we stepped out of the plane, we were on our own again, struggling through logistical nightmares. It soon hit home that straggling after the PM and his immediate entourage in rented buses and on terrifying middle-eastern commercial flights had very little charm.

In Egypt, while the PM and a couple of aides and officials swanned about in the Valley of the Kings, we sweated in fetid waiting rooms and hustled mountains of scattered luggage. Finally, at the famed Shepherd's Hotel in Cairo, there was a serious revolt. Two reporters found bedbugs and cockroaches in their rooms and refused to spend the night there. One of the jobs of a press secretary is to solve such crises quickly before the press consensus of the trip becomes totally negative, and bedbugs or other travel nightmares become the subject of stories for back home. Minutes later, I was begging the manager of the nearby Hilton for rooms.

For the next leg of the trip – Bonn via Athens – we had persuaded the PM to accept a reporter on board the Jetstar, John Ferguson of Canadian Press. It was a fight to get the PM to recognize the valid principle that, for such long hauls where the press could not follow or observe, he should be willing to accommodate a "pool" reporter, who in turn would tell his colleagues of any public statements made during their necessary absence.

So there was "Fergie," as he was known, in closer proximity to the PM and his son for a longer period than just about any reporter I could remember. I liked the gruff and forthright Ferguson, and Trudeau recognized in him a spirited interlocutor. He watched fascinated as the PM spent much of the flight giving Sacha his lessons, and patiently explaining to him the geography and personalities they were encountering. It was one of the rare chances

I had to prove to the press that the family side of the PM was immensely attractive and credible.

A Day in the Jungle

In January 1981, the PM set out on another North-South odyssey. The itinerary called for a trip first to Austria for a visit with Chancellor Kreiske, a leading advocate of a more imaginative approach to the debt problems of developing countries. Then on to a developing country, Algeria, and from there to Nigeria where, after seeing the President in Lagos, the PM would visit the northeast tribal region of the country. The next stop would be Senegal, one of the world's poorest nations, then across the Atlantic in one huge hop to Brazil, and home via Mexico. Because of the exceptionally long flights involved, Trudeau agreed to use the Boeing 707, if for no other reason than it provided the luxury of a private bed in the forward compartment!

This first-class prime-ministerial ramble was surely one of the most remarkable pilgrimages ever taken by a modern leader. A pilgrimage in pursuit of the rather abstract notion of bringing the rich nations' responsibility for the poor to the table where the powerful make world policy. The fifty or so aides and journalists accompanying the PM shared in what was really an extended study trip on a fundamental global problem. This time we had White House-style logistics, but the process was as far removed from Washington as Trudeau's approach was from that of the newly elected Reagan.

It was an exceptional group on all sides. Allan Gotlieb, then Undersecretary of State for External Affairs, lent his considerable intellect and leadership to the North-South exercise. The following summer, he would be the head of the Canadian delegation to the summit Canada would host. Gotlieb was backed up by the considerable clout and idealism of Marcel Massé, then President of CIDA, on the aid side, and by Robert Joyce from Finance on the economic side. The whole North-South effort was mothered over and guided by the immensely modest and humane Larry Smith from External Affairs. This group impressed me and the press alike. It was clear they stood for the best in Canadian care for and expertise on world problems.

We arrived in Saltzburg, our first destination, in high spirits, expecting to meet Trudeau, who had left earlier for a skiing holiday in Lech. The resort, however, had been cut off by storms and avalanches, and the PM was unable to get out. As the hours rolled by, the schedule became more and more confounded. To the intense embarrassment of the PM's high-powered entourage, this delay soon started to eat up events planned for the next stop, Algeria.

Trudeau was not about to let this divine intervention spoil his good humour. Neither were the press, for that matter, who found the unexpected vacation an enjoyable bonus, with nothing to file but yet another report of the weather in Lech.

I thought it would be a lark to have a news conference through a remote phone hook-up with the PM in Lech, using the PMO's portable sound system so that he could be heard and could hear questions from a room full of reporters. Trudeau readily agreed – it was snowing too hard to ski.

It was one of the strangest PM-press dialogues ever. I had a photo of Trudeau skiing and put it on the sound box, then I placed the call. "They're ready," I told the faint PM at the other end. "OK, let's go," he said, and I switched his voice onto the speaker in the crowded room. The TV cameras rolled, filming the still photo and the sound box.

The questions were of the "what's it like there" variety. I cringed as the PM's ebullient voice went on with this tongue-in-cheek description, "It's a nice place to be isolated. We haven't had our usual supply of fresh fish from the channel and avocado from the hot countries. We are probably going to run out of green vegetables if this lasts, and live on cheese and wine and bread . . ."!

The picture of me and the press crowded around the sound box was used front page nationally, as was the story, told straight, of the PM's "hardships"! This was hardly the way to gear up the media or the country to consider the plight of poorer nations.

After our third day of waiting, there was little left of the Algeria visit. We scrubbed what there was after anxious phone calls from the Saltzburg airport lounge where we were finally reunited with the ever-smiling Trudeau, fresh out of an Austrian rescue helicopter, skis in hand! A few more phone calls, and we were all lodged at Lahr, the Canadian Forces base in West Germany, where we hastily replanned the faltering trip.

We now travelled directly to Nigeria, coddled in our first-class capsule for the flight to Lagos. At the airport, we emerged into the heat and were greeted by a bizarre tribal welcome ceremony. Then we were dumped into armed jeeps and buses for a terrifying ride into the capital through the most indescribable slums. The real trip had begun. Suddenly exposed to Nigeria, we were all shocked – genuine culture shock. Despite the garish luxury of the guest residence and the mock-American standards of the Holiday Inn where the media stayed, this was Africa, grasping, dangerous, desperate, and, for most of us, an experience for which we were in no way prepared.

The press were aghast at having to get their stories out through telex operators who had not been sufficiently well bribed (the "dash" system that is mandatory for transactions of any kind). Trudeau, on the other hand, had travelled widely in this country years before when it was even more dangerous and desperate.

He was masterful in a pitch to the full Nigerian Cabinet, which we all witnessed. Trudeau was on a roll. He was greeted with the deepest warmth and respect. We careened out of the armed camp that was the presidential compound, knowing we were part of something important.

We were a somewhat dishevelled band of missionary-like Canadians when we flew into the heart of Nigeria, Maiduguri. There, in the motorcade from the airport, dozens of Peugeot 504s collapsed like an accordion in what must have been the largest such accident in Nigerian history. The hell-bent cavalcade quickly regrouped. As we entered the town, fields and dusty crossroads gave way to urban desperation – the decaying remnants of a colonial town where seemingly half the population lived in packing cases or cardboard boxes, which crowded the filthy boulevards and avenues.

That afternoon, the magnificent Dhurbar ceremony of hundreds of decorated horsemen, put on by tribes from the surrounding region, hardly distracted us from the tales of misery and danger recounted by the local Canadian CUSO volunteers, for whom the visit of the PM was a once-in-a-lifetime event.

By the time we arrived in Senegal, our next country, the press was beginning to respond to the problems seriously, huddling with Marcel Massé and learning about the challenges of devising appropriate aid and assistance for the conditions they had seen first hand. Even hardened reporters were sincere in their concern.

What they had seen had moved them beyond mere journalistic interest.

Trudeau was wonderfully accessible. He met with groups of reporters in the aircraft's forward compartment, and took time to discuss what we were all experiencing. This was his issue. He was doing the grass-roots work with Third World leaders to create some sort of consensus he could take to the Summit of the Seven in Canada, and later to Cancun, Mexico, where the Austrian and Mexican presidents were to host a true North-South meeting of heads of government.

The mood became infectious. Soon it became clear, as it would again during Trudeau's peace initiative, that the media were willingly collaborating in explaining an international challenge to the Canadian public. The trip proved to me that serious political will, applied to serious problems, evokes serious coverage.

To my delight, this mood of co-operation continued throughout the trip, and I did all I could to keep the PM and the press close together, even resorting on one occasion to some modest kidnapping.

After visiting Senegal, we had a long, though uproarious, flight across the Atlantic to Brazil, landing in Brasilia. The atmosphere was so relaxed that nobody noticed that the PM kept on the running shoes he wore in the aircraft when he emerged for his official airport welcome and review of the honour guard. This became a cause célèbre in the Brazilian press.

From Brasilia we flew to the confusion and madness of overcrowded São Paulo. Then, following a long flight across the upper reaches of central Brazil, the party was lodged in the magnificent resort at Manaus on the Negro River, a tributary of the Amazon, a state-run haven of charm and luxury in the jungle.

There, a trip downstream to the Amazon was planned. Two small steamboats, reminiscent of Canadian lake boats from the thirties, were moored side by side waiting for boarding. Vaughan Johnston of External Affairs and I decided we would arrange it so that the Canadian government officials, who invariably surrounded the PM, would be on one boat, and Trudeau, together with the attractive Brazilian foreign office guide, the press, and press officers, would be on the other. All we had to do to isolate the train of officials was to pre-load them on the nearer boat, then walk the PM onto the next boat where the media would already be aboard.

We did this with wicked efficiency, and, before the Ottawa mandarins knew what was happening, our boat, with the PM captive aboard, was steaming off. Their treasured afternoon of relaxing conversation with Trudeau was not to be.

The mandarins were not only isolated from their boss – their boat soon ran aground. A few of them determinedly tried to catch up with us in an outboard motorboat commandeered from the resort. Allan Gotlieb, Marcel Massé, and Bob Fowler appeared uncharacteristically forlorn as they looked for a landing spot in the middle of the jungle in their desperate effort to stay near the PM! But by this time, our boat had docked for our walk through the jungle and Trudeau strode off ahead at his terrible pace, easily showing us all up.

As we strung along the jungle path hooting and laughing, the raucous jungle sounds came up on cue. The path was narrow and tortuous, and soon the PM was well ahead. I gave up trying to stay near him while the press were around – for once. The path started to wind downhill, and, at the bottom, there was a small pavilion in a little jungle backwater where we had soft drinks. The PM stepped into a canoe and paddled off. Bob Cooper, our official photographer, was going crazy capturing these images. The rest of us hardly needed a camera to engrave them on our memories.

Back on board, notepads and tape recorders were stashed, shirts were peeled off, and even the rather frail looking Carol Goar of *Maclean's* finally relaxed for the balance of the voyage. The PM stayed on deck, chatting with various groups, and explaining to the CTV crew and others how his chronometer worked. Relaxed, we talked about his kids, and about his youthful experiences in Africa and South America.

Then Trudeau went below for a nap, emerging an hour or so later when we came to the confluence of the Negro and the Amazon rivers. Trudeau had assured us this would be one of the great sights of the world. He was right. There, the dark waters of the Negro mix mysteriously with the pale Amazon. Porpoises played, the sun sank lower, and the river boats chugged by. He really had become our tour guide, and his informed enthusiasm brought us all together. Later, at the incongruous and ornate Opera House in Manaus, we all listened attentively as he questioned the guide about the frescoes in the echoing lobby.

The "family photo" from that remarkable trip was staged later at the Mexico City airport. It shows as joyous, if disparate, a gang of expatriates gathered around a PM as you'll ever see, all saluting our experience in a straight-armed, fist-up salute we had learned is a good-luck greeting in Brazil. We had taken part in a valiant, if somewhat naive, attempt to understand the world better, and had discovered another Pierre Trudeau in doing it. We would make other North-South trips, but none would match this one.

Ralph Coleman and I closed the books on this trip with some pride. We had had no serious foul-ups. We had found ways for the press to get the news out in even the most absurd situations. At one point, we had arranged for the press to use the plane's radio to communicate to its home base in Trenton, and from there by phone patch to their offices. Peter Lloyd had done a "Canada AM" interview from thirty-five thousand feet above the Atlantic. But, perhaps most important of all, a good working relationship between the press and the PM had been developed and maintained for a few days. We could almost conclude that if you give the media a story and an enthusiastic leader, you can't miss!

ELEVEN

THE LANGEVIN REVISITED

Abroad, we had been introduced to the joy of travel with a PM ready to share closely his ideas and enthusiasms. But, back in Ottawa, the distance between his Centre Block office and the Langevin Building, where most of his staff worked, remained psychologically as great as it had been in his last prime ministerial incarnation. In the daily Ottawa routine, his manner of dealing with the rings of people around him and with the press changed little. Off the road, as it were, he was more determined and demanding than before.

There were some wonderful exceptions, of course. One involved the annual get-together of those who were in the Office of the Leader of Opposition on December 13, 1979, when the Clark government was defeated. Called "The Glorious 13th" society, its one meeting per year, on December 13, provided a rare occasion to socialize with a relaxed PM.

On one of these occasions, in a mundane backroom at the Ottawa steakhouse, Nate's, I entertained the assembled by reading part of my diary. It was the piece I had written about Trudeau's inner calm at a Liberal convention the year before when he had lectured a group of worshipful students from a precarious perch on a chair.

Clearly warmed by this memory, and the thought that someone had actually taken the time to write down impressions (Mr. Trudeau never did), the PM reacted in a touching and surprising way. One of my jobs during the 1980 campaign had been to

213

make sure Trudeau did not get carried away and speak too long at rallies and meetings. I invented a cueing system to tell him how long he had left. I would find a position in direct line of sight from his podium, catch his eye as he started, then catch it again as his predetermined time ran out, and hold up my fingers to represent the minutes left. He liked the comfort this system provided. During applause he would catch my eye and I'd give him his time. A trust had developed.

Towards the end of my reading at that reunion dinner, he suddenly raised his arms across the table from me and gave me the cues he so well remembered me giving him.

But this feeling of companionship gained through bygone battles did not translate into his giving any new priority to my real concerns – communications and press relations. If anything, the PM adopted a tougher, more unyielding attitude to the media in their normal day-to-day Ottawa manifestation. This classic Trudeau approach was evident in our first general meeting on how we would handle the press in the new regime. I was apprehensive that he would not forget that only a couple of newspapers across the country had supported us editorially during the campaign.

I was under great pressure from the Press Gallery executive to confirm that weekly news conferences would be reinstated. After all, they were a Trudeau innovation dating from the celebrated pre-1979 "agreement" that traded off the physically dangerous corridor scrums with the PM for a weekly meeting with the press. Clark had pretty well maintained the tradition.

I sat in the PM's hushed monastic office making my points, trying to persuade him of the communications value for the government as a whole of regular, formal dialogues with the press. "I really do believe there is merit in regular press conferences," I argued. My big error was to use the word "regular."

"Patrick," the PM answered politely, "you know those guys get tired of seeing me *every* week. They get lazy, the questions get bad, and they become pointless exercises. Why not just tell them we'll have news conferences on a *regular* basis, then we won't be locked into them every damn week." I was thunderstruck.

In the larger scale of things, this may seem to have been a perfectly reasonable suggestion, and my horror at his suggestion a tempest in a teapot. But for me and the Gallery, knowing the new government's pronounced tendency to secrecy, it seemed to be breaking a compact to use the press to communicate with the public on a *weekly* basis.

The weekly demands of facing the media impose a useful discipline, a kind of extra-parliamentary accountability. Every Thursday, or whatever day is chosen for the news conference, the PMO as a whole is forced to mobilize answers to satisfy the press's persistent probing. In terms of office politics, it gives the Press Office a day a week in the sun. A news conference is exclusively a Press Office event. A weekly commitment would assure me one lengthy meeting with the PM a week, a weekly opportunity to brief him on the moods and personalities of the Press Gallery.

But with the PM's wishy-washy commitment to a real routine, I knew my fate was cast. I knew I would have to beg, cajole, reason, use every known ally and every conceivable device every week or two to get Trudeau to consider meeting the press.

More typical of the impervious quality of his routine dealings even with senior journalists was his behaviour on a long-awaited interview with Barbara Frum on the CBC's "The Journal." That program, despite its appearance of being "live," gains its fast pace through careful editing and packaging during a long day of technical polishing. In order to give a clean end to an interview that is heavily edited, the format demands a neat little exchange of farewells and thanks, which is often taped separately. On this occasion, the PM, the interview in his office finished, was asked if he would say "Good Night Barbara," or "Thank you Barbara," or anything in response to her "Thank you Mr. Prime Minister" that could be edited into the end of the interview later. No matter how patiently this convention was explained to him, he refused to play along. "Why should I say that? The interview is over," he protested. For what should he thank Barbara? He was being awkward, and must have enjoyed it. With the press, he was once again proving the truth of the old adage that you can lead a horse to water but you can't make it drink!

So, charming as it was to have the PM's youthful executive assistant, Ted Johnson, usher me into the silent corner office to present press matters to the PM's razor-sharp mind, it was seldom that I could persuade that mind that the press's needs were important. I could almost see the PM's eyes rolling up into his head in a "well, what does Gossage want to persuade me to do now?" fashion whenever I came into the room.

It was no great mystery that my effectiveness as the latest press secretary to our reluctant Prime Minister Trudeau would be measured not by how much I was able to change the PM's "real" priorities to accommodate media matters, but by what I accomplished "in the margins" – by the kinds of operational reforms I could institute. I shared this objective with all my predecessors, whatever their titles, including Dick O'Hagan.

In fact, all occupants of that corner office in the Langevin suffer from White House envy. We dream of the White House Press Office, the focus of America's mature, policy-oriented press. We dream of briefings where reporters hang on every word and gesture from the White House spokesman. While we who worked for this PM knew that much of the dream was unattainable, we at least tried to model our services and operations on the plush and efficient White House systems.

Any press who go to Washington to cover a prime minister's visit to the president are overwhelmed by the hordes of helpful aides, the split-second timing, the sound systems set up everywhere, the platforms angled for the best camera shot, the fancy podium with the presidential seal which is carried to every speaking event, the roped-off press areas the leaders pass by, and so on.

There seems to be almost a corollary. If a major political leader is accessible and genuinely friendly with the press, they will put up with and forgive a lot of rudimentary or failed logistics and facilities. If he isn't, they won't. It was clear where we stood.

So, since the substance of daily "press relations" with the PM was tepid at best, we overcompensated by continually providing our journalists and cameramen with better and better logistics and staging to make their job as easy, as comfortable, and as predictable as possible.

During one particularly gruelling press stake-out at a premiers' meeting at 24 Sussex, we even set up a heated trailer with telephones and coffee so that the media did not have to wait in the cold and chill of the residence's cramped garage. (The PM did not like the press pawing his Mercedes 300 SL in any case.) We set up a workable press room in a more commodious garage near the old mansion at Meach Lake where the Cabinet meets for day-long planning sessions twice a year. Before, the press literally had to cool their heels on its sweeping veranda high above the lake.

We chose personnel for the Press Office to strengthen our logistics. Ralph Coleman, the career military officer with whom I had worked so closely until the defeat in 1979, was brought back from his enforced return to uniformed life during the Clark administration to serve again in the PMO, this time as absolute master of setting up events in advance of the Prime Minister's arrival ("advancing"). We hired Martha Durdin to specialize in setting up press rooms and other professional facilities on the road. In Ottawa we all worked together to polish the presentation and staging of the Prime Minister.

One of the first reforms was getting a proper podium built to replace the beaten-up portable version we had hauled about in two huge boxes during the 1980 election campaign. Ralph and I later felt our podium also needed some sort of seal or symbol of prime ministerial might, and decided to have an elaborate three-dimension coloured coat of arms cast in metal. The immediate excuse was the official visit of President Reagan to Ottawa in 1981. We were astonished at the cost of this adornment, but thought that the occasion merited a bit of extra show and ordered it anyhow.

We upgraded our sound distribution systems through which radio and television reporters get clean sound without having to string up their own equipment on the lectern. We even asked the Privy Council technical people to order foam "wind socks" for the new mikes similar to the tubular dark grey ones visible on presidential microphones. We made it routine for the Privy Council technicians to travel with us and set up the podium, sound system, even the lighting.

We restrained ourselves from installing a Canadian version of the President's miraculous prompting machines, which float moving text of his speech at eye level on either side of the presidential podium, allowing him to appear to be looking from side to side as he reads the moving words. This equipment, if used on the road, takes a truck and crew of three to move and install. Nevertheless, I was often asked why we could not look into one for the Prime Minister. Someone even suggested it might be installed for major speeches in the House of Commons!

We set up ropes and platforms and sound systems whenever the

217

PM met with a visiting premier or international dignitary. We made it all quite like the Rose Garden in the White House where the President makes his seemingly casual appearances in very controlled surroundings. When we set up White House-style camera platforms outside the residence at 24 Sussex, Doug Small of Global TV had fun accusing me of being a Ron Ziegler, Nixon's notorious media manipulator. The description hardly fitted. But, nevertheless, we *were* trying to emulate the White House skill at controlling the President's image. Moreover, since it was clear that neither the Press Office, nor anyone else for that matter, would dictate the substance of what the Prime Minister *said*, we worked happily away on the form, on *how* he looked saying it.

We never tried to have the press stand up when the PM came into the press theatre on Wellington Street for a news conference as the press does when the President comes to meet the White House corps, even though the PM enquired at least once why not.

We did hire Robert Cooper as the PM's official photographer. He had been doing some work at Government House, and Suzanne Perry, who stayed on with me after the election, asked him to shoot the swearing-in ceremony of the first post-election Cabinet of the new Liberal government.

"Coop, the corridor creeper" became a PMO fixture, shadowing the PM at every event. On foreign trips, the speed with which he made contacts with women was legendary. His role was a direct steal from the White House press staff, who for years have recorded every step, handshake, signature, meeting, smile, and yawn of the President. We didn't go that far, but we soon found Cooper's work of great public relations as well as archival value.

It was also important for us to see how we were doing. A computer system was set up to help us access Canadian Press wire service reports more quickly and efficiently at our desks. I arranged to have a revived and upgraded overnight media summary, "Mediaday," prepared by the monk-like Allan Fraser who had worked on our original media summary back in 1977 and then had been let go by Clark. He was immediately contracted to produce an even more thorough daily monitoring of press. We had the first copy of the new "Mediaday" hand-delivered to 24 Sussex at 8:00 a.m. so Trudeau could read the overnight press "reviews" on his morning drive to the Centre Block.

During the campaign, I had been stung by the fallout from a thoughtless remark I had made to Michael Valpy, then a senior reporter from the *Vancouver Sun*. I had denied his request for an interview with Trudeau saying, "We don't do regional interviews."

This virtual caricature of the worst possible central-Canada attitude to the West lost me a lot of credibility. My response to this self-inflicted wound was to prove that I had learned a lesson. We devised a series of "Visiting Editors" programs in which we gave senior editors and writers from outside Ottawa the same or greater access to ministers, officials, and even the Prime Minister, as reporters in the Capital. For a while it worked well, and got us some positive "ink," as we used to say.

We upgraded our transcribing service. We were soon able to turn around within a couple of hours a fully corrected transcript, in both languages, of anything the Prime Minister said publicly. We subscribed to a private wire service to get these transcripts to editors across the country within an hour or so.

It was relatively easy to get these reforms underway, and Trudeau and Coutts approved all of them. Everbody looked better – our photo service was great for egos at every level.

I "staffed up" in accordance with guidelines from Coutts that called for a much leaner and more efficient staff than had existed before the 1979 election. I even asked management consultants to look at a completely new Press Office structure. But I ran things casually – a little too casually in one respect.

Suzanne Perry stayed on from the campaign as number two. She was initially a tremendous asset, and I assigned her to shadow the PM at nearly every public event. As a result, there were a couple of predictable photos of Trudeau and his "pretty assistant" outside on Parliament Hill, and coming out of an event at the Governor Generals. The photos elicited a few wisecracks from the Gallery. At the time, I thought little of this, and even ignored the danger signs of a couple of calls inquiring about the lovely person beside the PM from British tabloids which had run the photos.

My naivety about image caught up with us later in London, England where we stopped after the spring Summit of Industrialized Nations in Venice and our visit to Rome. There, I found a distraught Suzanne reluctant to leave her hotel room. There had been calls and visits to our press room from British papers, desperate for a picture or statement from Trudeau's new "girlfriend." This was only the beginning of troubles for her, which eventually led to her seeking another career. But the troubles really started because of my insensitivity to how things *looked*.

I was very sensitive to how all of us in the Press Office behaved with the press. I felt we had to compensate for prime ministerial coolness to journalists in the most human ways. We had to have a spirited and helpful team. We found the right combination in the persons of two amazingly energetic and tirelessly upbeat women, Nicole Sénécal and press assistant Louise Lafleur.

Nicole was a refugee from the Department of External Affairs where she had been the departmental press spokesperson for a term. She was about to be shipped ignominiously to Haiti as a "reward" for her first-rate reputation with the media. We caught her just in time, and she was seconded to the PMO with guarantees that she would never have to tarnish her public-service status by doing partisan Liberal party work.

A diminutive blonde, she was often to be seen at major affairs with a walkie-talkie that seemed half her size bent to her ear as she tried to unravel some logistic nightmare.

Louise, though young, was blessed with an infectious self-confidence. She had absolutely no fear of the PM, and was often heard to shout at him in a busy press situation, "Monsieur Trudeau–par ici!" She also had a gift for turns of phrase in both languages that often brought hoots of laughter to horrible situations. She coined and endlessly promoted the ultimate Press Office slogan, noisily shouted and repeated enthusiastically during all tense or crazy times in the life of the office, "Je m'en fous!" which, roughly translated, means, "I've had it up to here," or "I don't give a damn!"

We beavered away at being organized and charming. The official subplot of our media relations campaign remained upgrading our "packaging" of the Prime Minister to White House standards. We kept the press operation small and cozy, and deliberately tried to be more open. Early on, we invited the eight or so members of the Press Gallery executive to a white tablecloth lunch for a discussion of mutual problems.

As for policy coming out of the new government, we had little to worry about at first. The first Speech from the Throne had been relatively easy to sell. It elaborated on themes and programs carefully constructed during the campaign. "Just tell them we are keeping our promises," was Axworthy's advice to us in dealing with the press.

The Garden Party

Life in the Langevin Press Office under the revived Trudeau did have some rare moments of bliss, even in Ottawa. The PM made a few rare gestures towards the Press Gallery, for which we took full credit, basking in these temporary outbursts of goodwill all around. But I knew, secretly, that such gestures invariably were more a result of his own mental processes or taste for the unexpected than of my attempts at persuasion.

A perfect example of this occurred in late April 1981, high over the Rockies in the tiny capsule of the Jetstar. We were just finishing a particularly good chinese dinner, catered by Trudeau's favourite Szechuan restaurant in Vancouver. We had been discussing food, and were sipping on a glass of wine, rare for these usually ascetic trips, when, out of the blue, Trudeau said, "You know, the blossoms will be out at Sussex in two or three weeks. Why don't we invite your friends from the press around to the house to see them?"

I nearly fell into my hot and spicy sauce. Relations had been at a standoff with the Gallery; there had been no radical warming to provoke such an excess of generosity from the boss. In fact, the PM had come close to directly insulting the Gallery by refusing either to attend or to speak at their infamous Press Gallery dinner just a few weeks earlier. In a sense, the *grippe diplomatique* that prevented his attendance was consistent with the "I'm setting my own agenda this time" attitude we were all learning to live with. Sometimes it seemed as if the simple fact that doing something was a "tradition" was enough to motivate him to break it.

The PM simply was not attuned to these annual dinners that were supposed to offer a relaxed opportunity for press and political fighters to enjoy a short truce. Moreover, he was expected to get up and make people laugh, and however easy this might have been before an audience already self-amused, stand-up humour was not one of his most developed talents.

At the Press Gallery dinner the year before, the first after the 1980 election, the Press Office's attempts to provide him with something funny to say had not been successful. Suzanne Perry and I, aided by the clever Press Gallery radio reporter, Jim Maclean, of "Poetry Wars" fame from the election, had laboured mightily to craft a speech in verse.* It had made for a difficult evening. I had the excruciating task of painfully working over the exact scanning of each line with a very professorial Trudeau in a tense afternoon session on the sunporch of 24 Sussex.

Nevertheless, his refusal to attend in 1981 was hard to understand because the invitation was from the new Press Gallery President, Jim Munson, a tough and plucky admirer of Trudeau, and one of the few journalists Trudeau felt any warmth toward.

Munson was the star of a legendary shoving match with the PM in 1976, before corridor scrums with the PM were outlawed. The PM was impressed with Munson's insistence on treating him the same as any other street adversary. The PM would go right up to Munson, waiting in a pack of roped-off reporters, and say, "Well Jim, what do you want to know?"

On this occasion, with a good deal of dignity under the circumstances, Munson had written me saying that Trudeau's refusal to honour the tradition of the Prime Minister speaking off the record at these affairs was particularly upsetting since it seemed to "reflect on his presidency." Despite the fact that the PM had handwritten "the dinner will be more fun for all of us this way" on the reply I had drafted, and had signed with the uncharacteristically personal "Pierre E.T.," there remained hard feelings.

* Here are a few of Maclean's verses:

The Rime of the Ancient Leader

I am an ancient leader
And I'll tell this rime to thee
So down sour beer and swill your wine
And listen now to me ....

I'll hold you with my glittering eye
Right here upon the Hill
You'll listen like a three year's old child
The leader has his will.

The press sit here upon their seats
They cannot choose but hear
Mike Duffy shakes, Bruce Phillips wakes
Jack Webster sheds a tear.

The Liberals cheered, the Commons cleared
The Tories we did drop
I hid my smirk upon the Hill
You thought I'd be a flop! . . .

Higher and higher every day
The polls showed us ahead
Stevens and the Globe and Mail
Proclaimed that I was dead . . . .

Perhaps to make up for this awkward situation, the PM wanted to create something unusual for the press in the year of the Munson presidency, hence his uncharacteristic suggestion to receive all the media at the "residence."

My reaction to this incredible proposal? This was one of those times when you just have to quietly accept the best with the same equanimity that you accept the worst.

Friday, May 14, 1981, turned out to be a brilliant day. The wonderful garden at 24 Sussex, overlooking the Ottawa River, looked at its best – cherry trees choked with blossoms, beds drenched with flowers. Bars and food were set up outside.

A large crowd was expected as we had invited not only Press Gallery journalists, but the cameramen, the technicians, and the still photographers who are equally responsible for the PM's image in the public marketplace. (Such an attitude is heresy to all but the most realistic print reporters.) We even persuaded everyone that it would be a lot more fun if cameras and tape recorders were checked, like weapons, at the gate. Only Bob Cooper, our official photographer, was armed with his equipment to immortalize this unprecedented camaraderie.

Only one misguided TV reporter from BCTV, Harvey Oberfeld, railed briefly at the gate, insisting on his right as a reporter to cover this "public event." Everyone else was soon too busy drinking, or trying to find something tasteless or extravagant about the pool and sauna, to care.

Nobody from the press had *ever* before seen the infamous swimming pool, the gift of still-anonymous businessmen. Nor had Trudeau, since I had been in the office, ever invited journalists socially to 24 Sussex. This was history.

The usually blasé corps actually rose to what they realized was a rare occasion. The Global TV crew, led by the ever-winsome Doug Small, rented a white Cadillac limousine and arrived in style decked out in white Global T-shirts.

Jim Munson, the Press Gallery president, strutted about in a deliberately tasteless Aloha shirt. The Prime Minister thought Pamela Wallin and Fiona Conway from CTV looked particularly fetching (they did), and almost agreed to their request for an interview on "Canada AM" on the spot!

Trudeau mingled easily, moving amongst the scattered knots of reporters, cameramen, and photographers. Nicole Sénécal and I took turns shadowing him to remind him of names. Taking me off briefly to the side, he enquired about several of the more attractive female reporters.

We realized that, in a sense, he knew this group far better than we had assumed. Even though he had not made an effort to befriend them, or develop a real relationship with any individually, he had been closely exposed to them on countless trips abroad in innumerable scrums and news conferences. Moreover, he outranked the vast majority of them in straight seniority, in years of service in Ottawa. Only a few, like Charlie Lynch, had been reporting through all the years he had been Prime Minister. So, for one verdant afternoon, he could well afford to be fatherly in a nice way, instead of stern and impatient as he normally was with this group.

In the Press Office, we also took advantage of moments with him on the way to or from news conferences or interviews to keep him up on enough personal gossip about some of the Gallery's more colourful members to put a more human face on them.

Perhaps that day we were at last seeing the results, however fleeting, of our endless efforts to build some sort of fragile bridge between PM and his media communicators. We were being rewarded for years of bending over backwards to humanize the Press Office and to make the press feel warm and welcome, even in the sacred Langevin Building, when they knew full well the top man did not hold them in the highest respect.

It was appropriate that when my PMO colleagues picked a photo of the Prime Minister to have signed and presented to me they picked a great shot of the PM and me strolling in step and chatting at the famous garden party for the press. It is best to remember the best.

TWELVE

LOOKING OUT – THE PMO AND THE WHITE HOUSE

A Presidential Visit

*P*resident Reagan's state visit to Ottawa in the early spring of 1981, followed by the Summit of the Seven Industrialized Nations at Montebello, near Ottawa, in midsummer of the same year, provided the supreme test for the Prime Minister's skill and idealism as a senior statemen concerned with the problems of rich and poor. It also put to the test the Press Office's support for this idealism and our ability to communicate it through the press to Canada and the rest of the world. On both occasions, we were head-to-head with the much-envied White House communications and press relations juggernaut.

When dates were set for the President's visit, his first foreign excursion since being elected the previous November, our first response was to polish up the packaging of the visit, to make sure every step was planned to logistical perfection, and to dazzle the White House with an Ottawa stage of impeccable beauty. This was to be accomplished by a secret task force that met every morning for a month under the competent direction of External Affairs' de Montigny Marchand.

The task force included everyone whose area of responsibility could possibly effect the visit. The National Capital Commission reported regularly on the progress of facelifting along motorcade routes, and Public Works ordered an unprecedented number of flags and bunting for everywhere the President's eye might fall. Don MacSween, head of the National Arts Centre, was not only to host a gala performance for the President but was to be generally in charge of all matters of taste, from checking the wording of toasts, to the most picky improvements on facades of buildings along important motorcade routes. We discussed everything from parking for guests at the gala to how to prevent ugly demonstrations on the Hill.

The redoubtable White House advance corps arrived in due course. Pussycats to start with, later they turned into tigers who demanded to check even the script of the gala.

There were also the rather ugly and recurring substantive alarms over the increasingly controversial National Energy Program. A couple of weeks before the visit, Reagan's Secretary of State, Alexander Haig, sent a diplomatic note clearly demanding major changes. Its existence leaked out, and while some of us were working day and night trying to book the President's favourite performer, Anne Murray, and convince her to sing more than one song for the outrageous amount we were being charged, the Americans were behaving as if they could reverse the domestic policy that had won us the election.

March 10 was finally upon us. We were assured by our RCMP Security and Intelligence friends that there would be no demonstrations to disrupt the atmosphere of peace and love. The RCMP were discreetly discouraging the odd activist from carrying a placard on the Hill. But, as anyone who watched television anywhere on the continent that evening knows, there was a demonstration – about acid rain – a noisy and visible one that nearly drowned out pleasant Ron. The PM gave a brisk lecture to the demonstrators on being polite, and all the networks had their clip. Folded and rolled signage had foiled the Force!

When the first meeting between the President and his staff and the Prime Minister and his took place, I was outside the Cabinet room. To my chagrin, my opposite number, the popular and portly presidential press secretary, Jim Brady, had Cabinet rank and was inside!

Ten minutes after the meeting started he swept out on the way to the U.S. press room in a downtown hotel with the news, "The chemistry [between Reagan and Trudeau] is good"! This bit of "atmospherics," as the White House would say, was apparently all the immediate news the U.S. press corps needed from the first encounter between right-wing Ron and socialist Pierre. Whatever the truth of this capsule reassurance, out it went as the early "lead" on most news stories from the first day of the visit.

For our part, we tried to impress with Canadian talent. A huge effort had been made through our old pal, Paddy Sampson, who produced the gala performance for Reagan at the Arts Centre, to have it broadcast nationally. Of course, we made elaborate arrangements should, just by some chance, any U.S. network wanted to pick up part of it.

We also went overboard for the visiting U.S. press, providing a lavish after-gala "Cast Party," hosted by then secretary of state Francis Fox, in the restaurant of the Arts Centre. This was all wonderful, but nobody from the American networks ran more than a short clip of the gala, and no U.S. media "stars" attended the party. You have to live and learn when it comes to trying to impress the most powerful.

But the positive "atmospherics" between the two leaders and all our elaborate packaging failed to detract from the very serious intent of Haig, whose final news conference I chaired. The administration did not like our NEP, an independent act on our part, and despite Haig's apologies for his letter, which had been withdrawn, his impatience with us was obvious. Lessons for later.

A Summit on the Ottawa River

The President's gleaming 707, Air Force One, had barely cleared the end of the runway at Ottawa's modest little airport when new task forces and committees were being struck to welcome back not just the President, but the presidents and prime ministers of Britain, France, Japan, Italy, and West Germany as well, who were to gather at the Summit of Industrialized Nations scheduled to meet in Ottawa in July.

At the Venice Summit of Industrialized Nations, the PM had agreed to host the next summit in Canada, in 1981. The event was not a surprise, only the location. The PM's friend, West Germany's Helmut Schmidt, strongly favoured a wilderness or mountain location such as Lake Louise, a choice which only gave us nightmares of huge tents on mountainsides filled with unhappy journalists. At first, there was much discussion about impressing the leaders of the seven most powerful industrial nations with Canada's most spectacular scenery, and for a few weeks a site in the Rockies was indeed seriously considered. In the end, the Château Montebello on the Ottawa River, a half hour from the capital, was chosen.

The PM's personal goals for this summit were to get a discussion of North-South problems on the agenda. The hopes of many leaders of the poorer countries he had visited during the past year's pilgrimages to Nigeria, Brazil, Algeria, North Yemen, and Senegal rode with him. President Reagan was known to have little understanding or sympathy with this, or nearly any other complicated issue. It was clear in our meetings with the new wave of carefully dressed advance people that they wanted to keep situations where he would be on his own with the other leaders to a minimum, lest his shallow understanding of most world issues show.

The PM had long-held ideas about how summits should be run. His ideal was one during which the heads of government or state were freed of their armies of aides, released from pre-cooked communiqués, and kept away from pressures of the press. He firmly believed that only then would they be able to discuss real problems like adults, responsible leaders, and intelligent caring citizens of the world. The Montebello site had been chosen to maximize isolation, to minimize regular press contact and the minute-by-minute pressure to make news.

Only essential personnel would be accommodated at the lodge at Montebello, the world's largest log structure, as someone discovered. I was among the lucky few senior staff who was actually to have one of the lodge's rustic bedrooms, a pleasure that was somewhat diluted by the presence on site of two female aides to Secretary of State Mark MacGuigan, who seemed to spend much of their energies organizing his tennis and jogging.

The media would be thirty miles away in Ottawa, along with the vast majority of hangers-on. Consequently, getting the news out of the riverside site, or newsmen into it, became the major preoccupation of all delegations. Even as the patient and diplomatic Canadian summit press organizer, John Robinson, drafted rules forbidding any interviews with leaders during the summit, and restricting *all* interviews on the summit site, wily press officers from various countries started thinking of ways to circumvent them.

I had learned at Bonn and Venice that summits are enormous exercises in providing a suitable backdrop and environment for the various national media to show their particular president or prime minister impressing the other six leaders.

Communicating a particular Japanese, or British, or even Canadian version of what had transpired in hours of closed discussion to the appropriate national press corps and thence back home becomes a vital operation, for which difficult time-zone problems and the risk of the other nations' versions dominating are potential spoilers of the best-laid logistics. The host's job is to make sure facilities are laid on that are scrupulously fair to all participants.

The White House is obsessed with getting the U.S. version out first and dominating not just the U.S. news agenda but the world press. The President must be seen to be leading the group, leading, in fact, the world. The White House advance people started plotting for Montebello three months before and continued their dark strategizing throughout the summit, often in the back corner of the timbered basement bar in the lodge.

At the end of each major session, most press secretaries or officials who were assigned to brief their press ("briefers"), the Brits, Japanese, Germans, and myself, were content to use the helicopter shuttles timed to get information to journalists waiting at national press centres in Ottawa.

Not so the redoubtable White House pros under the leadership of the tiny, energetic Joe Canzeri. He and I became friendly, and I used to threaten to bring girls from nearby Pointe Gatineau to distract his singleminded pursuit of getting White House news out first. "Bring 'em on, Gossage!" he'd yell, adjusting his walkie-talkie earpiece.

It was he who set up a briefing location in a house just outside the gates of Montebello – a most imaginative bending of the rule that forbade briefing on the summit site. An aide would rush there during or just after a session to give the good news of how well the President was doing to a "pool" of a dozen or so select U.S. newsmen, who relayed their stories, videotape, and film instantly back to the main group of U.S. press in downtown Ottawa.

So, while the U.S. version of events was already pulsing out to the world, I would be escorting some grumpy minister or External Affairs briefer onto a helicopter for the twenty-minute lift downtown to brief the Canadian press waiting patiently in a room set up at the Château Laurier! And all this effort, in my case, to produce a generally boring and inadequate Canadian briefing in which the PM's role was often barely mentioned, even though he was chairman of the meeting!

Trudeau's great moment (and mine, for that matter) on the world media stage was on the afternoon of the first day of the conference when he alone of the seven leaders reported to the media on where the summit discussions were going (the other leaders were completely silenced by the "no interview during the summit" rule). We had a lavish flag-bedecked press conference set up in the National Arts Centre where the PM faced the hordes of world media alone.

After their dramatic arrival in an "Apocalypse Now"-like display of military helicopter might on the pleasant front lawn of the Château, the seven leaders posed and puffed for cameras in the specially prepared plenary room in the lodge – a former small theatre that had been tarted within an inch of its life to resemble a UN style meeting facility. But then, as that first full afternoon of discussions rolled on, the sky darkened and it became clear that the PM's chopper lift to Ottawa for the news conference, which was squeezed between the end of discussions and the beginning of the evening reception, might be in jeopardy.

This thought did not bother in the least Derek Burney, the gruff Canadian chief summit organizer. He seemed to see this as simply an inconvenience for the press and a good opportunity to make some space in the schedule, while at the same time alleviating one more logistics problem.

I found myself in the Montebello basement operations centre begging, shouting, and finally demanding that the PM at least *try* to keep his appointment with the world press even if the cloud ceiling, as one military type told me with glee, was "marginal." I knew the PM had no qualms about flying in bad weather, and that the risk was minimal in any case.

I barely won, and finally the PM and I settled into the cramped seats of the drab green Huey helicopter and were soon skimming treetops as we wound along the banks of the Ottawa River to the capital. The helicopter's huge windshield wipers scarcely kept up with the sheets of water that seemed to engulf us. We had been told that there were half a dozen spots along the way where we could come down and continue by car if things got too miserable, but this information did little to alleviate the anxiety in my stomach. In another ten minutes, we were threading through downtown highrises at about the eighth-floor level to the landing pad just behind the Arts Centre.

Throughout the flight the Prime Minister, typically, had been a model of complete calm and concentration as he hunched over his notes. He barely acknowledged the short briefing I gave him over the intercom headsets.

After scrambling out of the helicopter, he strode purposefully onto the Arts Centre stage and performed as if he had just walked down to the press conference theatre from his Centre Block office on a sunny day. He did his best to be the first day's newsmaker, even though we found out later that the White House "scooped" the summit story with the non-summit announcement of a bombing raid on Lebanon!*

On the press coverage of the conference overall, the Americans did us one better on nearly every front. They organized their bilateral or individual one-on-one meetings with other leaders with such flare that, for instance, a shot of Reagan and Schmidt laughing at each other during a golf-cart ride upstaged many of the formal photos we had so laboriously arranged.

What little glamour the whole affair had for me soon vaporized as I read the "reviews," as we called the press clippings for such events. Our Press Gallery complained formally about our briefings, particularly their lack of even indirect quotes from our PM and the Canadian delegation, and the absence in them of the colour

* The summit competed for attention with the escalation of violence in the Middle East. The Israelis had bombed Palestinian positions in southern Lebanon heavily the preceding week. On July 17, they hit the headquarters of the PLO in downtown Beirut. It was the first air strike on Beirut since 1974 and the first time the Israelis had hit targets in populated areas. The raid was widely criticized both in Israel and the United States.

On July 20, the day Trudeau met the press, Secretary of State Alexander Haig held a news conference of his own. He announced the U.S. was extending suspension of shipments of F-16 fighters to Israel because of the renewed hostilities, although he denied the raid itself was the reason. Earlier that day, the summit leaders issued a statement condemning the bombing.

that brings such events to life for readers. Many Canadian newsmen deserted our dull briefings entirely for the U.S. nirvana of welcome, quotes, and colour down the street.

It became increasingly clear to me that when it came to communicating a message to the public, many of our officials and PMO advisers were prone to confusing technique with content. They thought they did not need much special presentation or skill for reading out to the press what had happened. How wrong they were.

The Press Office, too, had fallen into the trap of believing the use of White House-type paraphernalia would solve a problem whose roots were more our lack of concern for real communication than any lack of tools.

There were indeed tricks like Canzeri's briefings in the house outside the gates of Montebello, or as the Americans did at another summit, smuggling a pool of reporters into the highly restricted delegation hotel with delegate passes. But the U.S. strength extended beyond these "dirty tricks." They had something to say once the vehicles were in place, and they said it with enthusiasm and conviction. Canadian briefers continued the tradition of bureaucratic neutrality and modesty, which, in the case of mandarins from the Department of External Affairs at least, was grossly out of proportion to their expertise and influence in the world.

Canadians have always seemed to possess an ingrained lack of flare or care for press, a problem that has deeper roots in not giving enough priority to communicating messages efficiently even when the messages are good.

I determined to do something about this. At the briefing by an unusually modest Prime Minister Trudeau for Canadian reporters at the end of the summit, it was clear our journalists did not have enough solid evidence of what he and we had accomplished. The PM was ready to leave, and we had not targetted any official for a supplementary briefing. As I was at the mike and thanking the PM and press, I spied Allan Gotlieb (the Canadian "sherpa," as the senior summit official for each country is called) sitting flanked by a half dozen officials in the middle seats of the briefing room. "If you have any more questions, I'm sure Allan Gotlieb would be happy to answer them," I blurted out, and thirty hungry reporters descended on him.

Later, I found out, after some deeply unhappy experiences trying to get Canadian ambassadors abroad to help brief on aspects of prime ministerial trips, that many thought they should not, or were prevented by diplomatic tradition from talking "on the record" to the press at all! I raised this pointedly with Allan Gotlieb later, while he was Undersecretary of State for External Affairs. Indeed, a memo was crafted in the fall of 1981 reminding ambassadors that they could and should have open dealings with the press!

THIRTEEN

Looking In-Coutts
and the Constitution

Jim Coutts

W hile the PM tried valiantly to sell the notion of the North-South dialogue to an indifferent world and an even more indifferent Ronald Reagan, the government's domestic agenda was being overseen in the PMO by Jim Coutts and his number two, Tom Axworthy, and implemented by strong ministers like Allan MacEachen, Marc Lalonde, Herb Gray, and Ed Lumley. The PM himself only put his heart into such high-profile successes as signing an energy deal with Alberta, an accomplishment that he was particularly ebullient about as it had eluded Joe Clark when he was prime minister. On the domestic front, his imagination was mobilized only for the constitutional reform battles, which were soon to be joined.

In some respects, this ability of the PM to focus on only those subjects that really galvanized him was a tribute to his absolute faith in Jim Coutts's political judgements and ability. It was Coutts who concentrated on the domestic program devised in the short weeks between the defeat of the Clark government in 1979 and the January election campaign.

The program was largely the work of the Liberal Platform Committee under Coutts's friend, Allan MacEachen. Tom Axworthy, who had crafted much of Trudeau's substantive words and policies during the campaign, provided further guidance for this

234

exercise. In a sense, Coutts and MacEachen, with whom he talked endlessly on the phone, and the resurrected Michael Pitfield, who was a constant voice on the intercom in Coutts's newly decorated office (whenever I had an audience I was always amazed how much of his good Canadian art he had squeezed into the inner sanctum), pretty well ran all those domestic policies and political issues that might have distracted Trudeau from North-South dialogue, summitry, and now, constitutional reform.

By 1981, Coutts was coasting. He had been instrumental in bringing Trudeau back; election promises had been largely kept; the party was reasonably happy; and Canada's most polished political pro played statesman. He invited his cronies to Montebello summit dinners, and, on some of our travels, came more as a tourist than adviser. All the while he prepared his departure from the PMO and entry into riding politics – a decision that became more and more obvious during the spring of 1981.

The Coutts we were about to lose was a far cry from the pre-1979 version. He remained much more accessible after the 1980 victory than before the 1979 defeat. He actually gave advice rather than throwing back press problems with some sort of oblique remark like "I think you are doing a good job, Patrick – just keep it up." It was Coutts who insisted that the close, lean, mean staff, which had made our time in Opposition so pleasant, be maintained when we came back to power in the Langevin Building.

When Coutts started to be able to see the legendary light at the end of the tunnel, he became even more relaxed and accessible. More expansive, he took to calling me and asking, "How are we doing, Patrick?" I would answer with two or three balanced pieces of evidence of press wickedness or virtue. He would be appreciative. He was also enormously more helpful and open to my number two, Nicole Sénécal, than he had been to me when I was number two or three in the Press Office. He was now for me Jim Coutts, professional politico and somewhat of a friend – someone to whom I could say what I felt, and who supported his small staff actively.

I felt that his reputation for being distant, manipulative, even ruthless, was really a well-honed posture put on for the benefit of official Ottawa. He was another man away from the office, with real friends, or entertaining in the diminutive Toronto home which he hung on to as a refuge of calm and civility. When his friend Michael Pitfield rented the elegant Victorian house of Arthur

235

and Ginnie Birks next to us in Ottawa on returning from exile in Harvard, we became, for a few months, part of the extended Pitfield family which included Jim Coutts. We saw him as a warm friend of that family, a sort of benevolent Uncle Jim figure to the Pitfield children.

This proximity brought Coutts into our house. He immediately took a fancy to my wife, Helga, and was charming with our daughter, and son, Sean, for whom he was able to produce a summer job with one phone call.

I might have anticipated discovering this side of the Coutts persona. Some years before, at a time when I felt the pressures and preoccupations of work in the Press Office were denying me a chance to know my daughter Susanne, I had appealed to him to let me take a trip to visit press in Vancouver that I could combine with a skiing holiday with her. His answer was an unhesitating "yes."

Coutts's loyalty and devotion to Pierre Trudeau extended to sharing or adopting some of his boss's characteristics and habits. Like Trudeau, Coutts imposed a strict discipline on himself, and was not seen out with "the boys" except for a very routine weekly poker game. Lunches and dinners in Ottawa were purposeful. Like the PM, he measured his time and made sure his private life was private, he took holidays, travelled, saw interesting outsiders, and changed his views. I remember an argument he had with Michael Pitfield on the benefits of his holiday policy. Trudeau would have been on his side. No self-righteous "I haven't had a day off in three years" from Jim Coutts. He would take time on a trip to scour galleries for art, becoming a totally different and more relaxed person. And he was a better servant of the PMO for that attitude.

Years before, a cruel thing was done to Coutts by the magazine *Saturday Night*. They sent a photographer to shoot one of their exaggerated and stylized posed photos for a relatively decent feature piece they were doing.

Coutts did not, as did some other senior staff, have me present to make sure that poses were flattering. Unbeknownst to Coutts, the photographer used his widest of wide-angle lenses (beware of skinny lenses!), distorting the admittedly short and slightly rotund Principal Secretary into a carnival-mirror caricature. In the two horrible photos that accompanied the resulting article, Coutts looked bloated and self-satisfied. The photographer, through his medium, had provided the current image. But nothing could have been a greater disservice.

Coutts was a paradox nevertheless. The same man relentlessly pursued Allan Fotheringham for writing about alleged cheating in one of the endless late-night poker games of the 1980 campaign. All he claimed to want was a grand piano to compensate for the insult to his honour.

In late spring 1981, I received a call from his longtime secretary, Thérèse Horvath. "Mr. Coutts would like to see you." As I had so often, I dropped everything and went up. This time it was for a short announcement that he would be leaving to run in Toronto. He avoided my eyes, uncharacteristically, politely thanked me, and asked that I serve his successor, Tom Axworthy.

I refused to believe it. Coutts had granted me, an outsider, credibility in his circle on the Second Floor, and now this man who was my key to the world of realpolitic was deserting me. I said, "No, no, you can't. I don't believe this." It was more painful than anything I could have anticipated. How could he do this – to me! I took it very personally indeed.

As it turned out, the manner of his running in the Toronto riding of Spadina hurt me too. Appointing the comparatively young incumbent MP Peter Stollery to the Senate to open a seat for the Principal Secretary to the Prime Minister did not, I felt, provide a suitable transition into active politics for someone I liked. There were undoubtedly things I did not understand, and didn't want to.

Coutts, surrounded by the comforts of power and with everything going for him, in the end made a free choice to do battle with an unpredictable force that he knew could devastate him – the voting public. It did.*

---

* Coutts left Ottawa with a flourish. The government announced on July 2, 1981, that it had named Peter Stollery, the MP for the Toronto riding of Spadina, to the Senate. At the same time, it called a snap by-election for August 2. Coutts immediately flew to Toronto to announce his candidacy for the Liberal nomination. The riding had been Liberal for thirty-six years. Coutts was seen as a shoo-in. But, in a surprising upset, he lost the seat to New Democrat Dan Heap, a four-time loser in federal and provincial elections. Coutts worked the riding assiduously for the next three years and tried again in 1984. He did no better.

The New Team

I felt a strange detachment during the following months in the PMO, months that, because they were marked by the signing of the constitutional accord, could have been among the most stimulating of my career. But the electricity I had felt so consistently through the 1980 election and through the first year back in power I no longer felt in my day-to-day running of the PM's Press Office.

This detachment during those months was exacerbated by the appearance on the scene of what could be called the final-wave Trudeau PMO staff. There was a different, more boisterous style under the young new principal secretary, Tom Axworthy, who was brilliant and consistent in his advocacy of core Liberal policies, but lacked the clout and maturity of his predecessor Jim Coutts.

Tom Axworthy had come down to my office within hours of Coutts's announcement of his departure to tell me that he wanted me to stay on. He thought he was doing the right thing to confirm me in a job I had no reason to think was in jeopardy, but I felt slightly demeaned. I knew my days in the office must now be numbered. Coutts, in his own way, had won me, and I felt somehow disloyal turning to someone else.

I felt suddenly old. A veteran. Not the press whiz kid anymore; not the "boyish" Patrick Gossage the Ottawa *Journal* had pictured riding his bicycle to work. Now, a whole new younger, more collegial group started filling offices on the Second Floor. Meetings were regularly called where, before, there had only been one-on-one sessions behind closed doors. Coutts's plan for a lean, mean staff was abandoned. Papers and memos started to choke in-baskets where the intercom had sufficed. Studies, polls, policy options, expertise poured in. I felt weary of it all.

The strict hierarchy I was comfortable with broke down, and the PM, with his own end-of-the-era agenda, increasingly used whoever was bright, determined, and appropriate to help him accomplish it inside or outside the PMO. This explains the rise to some prominence of a former neighbour, Nate Laurie, whose bright, good-news approach to economic advice became a feature of the PMO. People like Michael Kirby on constitutional matters, Allan Gotlieb on foreign policy issues, and Hershel Ezrin on unity promotion could "end run" (a good White House expression we liked to use, adapted, like many, from football) the new Principal Secretary and the office.

On the Second Floor, only Marie-Hélène Fox remained from pre-1979 days along with the veteran Diane Scharf, whose loyalty as the PMO's most dedicated assistant and secretary was almost saintly. George Wilson, who ran interference for Coutts, and with whom I had a running electronic exchange of gags on our desk computers, went with him to Toronto to help him win Spadina.

The Second Floor was now dominated by an energetic group of event-and-promotion-minded professionals led by nobody in particular but including Peter Larson, Dennis Mills, and Jeff Goodman. They were affectionately known for their noisy hustle and bustle, and their almost entrepreneurial approach to politics.

I found it increasingly hard to keep up. I was more accustomed to an office that ran from the top down, and where lines of authority were more direct. Axworthy threw open the doors, set up teams, and generally democratized the office. I felt strangely out of place!

The Constitution

The historic constitutional debate was, for me, a succession of late-night staff meetings, and endless drafts and releases of telexes that culminated in my sitting outside closed upper rooms where "history" was being made, walkie-talkie at the ready to galvanize the dozing media in the Conference Centre press room below for the latest tidbit.

In this seemingly endless exercise, I had almost daily dealings, not with the PM or the PMO staff, who were at best accessories to the boss's central preoccupation, but with a small band of exceptional mandarins led by the deliberately Machiavellian Michael Kirby.*

The group met at the call of Kirby's Katie, a secretary who probably had read, through typing, more about the constitutional debate than the PM himself. When Katie buzzed, the people who were

---

* Just after Christmas 1981, I received a unique Christmas card cum thank-you note from Kirby. Specially printed, the card's face prominently featured the Kirby motto, " 'It should be borne in mind that there is nothing more difficult to arrange, more doubtful of success and more dangerous to carry through than initiating changes in a state's constitution.' Niccolo Machiavelli, *The Prince*"

going to give Canada a new Constitution came running. Whenever I heard "Mr. Kirby wants to see you," I'd drop what I was doing, take the elevator up two floors and would stretch out in the comfortable lounge area in Kirby's office. There would have been a development in the endless jostling with the provinces, and we would discuss the media strategy.

The informal group usually included Roger Tassé from Justice; Fred Gibson, the patient, kind, and tireless engine of the group; James Hurley, a solid thinker and drafter, who had a rare and often macabre sense of humour, from the Federal Provincial Relations Office; David Cameron, a quiet but immensely effective academic, also from FPRO; Gérard Veilleux, from Finance; and, of course, the fiercely loyal and ever-smiling and bouncing Eddy Goldenberg, Chrétien's long-time trusted aide and the Justice Minister's alter ego in all strategic discussions.

Hershel Ezrin, the determined head of the Canadian Unity Information Office, would come in from time to time when we needed to mount a dramatic public communications action. His own smoothly run and well-financed propaganda machine was one of the best kept secret wonders of Ottawa of the time.

The deceptively diminutive Michael Kirby provided constant and unflagging leadership. His slim frame neatly clothed in one of two or three perfect little suits, he exuded a kind of junior league hockey coach's confidence with his colloquial drawl, easy-going, open-door familiarity, and readiness to encourage and compliment.

I was always amazed that Kirby had left his wife and children in Halifax to take on this assignment. Their framed colour photo was prominent on his side table, and a call to them would often punctuate late-night sessions. He became a virtual monk in the service of bringing a constitutional compromise into being by a combination of pure faith and scholastic dedication.

During those months, it seemed the main tool in the slow advance towards a solution was the telex to the premiers that announced one or other compromise or ultimatum. These intensely laboured-over documents would be followed by endless calls to the network of Federal-Provincial officials, many of whom became close and valuable telephone cronies of Kirby and his team.

I developed my own contacts with the premiers' press secretaries to make sure bad public communications didn't make tense situations worse. Sally Barnes in Premier Davis's office was particularly helpful whenever I called.

I was often summoned by Kirby to do some final checking of the documents and excerpt passages to be given to the press. We released them, and waited for the inevitable response the next day.

The group was endlessly flexible and pragmatic – a quality in the top mandarinate that never ceased to amaze me. They prepared foot-thick arguments for unilateral patriation, then, after the Supreme Court's ambiguous September 1981 decision on the constitutionality of this route (legal but unconstitutional in the conventional sense), they set to work creating new foot-thick arguments for a negotiated compromise.

Kirby even found ways to make a virtue out of the leaking of the secret and deadly serious strategy document, the infamous "Kirby Memo" to Cabinet, by telling us that at least everyone now knew how serious we were.*

From the perspective of Kirby's office on the third floor of the Langevin Building, there was little mystery or sense of awe at being present at an important political birth. After a long day of negotiations, Kirby would come to an agreed position with the team and call Trudeau, often at the residence. I'd listen as he would say, "Prime Minister, we've talked to Davis's people and they'll buy such-and-such." There would be a brief silence, a curt "OK" from Kirby, and he would hang up the phone. "He buys it, let's go." This was a club of technicians crafting compromise.

It was clear to those who, like me, had some role in that coast-to-coast network of Federal-Provincial bureaucrats that they were setting the parameters for the finish to the prolonged and frustrating debate. Their political masters publicly indulged in rhetoric,

---

* In September 1980, on the eve of a federal-provincial conference on the constitution, a lengthy memo by Michael Kirby was leaked to Southam News. The memo reviewed the summer negotiations, proposed ways of playing off the provinces against each other, and discussed in detail the prospect of the government patriating the constitution unilaterally. It cited several reasons for unilateral action, including the popularity of the newly-elected government and its commitment to constitutional reform in the Quebec referendum.

The Kirby Memo, as it became known, was a political bombshell. The provinces immediately seized on it, saying the government had no real intention of consulting them and would use the failure of the conference as a pretext to act alone. The publication of the memo poisoned the political atmosphere at the outset of the critical talks.

while a few, particularly Chrétien, and Romanow of Saskatchewan, were solidifying the friendships necessary to accomplish the final deal.

The fact that a few ministers one November night could sketch out the final package is a tribute not just to their political skills, but also to the skills of that clique of apolitical technicians who had been talking, compromising, and planning for that moment for months. During those sleepless days and nights, Kirby never showed any more than his routine enthusiasm. He just had the paper with the details of the agreement ready!

I felt curiously detached from what turned out to be the final major event of my years as Trudeau's press secretary. I reflected perhaps the same mood to the media. In many ways, I had found it a tiresome story to follow. Although most of the press loyally favoured patriation of the Constitution and the new Charter of Rights, they paid increasingly fatigued lip service to the process.

Charlie Lynch, bless him, my own favourite bellwether columnist for all his folksy self-flattery, personal quirks, and romantic idiosyncrasies, was a consistent supporter of the reform. He, and we, knew that the majority of Canadians wanted to bring to an end the constitutional debate and to get on to other things.

Trudeau had cranked up our media clients too many times with his splendid rhetoric on the need for collective will to enshrine a national vision into an almost sacred document. After the document was finally signed by the nine premiers, the media denied the PM the satisfaction of congratulatory victory reviews. They immediately criticized the weaknesses in the compromise, reporting the alarm of women's and native organizations over their exclusion from the Charter, and adding their own on the perceived threat to the freedom of the press.

How typical it was of that whole operation that even the printing and distribution of the long-fought-over Charter of Rights and Freedoms itself became a major problem. The first problem was that the Charter was terribly long, and only in places did its prose soar to any height. The print would have to be small, no flourishes!

A problem for the unflagging Dennis Mills, who was in charge of getting millions of these documents produced and out to the waiting public, was that there appeared to exist no readily available few lines in which Trudeau had encapsulated his constitutional and national vision.

Dennis and I spent a good deal of time combing the dozens of speeches and interview material available on the subject for a likely statement. Finally, in frustration, I spliced material together from about four different sources. Trudeau quickly approved the sentence. He had used all those phrases before, just not quite in that order! This was really my most important service to the Charter, and, I felt, my own fitting epitaph for years of PMO service.*

My Final Year

As I was walking out of our home for another period of absence during the 1980 campaign, I remember asking my nine-year-old daughter flippantly not to cry too much while I was away. "You are away so much, Daddy, there are no more tears," she said perfectly seriously. I only appreciated this piercing honesty a year or so later. I realized that not only was I still almost always physically removed from family and real friends, but even while at home or in their company, I was mentally removed.

One of the more ugly delusions many of us in the PMO suffered from also became clear. This is the unattractive vanity, which develops amongst those who work in tense situations with the powerful, the belief that nobody can possibly understand what they are going through – certainly not lowly mortals like wives and children who appear to lead routine and undemanding lives! If a common cause links the broken relationships of people at the top of politics – this is it.

This isolating vanity is fed, of course, by the fact that "outsiders," including one's own family, often treat you as a "position," not a person. I was often seen as the Prime Minister's press secretary, not good old brother Pat, husband Patrick, or the Pat I knew at university. One brother expected me to get him a government appointment, admitting in the same breath that he couldn't possibly support the Liberals. I tried to explain to him that the appointment he wanted usually went to someone who had at least some

---

* "We must now establish the basic principles, the basic values and beliefs which hold us together as Canadians so that beyond our regional loyalties there is a way of life and system of values which make us proud of the country which has given us such freedom and such immeasureable joy. (signed) P.E. Trudeau"

connection with the party. In frustration I added, "Put a sign on your lawn next election and I'll see what I can do." He wouldn't think of it, of course!

Our names were now on coveted foreign Embassy "A" lists in Ottawa and we were regularly invited to Embassy parties and other important Ottawa social events. But, at these events, I constantly risked being exposed to ridiculous anti-government or anti-Trudeau outbursts. A friend of my wife's cornered me at a party once to tell me, with a murderous glint in her eyes, that she almost drove Trudeau's limousine off the road into the Ottawa River on her way to work a few days before. This tweed kamikaze's loathing of my boss was so deeply shared by her husband that we terminated a friendship, which, for my wife, went back fifteen years.

I was equally unsettled by the bloated proffering of friendship from a certain circle in Ottawa who had cut us dead after the 1979 defeat. They now saw me as a different, more friendly, and personally attractive person now I had title and "position." Helga, being of far more constant opinion in her friendships, rolled philosophically with this revelation of mores in a small capital. I didn't. This discomfort, combined with a sense of alienation in the "new" PMO, made me highly vulnerable to suggestions of escape.

In the summer of 1981, O'Hagan, now a Bank of Montreal vice-president, urged me to "go for" what was, in his estimation, one of the best government political appointments – head of the well-staffed public affairs division of the Canadian Embassy in Washington. O'Hagan had held this appointment for years before coming back to Ottawa in 1975, to serve the Wages and Incomes Commission and then the PMO as special adviser on communications.

Dick reminded me that the job had been created for him when, after his years as Pearson's press secretary, he faced a similar desire to leave the PMO. We talked about hospitality allowances and other perks that make life so pleasant in senior foreign service postings.

Allan Gotlieb, the Undersecretary of State for External Affairs, was named the new Ambassador to the U.S. in the late autumn of 1981. One day, I saw that tall, somewhat stooped figure loping by my office door. I ducked out into the hall and told him that if he was planning to restaff the public affairs position, I was interested.

He was also interested, and, before I knew it, Gotlieb and his minister, Secretary of State for External Affairs, Mark MacGuigan, were lobbying to wrest me from the PMO. There was some opposition from Axworthy, and Trudeau himself was not quite sure I deserved such a generous reward. I think he felt I had not been of such meritorious service, that, perhaps, I had paid too much attention to the press's needs and too little to the PMO's. He used to tease me about liking "them" too much.

I was told by Gotlieb that I had to plead my case directly to the PM or risk not having the appointment go through. So, with some trepidation, I told Ted Johnson I needed to see the PM to "discuss my future."

A day or two later, I found myself, for the first time, being excessively personal with Pierre Trudeau. I told him I had to have a change because my home life was endangered. The Washington post would be a perfect way to continue to serve him in a more manageable position. He listened intently, then asked how long I had been in the office. I told him over five years. He was impressed. "That long, eh?" he said. Then he demurred about the appointment. I couldn't believe I'd have to beg!

He said he had been thinking of Iona Campagnolo for the Washington job, and that other ministers might have other ideas. Iona indeed was more deserving of a break because her West-Coast career as a talk-show host was on the rocks. But he finally said, quietly, that he would support my candidacy. This was not how I thought appointments worked when the PM was involved.

Michael Pitfield, far from being enthusiastic, thought that it was not such a great idea, but refused to say why. I think he worried about how I would survive under the demanding Gotlieb. At that time all I could see was a worthy outlet for my talents at a safe distance from Ottawa.

Then my family started to waiver about the dislocation. In a short meeting in which I told Gotlieb about this problem, he made it crystal clear that I had to take it or leave it. I had to join him in Washington right after Christmas, even if it meant leaving my family behind, or I had to forget it. I refused to forget it.

Finally, the Order-in-Council was signed and a date to start in Washington in the new year was fixed. One of my last meetings was a rare (for me) tea with Senator Keith Davey, who warned me not to forget what Liberals stood for, and to watch out because Gotlieb's commitment to "our" brand of economic nationalism was somewhat uncertain!

Ceremonial sendoffs for me were organized by both the PMO and the Press Gallery. The PMO affair was held in the Four Seasons Hotel and organized with great imagination and military precision by my old comrade-in-arms, Ralph Colemen. Marvelous mementoes were created, including a wonderful red T-shirt with the office's brave *cri de coeur* – "je m'en fous!" emblazoned on it – by far the most fitting motto of the office I was leaving. I spoke, following just about everyone in any position of either friendship or authority, and in listing those to whom I was grateful over the years, stupidly forgot my wife. I knew she was hurt, and this uncorrectable gaffe shadowed the evening.

The Gallery's affair in the dining room of the Press Club was more easily sentimental for me – Luc Lavoie was particularly touching in his remarks and presented his text to me afterwards with a handwritten – "Patrick, l'amitié va bien au delà de la politique." Now that I was leaving I was able to express openly the same feelings back to Luc and to a few others amongst the Gallery members. We had experienced a friendship well outside politics, and I was grateful. I publicly thanked Helga and started to get really misty about the departure.

Everything started to become sentimental and difficult. In late December, on the way back from taping the regular New Year's message with the PM, we talked warmly in the back of his limousine. I tried to say that really I was leaving his office only to serve him in another way. I don't think he was convinced.

Then I raised a final interview request, a difficult subject at the best of times. But I felt this one had important historic possibilities as the interviewer was David Frost, one of the most probing in the world. A friend of mine from CBC days, Bruce Raymond, had cooked up a TV series to be called "Frost over Canada," and the PM's appearance on the series had become as important to me as it was to him.

"I'll do it, for you!" was the PM's pointed reply. It was an interview in which the wily Frost got Trudeau to talk even about abortion. And, although the PM made a much appreciated appearance at my goodbye party, the Frost interview, in a more real sense, was his farewell gesture to me.

FOURTEEN

WASHINGTON AND PEACE, TRUDEAU STYLE

*D*espite the comfort my streak of Canadian chauvinism afforded, I faced a tour in Washingon in my country's service with some emotion. Like so many Canadians, I both feared and secretly longed to be seduced by the U.S. of A. We are a strange lot, we Canadians. Most of us live vicariously in the daring, dramatic, powerful, and glamorous world we perceive to exist south of the border.

If we are newsmen, our role models are the U.S. superpower media, the networks, the *New York Times* and *Wall Street Journal* – technically omnipotent, editorially consulted by presidents. In business, our dreams are of markets and profits tenfold as big, and of the alleged pro-business slant of U.S. governments. If we are politicians, we live in either outright rejection or blind embrace of U.S. policies and political mores, domestic and international. Only a few of us, like Trudeau, have entirely escaped the huge shadow cast by the U.S. and have set their own course.

These were my thoughts as I left Ottawa, my family (temporarily – they would join me later), Pierre Trudeau, and the PMO breadbox with a sigh in January 1982. At the crack of first light on one of Ottawa's coldest, crispest mornings, I looked back through the frosty rear window of my departing cab at our silent New Edinburgh home. The heat and smoke from hundreds of furnaces struggling with the cruel, piercing Ottawa winter stood straight skyward in the intense early blue as I taxied to the airport for the Eastern flight to the Baltimore-Washington Airport.

Washington greeted in its so-called winter garb, as if fixed in an extended Canadian late fall. I was met by Darryl, one of the Embassy's more attentive drivers, who made my entry into power city slightly more friendly.

My exposure to Washington realities was quick and decisive. It took me only a few days to discover the most salient home truths about Canadians in Washington. The first is that Canada does not wield much real influence in the southern capital.

Both Allan Gotlieb and I prided ourselves on a degree of sophistication bred through years of world travel and assignment and from mixing with world figures at the highest level. The Ambassador may not see my experience as equal with his, and in terms of breadth, if not pressure, he is probably right. But nothing could have prepared either of us for the impotence one feels in Washington, the palatial and historic Canadian Embassy installations and lavish staff notwithstanding. Sondra Gotlieb, "wife of," and a nationally known satirist and writer in Canada, has made a career out of mocking variations on this impotence theme, but it is real nevertheless.

It is one thing to read about the harsh reality of a seriously unbalanced Canada-U.S. relationship; it is another to live it. Since we are a calm, small, and peaceful neighbour we merit and get about the same attention as Sweden.

A second truth was soon forced on me. Even if I was fresh from serving Trudeau, and thus at least of some folkloric interest ("What's his situation now with Margaret?"), my title, Minister-Counsellor, was not quite high enough in Washington's pecking order to ensure instant respect. "I don't speak to anyone under the rank of Minister," I was told by one snooty guest at a party early on!

The tradition for most Canadian Ambassadors and their advisers had been to accept being minor, if familiar ("you speak American"), and warmly appreciated bit players in world power central. Not the Gotliebs. They wanted to get into the Washington fast lane quickly, and I was ready and willing to help them.

To their eternal credit, the gangly and sometimes awkward new Ambassador and his quirky wife decided to accept any advice, and go to any lengths, public or private, to put Canada on the map. This meant they agreed with me on the importance of "getting ink," of being noticed by the all-powerful Washington press. They made a battle cry out of my pseudo-professional line, "We need to get ink . . . !"

We moved quickly to make the Washington press part of the Gotlieb's social surroundings, and decided to invite the press to an early dinner. But who? We knew almost nobody.

I consulted my efficient and enthusiastic press officer, Marc Lortie, on which "heavies" might make an "A" list anywhere else, and we compiled a working document, adding big media names almost at random. They were unknown to myself and the Ambassador. Within a year, most, if not all, of these media stars had been in the residence. Finally, even veteran TV superstar David Brinkley could not resist the Gotlieb lure.

We continued a policy of "get them any way you can." Later, when Canadian Peter Jennings became ABC's Evening News anchorman, I suggested we do a party in his honour. When the Gotliebs grasped that he was a Canadian who had made it to the top three in U.S. television, they readily accepted the idea and put on one of the more glittering parties of that season.

We almost abused this strategy of using celebrities who were Canadian or had a Canadian connection to attract Washington "influentials." One such Canadian star, Norman Jewison, a film maker with a major reputation in Hollywood, willingly added glitter and clout to Gotlieb parties. The first time I tracked him down, I found him shooting a film with Goldie Hawn in a Washington suburb. We quickly authorized an invitation to her as well. She arrived in baggy purple pants with a boyfriend shod in running shoes and stunned the Georgetown set.

My own entry into some sort of state of social grace was signalled when the government bought me a dinner jacket to attend my first formal dinner at the Ambassador's residence, this one for Secretary of State for External Affairs Mark MacGuigan the second day after I arrived in Washington. At this event, U.S. Secretary of State Alexander Haig recognized me from the President's visit to Ottawa, and I thought I had gone to heaven! I bought another "representational suit" (grey pinstripe), which the government also paid for, to look the part in all circumstances, and I never looked back.

For the first six months, until my family joined me and we moved into a large and gracious house, I lived alone in an apartment with rented furniture. About the only sentimental reminder I had of my family in frozen Ottawa was a sewn padded heart my daughter had made for me in her Montessori class. I rented a TV and religiously noted down names of the TV news heavies for future invitations. I was innocent but unafraid, ready to flog my new boss anywhere to anyone.

The Gotliebs' press personae received a gratifying amount of newspaper notice almost from the beginning. One of the secrets of accomplishing this was to be nice to the *Washington Post*'s "Style" assignment editor, Robin Groom. I never met her, but she did more than she will ever know for Canada in the U.S. Chuck Conconi, the ever receptive writer of the *Post*'s "People" column, should also be mentioned.

Sondra Gotlieb quickly established her offbeat and irreverent approach to official diplomacy as an immensely amusing foil to the rather stuffy and orthodox Republican social atmosphere of Reagan Washington. She got so good at it that she was even able to loudly insult a journalist with whom she had crossed swords at a White House reception and not have it reported.

After only a year in Washington, the Gotliebs had achieved social power. They had a jet-assisted takeoff, the extra thrust provided most notably by the columnist Joe Kraft and his wonderful artist wife, Polly, who were Washington and Georgetown power brokers. They took the Gotliebs under their wing and genuinely liked them. Equally helpful were Reagan's Californian friends, the charming Attorney General William French-Smith and his attractive and friendly blonde wife, for whom the Gotliebs gave an early party.

Canadians are generally overwhelmed by Washington, and approval in U.S. circles tends to be the touchstone of credibility and importance for Canadian efforts, however well perceived they are in Canada. Given this sad fact, it was doubly delightful to overwhelm Washington right back, in a social sense at least. And we did.

Soon Cabinet secretaries, White House aides, and senior State Department types seemed to be eating out of our hands–socially, at least. But, whatever the Gotliebs' status in social Washington, however many times the media covered an Embassy event or put the Ambassador's views in print, however many times Sondra did her innocent-abroad act on U.S. radio or television, or however popular her weekly letters in the *Washington Post* became, some of us wondered in the dark of humid Washington nights how much real respect in Washington or the White House this bought Canada or Prime Minister Trudeau.

Such soul-searching was made no easier by the difficulty of tracing a consistent Canada-U.S. philosophy in Trudeau. He simply never displayed the kind of strong feelings towards our neighbours that most of us do who are less certain of our identities. He treated the relationship much like any other–pragmatically–and, so, often we were not certain what we were representing. An example of this was his surprising support for testing the U.S. cruise missile over Canada.

At the height of the cruise-missile debate, I watched from an alcove of the pristine ninth floor of the External Affairs Building as Vice-President Bush worked his Eastern Establishment charms on Trudeau over lunch during Bush's official visit to Ottawa.

At the state dinner for Bush that evening in the ornate Château Laurier ballroom, I saw the horror on the faces of External policy-makers as Trudeau departed from his prepared text. All over the room eyebrows went up as the PM, the man who once severely cut the number of Canadian troops in Europe, stated flatly and with striking sweet reason, that we should quit NATO if we weren't ready to agree to test the cruise! I appreciated the drama and surprise of this uncompromising endorsement of the U.S. request, but knew it would be hard to explain.

Trudeau disliked the endless Washington sniping at certain provisions of the National Energy Program, yet when the U.S. Ambassador to Ottawa, Paul Robinson, the President's former Illinois fundraiser-turned-diplomat, was at his most outrageous, Trudeau sensibly told the House that such outbursts simply made it easier for Gotlieb to say what he thought in Washington!

Years before, I arranged and sat in on an interview between the writer Heather Robertson and the PM. It was for one of the now-defunct weekend magazines that were inserted in various newspapers, and focused on the PM's views on nationalism. Robertson was then considered a somewhat radical writer. After half an hour knee to knee with the PM in a Royal York Hotel suite in Toronto, she told me, "You know, he really isn't a nationalist at all!"

Yet, for those who cared to seek beneath what seemed to be contradictory signals, Trudeau was consistent. On a practical level, his forays into economic nationalism were to protect or develop only those sectors he considered vital to a separate and sovereign nation. It was easy for us to say in my early days in Washington that there would not be another National Energy Program for, say, computers, as a mischievous article in *Fortune* had suggested; that sector did not fall into a Trudeau "vital" category.

But, more profoundly, he was proud for Canada. He would not tolerate being patronized, or having his views treated as second rate because they did not come from the platform of a major power. He believed his views on world affairs were as valid as those of any other world leader, and that a nation's influence should not only be measured by the strength of its armies, but also by its intelligence, understanding, and will.

In Allan Gotlieb, too, there was much of the same intellectual pride, to which he added his own brand of social and political acuity. This, in large measure, explains the significant impression he left as he moved around Washington. He shared with Trudeau the feeling that, in his mental abilities, he was second to few.

I saw Gotlieb's impatience with evidence of American stupidity, vanity, and chauvinism in those days, over everything from not being informed of the unannounced invasion of Grenada to the U.S.'s chronic inability to understand that we had a different society north of the border.* This impatience could equally have been Trudeau's.

The stage was set for a confrontation of sorts with Washington, which in effect would highlight the end of my public service. It would not be over the cruise missile or over our "unfair" exports of lumber to the U.S. It would be over Canada's right to say something about relations between Washington and Moscow.

* Gotlieb coined a wonderful phrase to describe American attitudes at a staff meeting soon after my arrival in Washington. He said, "Americans are very parochial, but they consider the world their parish."

There were now two powerful forces in my working life, Gotlieb and Trudeau, and the influences they wound about me came together in an unstable chemistry as soon as Trudeau decided to do something for which Washington approval was a key ingredient. Then I would be put to a final test for both my old boss and my new one. For even as the Gotliebs were zenithing in Washington in the fall of 1983, back in Ottawa Trudeau was clearly looking for a final chapter to his career as prime minister and had decided, with, it seemed, some prodding from one of his friends, the lovely Canadian film actress and activist Margot Kidder, to start a full-time peace quest.

The PM had made a curtain-raising effort on this issue at the 1983 Summit of Industrialized Nations, which the U.S. mounted at Williamsburg, the restored colonial town in Virginia. There the PM made himself very unpopular by fighting for conciliatory language towards Russia in the joint communiqué.

That summit had been a strange experience for me. For years I had relied on our local Embassy staff when travelling abroad with the PM. Now, I was an Embassy helpmate for the PMO on the road. My old boss was being looked after by Nicole Sénécal, who had succeeded me as press secretary. Marc Lortie and I were getting pretty good intelligence via walkie-talkie from the sealed-off summit site and were passing it on as fast as we got it to our carefully coddled contacts at the *New York Times, Newsweek,* and the *Washington Post.*

This time we had something to tell. Trudeau was definitely an isolated peacenik as anti-Soviet rhetoric increased amongst the other six leaders cloistered in colonial splendour at Williamsburg. Trudeau finally told Thatcher, Reagan, and the other four leaders that they should be "busting their asses for peace" (his exact words in the closed meeting of heads of state and government), and a fearless External Affairs spokesman, John Noble, had the temerity to report this verbatim to the waiting international press.

Our Embassy colleagues there had heard from their State Department contacts that Secretary of State George Shultz (who had replaced Alexander Haig), among others, had found Trudeau's harping on commitments to seeking a reduction of tensions with the Soviets "tiresome."

Then, in early September 1983, the Soviets shot down the Korean jetliner.* This provided the immediate impetus for the peace initiative, and also gave us an unexpected and unusual honeymoon with the Reagan administration.

How differently things appear depending on which capital you are in. In Ottawa, Reagan's ill-considered remarks about Russian murderers gave Trudeau the proof he needed about how dangerous "megaphone diplomacy" could become. Canadians were almost as worried by Reagan's warlike blustering as by the incident itself.

Nevertheless, our Secretary of State, Allan MacEachen, when finally reached and informed of the tragedy, was quick to announce suspension of landing rights of the Russian airline Aeroflot in Gander.

In Washington, this provided a Canadian public-relations bonanza. We played it for all it was worth. Aside from Reagan's and the administration's expressions of shock and bile, there had been little movement on the story the day after the shooting down, so Canada's prudent little act became an important piece of U.S. news.

I received a call at home (it was a holiday) from the beautiful CBS TV White House correspondent, Leslie Stahl! This was the only time I ever received an unsolicited call from a major network correspondent. Clearly it took an aggressive act to get the attention of the U.S. networks. We were heroes. We did not argue with the U.S. impression that the suspension of landing rights was in direct support of the President!

In Ottawa, Pierre Trudeau decided to devote much of his time for the next few months making sure that such incidents did not

---

* Korean Airlines' Flight 007 was shot down on September 1, 1983, over the Soviet Union. Canada condemned the act, and suspended landing rights in Canada for Aeroflot, the Soviet airline. While Trudeau abhored the loss of life, his statements were far more moderate than those of the Conservatives. He worried about the response of both the U.S. and the Soviet Union, saying "the world is teetering on the brink of disaster."

When Margaret Thatcher addressed the House of Commons later that month, Trudeau distanced himself from her hawkish remarks, saying western leaders should show "the courage and even the audacity" to pursue a relaxation of tensions between the superpowers. "For my part, I can think of no personal endeavour, no other priority, that is more deserving of my full attention than the pursuit of peace," he said. The peace initiative had begun.

trigger a major U.S.-Russian confrontation. Less than a month later, Trudeau was set firmly on a peace track that would put him on a sideswipe, if not collision course with Reagan's Washington.

While the PM's abrasive reaction to the U.S. "liberation" of Grenada was almost acceptable, his attempts to insert Canada into Russian-U.S. peace and security issues were not.

He assembled a "secret" task force, who prepared a blueprint for a personal crusade that would inject some political will into reducing East-West tensions. He told the group, augmented by Cabinet ministers and Canadian ambassadors to NATO countries, including Allan Gotlieb, at a remarkable meeting October 7, 1983, at Meach Lake, to accept as a working hypothesis that "Canada would like to play a role in de-escalating nuclear war."

He emphasized to officials that it was to be a political initiative and not to worry about him if he "got egg on his face." In a rare and revealing moment, he blurted out, "I could kick myself for not starting earlier."

When the PM's Principal Secretary, Tom Axworthy, asked the Ambassador if I could be borrowed to come to Ottawa for a few days each month to work on international press for the task force, the operation was already in full gear. They already had a near-final draft of the speech that would launch the initiative in Guelph on October 27.

Great secrecy surrounded the work, even the existence of the task force. I enjoyed teasing its elegant leader Louis Delvoie about how I could so easily make him and his dedicated group media stars. It was only a couple of weeks after the Guelph speech that I finally decided to demystify the "secret" task force for the Ottawa media, who rightly thought it a bit much that such an important initiative was being run by nameless and faceless officials. I gave out a few names, the "secret" story vanished, and a certain amount of celebrity did start to accrue to that worthy cell.

It was clear that the Canadian press wanted to believe in the PM's peace crusade. The ghost of Pearson seemed to animate some of the more mature Gallery types like David Halton of CBC television. Even though many of them were not quite sure the initiative would have a large impact on the superpowers, they suspended disbelief and continued to report from their hearts, just as the PM and his tacticians worked as much from their guts as from their heads. Trudeau's famous slogan "reason over passion" was being stood on its head. It was exhilarating.

We ran a pretty effective peace propaganda machine. We printed up copies of the opening Guelph speech and sent them all over the United States and to many Canadian Embassies and Consulates abroad the day it was delivered, together with briefing and background notes. Soon, positive notices started to appear from places as far flung as Bonn, The Hague, Duluth, Dallas, and L.A. It even received a kindly nod from Pearson's old friend and admirer, the *New York Times* columnist, James Reston.

A very upbeat Prime Minister was off promoting the initiative in Far Eastern capitals when the seamless veil of support started to show some small tears. There had been ominous foreshadowing in Canadian Press reporter Roger Smith's report of the State Department's warning to Trudeau not to "meddle" in Russia-U.S. negotiations.

Then at an America's Society conference in New York in early December, after the PM's pilgrimage had received positive encouragement from Commonwealth leaders, and while he was off seeking Japanese support, a couple of Pentagon panelists, discussing North American defence in an off-the-record affair, called the peace initiative a "cop-out" for a PM who had paid so little attention to bolstering Canada's NATO contributions.

Trudeau answered shortly after that he was not at all disturbed by utterances of a couple of "pipsqueaks in the Pentagon" who were not, after all, well known for their dedication to peace.*

---

* Trudeau was referring to critics in the Pentagon and the State Department. In late fall, as he was gathering support for the peace initiative, the *Toronto Star* reported on November 18, 1983, that senior American officials said Canada had no credibility to discuss defence because of its "shameful" contribution to NATO. "It's a cop-out," one official said in an off-the-record session at a conference in New York. "Even Europeans who aren't as crass as we are think Canada should put its money where its mouth is."

Predictably, Trudeau scorned his detractors. At a fundraising dinner in Toronto on December 14, the night before his visit to Washington, Trudeau dismissed "pipsqueak Pentagon critics." The next day, as he was leaving the White House after meeting Reagan in the Oval Office, Trudeau snapped at a reporter who asked if the criticism had come up in conversation with the President: "The kind of third-rate, third-level pipsqueaks who say I'm not allowed to participate in the peace process because we don't contribute enough to NATO – that's baloney."

This peek into what the real U.S. attitude was got wide play in Canada. My life became miserable, and it became hard to keep a straight face while telling Canadian reporters that yes, the Americans were delighted to invite Trudeau to play in their arms-control sand-box.

At a party at the Ambassador's residence around that time, I talked with the handsome but arrogant Richard Burt from the State Department, a Gotlieb "A" list regular. He was important to talk to as his security advice and contacts in the White House were excellent, and he also had final responsibility for Canada as well as Europe and NATO. He had some credibility with the press, moreover, as he had been a senior *New York Times* writer.

Burt wasted no time telling me what a waste of time he thought the Trudeau peace effort was, lacing his comments with some four-letter words that I found more than a little insulting. I could only hope that his Department's mild public support for the peace initiative would hold against such private dismissals.

At about the same time we were running into some heavy weather trying to finalize arrangements for Trudeau's key visit to Reagan at the White House, December 15. It was the President's invitation to have the PM brief him on the initiative so far. Even so, the President's National Security Council people, who were in charge of arrangements on the U.S. side, were digging their heels in about having the President appear with the PM after the Oval Office meeting to say a few words.

We were adamant with both White House press people and the National Security types that a few presidential parting words were essential to give at least the visual appearance that the initiative was being taken seriously. We were told in no uncertain terms that this would necessitate upgrading the visit from "private" to "official working." The PM had already had an official working visit that year. It would mean setting the precedent of two!

Even as we were trying to wrestle a little cosmetic respect out of the White House, across town at the Carnegie Endowment's regular luncheon-speaker series, a high ranking State Department official was answering a question, off-the-record of course, on what he thought of certain of the PM's proposals.

"Whoever thinks we would agree to that must have been smoking something pretty funny" was his reply. A number of atten-

257

dees were outraged, but the respectful Washington reporters present observed the off-the-record rule and nothing appeared in print.

The PM's visit provided the acid test for his peace initiative. I was on the "ramp" as the PM's Challenger jet pulled up. A warm handshake from a bouncy looking Trudeau, and we were off in "Marine 1" helicopters to the reflecting-pool landing pad, smack in the middle of the Mall.

While cruising low over the monumental capital, I thought how often I'd seen these immaculate birds swooping in with yet another state visitor, and how smooth the logistics machine was that wafted impressed foreigners into the "world's most important city," as a Washington bank commercial called it.

Now I was aboard one machine with the staff, Trudeau on the other. The twin helicopters made a mid-air change of position to confuse any would-be missile-toting terrorist wanting to shoot down the chopper with the leader aboard.

Trudeau was a one-hour write-in in the President's schedule. No more, no less. There would be a farewell on the East Lawn which would include the hard-won brief remarks from the President; then a briefing or "readout" of the meeting by a State Department official in the White House press room; then on to the next photo opportunity.

Trudeau carried a lot of hopeful Canadian baggage with him that day. And it was Allan Gotlieb, as faithfully reported in a superb *Saturday Night* magazine piece by his friends Richard and Sandra Gwyn, who, minutes later, virtually dictated the final details of an Oval Office strategy to Trudeau in his suite at the Madison Hotel.

Canada's best foreign policy minds, including the usually loquacious de Montigny Marchand, listened in silence as Gotlieb told the PM not to harass the President with details of his initiative, but to appeal to his vanity, urging "the great communicator" to find a better way to communicate his desire for peace.

The visit was all over in a blink. As the PM got out of the limousine at the West entrance, ABC's Sam Donaldson shouted questions to the PM about his characterization of the Pentagon officials who had criticized the initiative as "pipsqueaks." The PM shouted something back, but only later elaborated on just what he thought of the "pipsqueaks" when he was getting into the limousine to leave. This amusing little exchange for ABC mikes provided the only network coverage of the visit.

There was a moment of excitement as we realized that the Oval Office meeting was going overtime. A good sign. Then, I bit my tongue at the President's lukewarm and condescending "Godspeed" to Trudeau at the hard-won departure scene. Later a pleasant, but lower-ranking, State Department officer boasted to me that he was the author of the "Godspeed" line for the President.

I rushed around for the White House "readout" of the meeting. In his off-the-record debriefing, Richard Burt was so enthusiastic about the meeting that you could hear the U.S. correspondents' pencils and pens being put down–they simply did not find what he was saying credible.

I made quick, overly positive notes of the briefing and met Trudeau at the residence, where we had assembled the cream of Washington media. I talked briefly with the PM in Gotlieb's guest bedroom, and down we went to meet the media guests in the salon below.

I felt in my stomach their disappointment that the PM was so mild, and would not openly criticize the President. Trudeau recounted how he had told the President that there was a communications problem, that the President's real desire to reduce tensions was misread or hadn't got out. He listed evidence that the initiative was already producing results. Those journalists were not convinced.

When asked what the President thought of some of the more imaginative and substantive elements of the initiative, Trudeau was forced to say he hadn't brought them up. Not much to write about! We got little out of this elaborate session, and the poor immediate coverage in the U.S. press fed the Canadian press's impression that Trudeau had been treated to a Washington brushoff.

Canadian journalists were rushing around trying to make up their minds if the Americans were taking the initiative seriously. They had some stake in a positive lead to their stories out of Washington. Many of them had spent thousands of dollars of their employers' money to accompany the PM around world capitals on this peace pilgrimage, and the American reaction was the key to it all.

259

The seasoned Washington-based Canadian reporters, Bill Fox of the *Star*, Joe Schlesinger of CBC TV, Hal Jones of CBC radio, Craig Oliver of CTV, and Carl Mollins of Canadian Press, were all pretty skeptical. Rightfully so, as it turned out.

The day before the PM arrived, I had heard the rumour about a "senior State Department official" making personal slurs about the PM in an off-the-record session. At that time this rumour was all that was in circulation about the incident at the Carnegie Endowment lunch. As Burt's remarks to me earlier had been of a similar nature, I felt that there was likely some substance to the rumour and, in an unprofessional moment, told a couple of my Canadian media friends, including Carl Mollins, as independent and tenacious a veteran Canadian Press reporter as one could imagine.

As we were wrapping up the trip, and trying to appear smug about quiet but "respectful" coverage in the U.S. press–(disastrously buried on page 8 in the first section of the *Washington Post*), Carl Mollins was holed up doing a day-and-night phone blitz to find out who had slurred the PM, when, and how.

At dinner in a little Mexican restaurant with him and his wife a couple of days later, I said that if he was going to "nail" this someone he had better be sure he had his facts right. Mollins said not to worry, he was hot on the trail. I asked if I could be the first to know the identity of the slurrer. He agreed.

Exactly a week after the trip, I was in Gotlieb's ornate office at the Embassy Chancery speculating on who in fact might have said such horrible things (Jean Kirkpatrick?–well . . .) when the phone rang. It was Mollins. "I've got him," he said. "It was Eagleburger!"* His tenacity had paid off. Gotlieb was ashen. It was like a slap in the face from a friend.

Larry Eagleburger was number three in the State Department,

---

* On Dec. 21, the Canadian Press reported that it was Eagleburger who had said Trudeau's peace efforts were akin to the mutterings of a misguided leftist smoking marijuana. CP said Eagleburger told a private dinner party three weeks earlier – a week before Trudeau's visit to Washington on December 15 – that only a PM high on drugs could believe anyone would take his peace initiative seriously. The next day, a spokesman at the State Department called the report "grossly distorted" and said Eagleburger had "the highest regard and respect" for Trudeau.

and had gone out of his way to take Canada seriously, presiding publicly over the upgrading of the Department of European Affairs, where Canadian affairs had once been anonymously located, to the Department of European and Canadian Affairs. He had also overseen the appointment of James Medas, an attractive and well-connected White House graduate, to the new position of Deputy Assistant Secretary for Canadian Affairs. He was an occasional guest at the Gotliebs' residence.

Aside from the slur, which indeed some present told Mollins was made jokingly, Eagleburger was reported to have said that relations with the Soviets were complicated enough without "interference" from others. It was the stay-out-of-my-sand-box attitude perfectly.

Eagleburger was painfully embarrassed when he subsequently talked to Gotlieb. Indeed, it was a hurtful moment for all. Mollins had momentarily torn away the Embassy's careful padding and packaging of the closeness and clout we claimed to be enjoying in the world capital.

Late one Friday a few days later, the Canadian press corps in Washington, led by Hal Jones and Joe Schlesinger of the CBC, Bill Fox of the *Star*, John King of the *Globe*, and Brian Butters of Southam, together with assorted others, presented me with a badly bandaged and wounded stuffed partridge "dove of peace" they had bought and decorated with signs, slogans, and even a "Godspeed from Ronnie" stuck in with a toothpick.

I then admitted to myself, and almost to that cynical but honest group of reporters, that what Burt had told me, and what Eagleburger had said to that audience about the initiative, reflected what they were telling their senior U.S. media cronies as well. "Off the record" of course.

How could the PM's best efforts find credibility with the tough Washington press if the State Department was dismissing it behind his back? The PM would not, moreover, confront the President directly, so that was the end of finding a media audience in the U.S. for the initiative.

He had done what he could. I talked to him before he left, and he was obviously satisfied. U.S. and Canadian press "notices" were not about to worry him. I told him we had done well. I could not bear to spoil his good mood as he got on the Challenger for the flight to Ottawa. In subsequent telexes we tried to smooth over

261

the Eagleburger incident. It was obviously of much greater concern to us than the PM.

I continued my flacking for the peace initiative nevertheless. I managed to make a connection between a more conciliatory tone towards the U.S.S.R. Reagan showed in a session with *Time* magazine and the PM's appeals to him immediately prior to the interview. Richard Gwyn bought this "proof" of how effective the PM had been, though few others did.

I wrote long telexes as some positive comment flowed in from around the U.S. – my conclusion was that we should reassess "the assumption widespread in Ottawa that the visit had little media impact."

"It is obviously difficult for the central media players to admit easily that Canada possesses significant international clout," I wrote in one of the understatements of the year, "but media outside the eastern establishment (i.e., outside Washington and New York) are more inclined to look at Trudeau's initiative on its merits." True, in fact, but small comfort.

My admiration for the Gotliebs' resilience only increased as they returned immediately to their ceaseless and energetic rounds promoting Canada. But, in a sense, I decided that all the goodwill and visibility we had so painstakingly constructed really only yielded results in the margins when real issues were at stake. Was this realistic assessment of our clout in Washington such a revelation? Perhaps not. But it took a week of hard work by Carl Mollins to hammer me on the head with the obvious.

Trudeau may have learned something about trying to overwhelm the Reagan administration with flattery. His subsequent tone certainly changed.

Later, he had the apparent gall to challenge a cornerstone of NATO doctrine, that the U.S. would use nuclear weapons to defend a Europe invaded by Russia. At a Davos symposium in January 1984, he questioned whether the U.S. would "start World War III in defence of Europe" in a stiff exchange with Deputy U.S. Secretary of State Ken Dam and ex-French PM Raymond Barre. This caused considerable shock in External Affairs.

Then, in June 1984, he had a harsh and widely reported exchange with the President at the subsequent summit in Bonn, West Germany, where he had told Reagan, "Ron, you have to do

262

more . . ." to promote détente with Eastern Europe. Reagan was reported to have pounded his fist on the table and said "Damn it, Pierre, what the hell can I do to get those guys back to the table!" This story, which came out of a well-detailed U.S. briefing, finally put the PM's views on the need for more attention to be paid to peace on the first page of the *New York Times*!

The whole process taught me other lessons – including a few about the real feelings and priorities of my adopted colleagues at External Affairs. Apparently many had lost patience with Pierre Trudeau as he escalated his outspoken advocacy of peace. Some bemoaned that the PM's harping on the subject was harming our relations with the U.S. I could not believe this attitude, and was even more incredulous when I read an intemperate memo from an official of the highest rank who should have known better. In print, he had the nerve to object to the peace initiative being cast as Trudeau's "personal" initiative and characterized the result-ing planning by the task force as "reckless as it is irresponsible."

Neither official Washington nor officious External Affairs were ready for Trudeau's "radical" views. I felt let down, but I should have known.

FIFTEEN

POSTCRIPT

Admitting Change

*D*uring a lonely walk in a raging snowstorm on February 28, 1984, Pierre Trudeau made his absolute and final decision to resign as leader of the Liberal party and as prime minister. He announced his resignation the next day. There was not going to be an afterlife this time as there had been in 1979. This was it. The official end of the Trudeau era. Since I had lived through the first "end" and seen how active and vital a national personality Trudeau remained even when off centre stage, I did not think through what this more complete separation of Trudeau from public life would mean for the country, or for myself.

Even if he withdrew completely from Canadian public affairs, I had visions of a television series with him that I might direct, of helping him strategize worldwide speaking engagements. Even if there was to be no political afterlife, surely there would eventually be equally alluring opportunities for those like myself whose lives were so accustomed to being shaped by his thoughts and run according to his timetables.

In June, I was among the PMO "old boys" invited to attend the tribute to Pierre Trudeau at the Liberal leadership convention. Old boys indeed; we were installed out of the floodlit area well below the boss's box, where he sat with his three sons, his sister, and other members of his family and a group of the current PMO

264

who were seeing him out along with their own careers. The evening, I felt, was staged to provide the kind of show someone felt that crowd needed, not one that reminded us what the Trudeau years were really about. Paul Anka's performance of a reworded "I did it my way," which ended the elaborate multi-media tribute to the outgoing PM, was about as appropriate as bringing on Claude Ryan to thank Trudeau for saving Canada during the October crisis of 1970!

Like many Trudeau old boys, I knew I would not be favoured by the regime of the real star of that convention, the new prime minister, John Turner. He made it clear that he wanted to distance himself from the former PM, and that meant his old staff too. While, like many, I would have responded to a call to help in the federal election campaign that followed, I was not asked. I assumed that Turner would win the election, and my plush life in Washington would be protected.

This assumption made it a gut-wrenching experience that summer, back in Canada for our regular weeks of summer-cottage bliss, to watch from my wicker chair as events unfolded on the cottage's tiny black and white TV, and see Turner and his people blow away their lead. I did receive an unconcerned-sounding call from a Turner staffer a couple of days before the televised leaders' debate to ask who might be useful to "coach" Turner. I nearly blurted out that if they were thinking of help only now, it was far too late! The resulting debate was excruciating for me to watch and simply showed that Turner had been told little of the demands of such an occasion.*

As we watched the results of the election, it came home to me that it was more than just the Trudeau years that were over; it was the end of the Liberal era as well. I returned uncertainly to

---

* The leaders debate took place in Ottawa on July 25. It may have been the turning point in the campaign. While Turner held his own for much of the first hour, in the closing minutes he made the mistake of raising the issue of patronage. Mulroney immediately took him to task for appointing a number of Liberals to government jobs. Turner responded weakly that Trudeau asked him to make the appointments and he had "no option" to preserve his parliamentary majority in the days before an election was called. Mulroney, seizing on his comments, said Turner could have "said no for Canada." The debate left Turner looking fumbling and ineffective.

Washington to see if I could serve the new PM, Brian Mulroney. I was not entirely ill-at-ease with the idea, at least for the interim. I had become slightly acquainted with him when he came for an elaborate visit to Washington as leader of the Opposition in June, before the election. On that occasion, the Embassy had turned itself upside down in a startling display of exaggerated bi-partisanship.

At that visit's end, just before getting into the Ambassador's car, Mulroney made a gesture to me that I had never experienced in all my years with Trudeau. With the kind of hearty *bonhomie* for which he is justly renowned, he grasped my hand demonstratively and thanked me for all my press efforts for the visit. Although I didn't conclude that I was about to become a Mulroney intimate, the gesture later lulled me into thinking perhaps my position would not be in immediate jeopardy when the hand-shaker became prime minister. I even sloughed off an early small item in the *Financial Post* that put me high on a "hit list" of Liberal appointees for the new government to replace.

The change from the Liberal years was dramatic, especially from the Washington perspective. We prepared for Mulroney's first lightning visit to Washington as prime minister and from that point of view, I almost enjoyed the love-in atmosphere generated by the September appearance of the new PM. The White House National Security and Press Office types we had dealt with so many times for Trudeau's visits were overtly delighted with Canada's new PM. Some of us were uneasily aware of the sighs of relief from our State Department and White House contacts. They were pleased that the irritating Trudeau, who insisted on forcing Canadian concerns and views onto their crowded international agenda, was gone.

They were relieved that the loveable Mulroney would be no problem; lingering bilateral problems with Canada would be quickly solved; the new Canadian government would support, not carp about U.S. foreign policy. Canada would no longer be a real issue, and the administration would have one less distraction from real world problem-solving.

As the two Irishmen charmed each other in the Oval Office when the visit finally got rolling, I sat in the White House press office with Mulroney's press secretary, Bill Fox (the same Fox who had been the *Star*'s Washington correspondent), and presidential spokesman Larry Speakes, a man who had been helpful to me since we first met at the Montebello summit. They exchanged gifts as was the practice. Speakes presented a real class "A" gift in the White House hierarchy of trinkets – not the usual paperweight, but a heavy White House medallion of the presidential seal in an expensive velvet-lined case! Clearly a new era in Canada-U.S. relations was being launched.

Later, in my office, I wondered aloud to Fox, a veteran reporter and long-time Press Gallery personality in Ottawa, whether I could effectively serve Mulroney; in effect, whether a leopard could change his spots. Could I willingly promote this new accommodating Canada-U.S. policy?

Soon, I began to miss the creative tension in Canada-U.S. relations that Gotlieb and I had successfully exploited when I first arrived in Washington. Then we had the National Energy Program and a bit of cultural nationalism to defend. Trudeau was irregularly naughty about U.S. foreign policy excesses, and on that basis you could lunch and wisecrack about the U.S. administration with senior U.S. reporters, some of whom still remembered and admired Pearson's courageous contributions. The two Irishmen, who now shared control of the continent, seemed determined to create a new *pax Americana* and, even from the point of view of professional press relations, transborder love was even less newsworthy than a well-meaning Canadian peace initiative.

I heard little of the former prime minister. He had moved to Montreal, and was apparently relaxed, happy, and spending more time with his children than ever before.

One day in that fall of 1984 I was called to the Ambassador's residence for an unlikely meeting. The Canadian actress, peace activist, and sometime escort of Trudeau, Margot Kidder, was languidly arranged on a veranda settee with her pretty and exquisitely dressed daughter discussing a party for Pierre Trudeau with a slightly uncomfortable pair of Gotliebs.

Trudeau had just won the prestigious (we were assured) Albert Einstein Peace Prize. There was to be a lunch in Washington in November at which the prize would be presented. Then it was proposed there should be a full-scale party at the Ambassador's residence, scene of so many affairs for Trudeau when he was prime minister. A guest list with a slight left-leaning tilt towards friends of Margot's was discussed. This wonderfully attractive and agile lady was taking charge of advancing Trudeau's first Washington visit as a private citizen. I remembered some confusion at an earlier party when Trudeau was PM, when we were instructed by the PMO to invite a stunning girl Trudeau knew in the U.S. Peace Corps, only to have him walk in unexpectedly with Kidder on his arm. There would be no confusion this time as to who was Trudeau's date!

I learned from Kidder, and from other sources, that my old boss was devoting a lot of time to the speech he would give, and when I called him to enquire about press arrangements for the visit (I knew I would be doing some work for him again, and this encouraged me) it was clear he was going to make a pitch that he would not have made when prime minister. As for the retired Trudeau, his good spirits and easy joviality were a nice change.

When we next met, he was ready to take on Washington as never before. It was at a small reception in his honour the evening before he was to receive the Einstein Peace Prize.* He was in rare form, and welcomed me and Pam Chappell from my office warmly. We went over his press arrangements. This time he was prepared to do a number of interviews.

At the award luncheon the next day, I was swept back to another era. Helga and I found our places in the stark underground ballroom of the Hyatt on Capital Hill. Ted Johnson, the former PM's executive assistant, was in Washington for the occasion, chatting up Lacy Newhouse, a beautiful Texan seen on occasion in New York discos with Trudeau. But Margot Kidder was definitely *the* date and was fussing over Trudeau at the head table. This was a great moment for her. She was really proud of her older friend,

---

* Trudeau accepted the Albert Einstein Peace Prize on November 13, 1984. In his speech, he urged the world leaders to become more involved in the "politics of peace" to keep the world free of war. He complained that leaders had too often failed to try to stop the nuclear race. The presence of ambassadors, functionaries, technocrats, and negotiators had put too much power in the hands of "nuclear accountants who hold the world to ransom."

"The politicians who once stated that war was too important to be left to the generals now act as though peace were too complex to be left to themselves," he said. He called on NATO members to make more of the alliance, to make it a place where negotiations could begin.

who seemed ready to say what he really thought this time. Trudeau faced a highly sympathetic crowd. There were lots of press present, and they were listening hard this time.

On his feet at the podium, he rolled into a classic Trudeau "barnburner," as we used to call his exhorting speeches that flowed out in long bursts of energy. He lashed out at the useless discussions that leaders indulge in at summits, he pleaded for a renunciation of first use of nuclear weapons, and warned that, although Reagan personally might want to make progress, he doubted if those around him would allow it.

If clout in Washington is at least partly measured by front-page coverage in the *Washington Post*, Trudeau achieved it with that speech. He finally exposed the shallow attention paid by western leaders to questions of peace at NATO and summit meetings. An old Trudeau theme was at last delivered with passion.

The subsequent dinner given by the Gotliebs for Trudeau brought me full circle with the man whose thoughts and actions had so measured my life for the past eight years. In my ultimate brush with him in a semi-official capacity he did not let me down.

It was a somewhat uneasy affair. The guests representing official Washington and their attentive suitors, the Gotliebs, had adjusted to Brian Mulroney and his radiant wife as the number-one Canadians of interest, and it was a bit awkward to be fêting someone who had entertained and fascinated in the past but who had also been, after all, a bit of a burr under the saddle. Trudeau took all this in, his behaviour not affected in the slightest, proving he remained the master of his inner space – the characteristic that I have found most fascinating about him.

There he was that November evening, Margot Kidder as stunning as ever on his arm, his "steely blues" glittering, enjoying the attention like a child who is still everyone's darling even if slightly badly behaved.

After the meal, we all retired to the living room to exchange toasts. Trudeau, customarily cool on these occasions, unexpectedly lavished praise on the Gotliebs for their consistently high standards of hospitality. He remembered their days in Ottawa, and called them his old "friends," even singling out Sondra for special praise.

I listened in amazement, and watched the Ambassador. He was clearly puzzled too, and doubtless apprehensive. Trudeau had nothing to lose, what would he say next? Why was he going on and on like this? Trudeau knew, like everyone else, that Gotlieb, whom he had appointed Ambassador to Washington, had made such a favourable impression on Mulroney that the new PM had told the President himself that Gotlieb was being asked to stay on to serve the new government. Was the wily former PM reminding the Washington crowd that Gotlieb had long been a Trudeau man? Or was he being genuinely appreciative?

He was less ambiguous with me. Earlier that day, to help my old boss prepare for an interview, I had given him what I thought was a copy of a telex from the time of the peace initiative that listed ten points on which he had felt the White House and the Kremlin might agree. We had called it the "decalogue." I was still being the perfect aide – anticipating every need!

It turned out he was delivered the wrong document. To my horror Trudeau now produced it in front of a group of Washington guests at the party, making quite a story about how I never got anything right. He even unearthed from his terrifying memory how I had put on the wrong videotape years ago at a screening at 24 Sussex Street. I was mortified, and only Helga's presence at my side saved me further embarrassment. He was absolutely charming with her. We talked family and passed to other topics.

Trudeau had fun with both Gotlieb and me that night. He knew that the circumstances were forever altered, so why not enjoy them: stick it a bit to old Allan, and remind Gossage that he isn't perfect. Clearly the former PM had cast himself loose from the apparatus of which both Gotlieb and I were still such intimate parts. His eyes told me he was loving it.

In his earlier speech, he enjoyed tweaking the Washington establishment who had treated him with only barely more than tolerance in the final act of his prime ministerial career almost a year before. He enjoyed the impact he was making, even in that stuffy overdecorated room in the Canadian Ambassador's residence. Most of the guests on the fringes of the circle that surrounded him were talking about what he would do or say next.

I was far too self-conscious to understand all this at the time; or to understand that the new Pierre Trudeau would indeed *not* seek international fame and fortune and take me along with him. Nor could I imagine then that he would do exactly what he had told

Alain Stanké years ago – lead a private life, enjoy the miracle of young people growing up, perhaps even know every tree in the forest.

Instead, the last eight years passed through my mind in a flash. I felt discredited. I could not admit after all these years of labour that my special relationship with power was finally altered forever.

A week later, on U.S. Thanksgiving, a holiday for Embassy staff, the phone rang at our home. I left my half-eaten breakfast with Helga and Susanne. On the end of the line was a voice I had never heard that identified itself as a person I had never met, the head of personnel at External Affairs in Ottawa. It told me curtly that it "understood" that later that morning an Order-in-Council would be signed appointing the veteran CTV newsman and commentator, Bruce Phillips, to replace me as minister-counsellor at the Embassy.

From one second to the next I, too, was cut loose, and I began the long, hard adaption to another sort of real life. I tried outwardly to mask my profound surprise and foreboding on being with no job and few prospects for the first time in my life. More than any other event since coming to work for Pierre Trudeau, this sudden turn of fate in Washington put to the test my own belief in his favourite maxim, a quote from Flaubert: "Un honnête homme, rien ne l'étonne," which freely translated means "Nothing surprises a good man."

I could have learned another lesson. At that final party at the Ambassador's residence for my former boss, instead of trying to hang on like a jilted lover to a life and to relationships that were gone forever, I might have learned from Pierre Elliott Trudeau's behaviour to cut myself loose as he had, to face up to the facts, and to make it an easy and accepted part of my life that things for me and for the country had changed forever.